THE FIRST ALBANESE GOVERNMENT

JOHN HAWKINS heads the Canberra School of Government at the University of Canberra.

MICHELLE GRATTAN is a professorial fellow at the University of Canberra and chief political correspondent at *The Conversation*.

JOHN HALLIGAN is emeritus professor of public administration and governance in the Canberra School of Government at the University of Canberra.

THE FIRST ALBANESE GOVERNMENT

GOVERNING IN AN AGE OF DISRUPTION AND DIVISION, 2022–2025

AUSTRALIAN COMMONWEALTH ADMINISTRATION SERIES

EDITED BY

JOHN
HAWKINS

MICHELLE
GRATTAN

JOHN
HALLIGAN

UNSW PRESS

A UNSW Press book

Published by
NewSouth Publishing
University of New South Wales Press Ltd
University of New South Wales
Sydney NSW 2052
AUSTRALIA
https://unsw.press/

Our authorised representative in the EU for product safety is Mare Nostrum
Group B.V., Mauritskade 21D, 1091 GC Amsterdam, The Netherlands
(gpsr@mare-nostrum.co.uk).

A catalogue record for this
book is available from the
NATIONAL
LIBRARY   National Library of Australia
OF AUSTRALIA

ISBN: 9781761170737 (paperback)
          9781761179389 (ebook)
          9781761178641 (ePDF)

Cover design Alex Ross
Cover image Prime Minister Anthony Albanese prepares to speak to the press
    outside 10 Downing Street, London, United Kingdom / © Tayfun Salci/
    ZUMA Press Wire
Internal design Josephine Pajor-Markus

UNSW
SYDNEY

CONTENTS

PART IV: GOVERNING CHALLENGES AND LEADERSHIP

We wish to acknowledge the traditional custodians
of the land on which the authors and editors of this book
live and work. We pay our respects to all Aboriginal and
Torres Strait Islander people as the First Peoples of Australia.

PREFACE

HON BILL SHORTEN
VICE-CHANCELLOR AND PRESIDENT, UNIVERSITY OF CANBERRA

The 2022 election win for the Australian Labor Party was even more of a triumph when you consider that after the 2013 election defeat the ALP had been reduced to just 54 seats, a long way from the majority it would have needed to form government.

When I accepted the role of Leader of the Opposition, I knew the Labor team had a Herculean task to make the party electable again. From 2013 to 2019 we drew the battlelines that would unite us, define us and rebuild us. And rebuild we did.

Prime Minister Anthony Albanese and the Labor team had a long 'to do' list when we came to government in 2022: restoring our reputation on issues such as climate change, repairing relationships with global leaders and trading partners – specifically China – and reinvigorating Australia's manufacturing sector.

Over the next three years, the Albanese Government navigated an Australia eager to return to some semblance of a pre-Covid equilibrium and tackle the cost-of-living crisis, whilst witnessing the rise of authoritarianism around the world and the Russian invasion of Ukraine, which was emblematic of the broader geopolitical instability.

I left my parliamentary career and Cabinet ministry in early 2025 to take up my current role as the Vice-Chancellor of the University of Canberra. In my time as Minister for Government Services and the National Disability Insurance Scheme (NDIS), I heeded the words of Kipling to 'fill every unforgiving political minute with 60 seconds of distance run'. It was a necessity if I was to leave the portfolios in better shape than they were when we took office.

Top of my agenda in Government Services was a Royal Commission into Australia's worst failure of public administration, Robodebt. On equal footing was the need to address the depleted staffing levels at Services Australia, which inhibited the ability of Australians to access services and programs to which they were entitled.

In the NDIS, I ordered a comprehensive review to find out where the Scheme had gone off the tracks. The Review's recommendations, based on consultation with Australians with disability, along with their families, carers and advocates, drove the legislation for reforming the NDIS, which was passed with bipartisan support.

The Albanese Government's first term was filled with ambition and steeped in ALP values; this book analyses the extent to which those ambitions and values were fulfilled and considers possibilities for the future. I commend this collection of articles by some of Australia's foremost experts on politics and policy issues and edited by John Hawkins, Michelle Grattan and John Halligan. In a world of misinformation and disinformation we need such trustworthy sources of information about these moments in history.

INTRODUCTION: A BUMPY FIRST-TERM RIDE TO A BIG SECOND-TERM MAJORITY

MICHELLE GRATTAN

Anthony Albanese led Labor to a narrow victory on 21 May 2022, helped substantially by the deep unpopularity of the Morrison Government. This was just three years after Scott Morrison had won his 'miracle' election. Albanese had been in parliament since 1996, and was a senior minister under prime ministers Kevin Rudd and Julia Gillard, rising to be deputy prime minister briefly in 2013 when Rudd overthrew Gillard. Later that year Albanese lost the race for Opposition leader to Bill Shorten, winning the ballot of Labor's rank and file but not the Caucus vote.

Becoming leader after Shorten's 2019 election defeat, Albanese made Labor a small target for the 2022 poll. The most dramatic example of that was having Labor immediately accept the Morrison Government's AUKUS agreement with the United States and Britain after its announcement in September 2021. In the election campaign itself, Albanese personally made early mistakes, but the country, coming out of the Covid years, was ready for a change after nearly nine years of Coalition rule, and Labor was a safe alternative.

The 2022 election brought in not just a new government, but a clutch of new high-profile professional women, the so-called 'teals', who took Liberal heartland seats. They had limited influence, given Labor had a majority, but they were a key feature of the new parliament. Their arrival underlined that voters were disillusioned with the major parties. Labor had won with only 32.58 per cent of the primary vote.

In his victory speech, Albanese began by committing his government to 'the Uluru Statement from the Heart in full'. A key element of that statement was to insert into the Constitution an Indigenous 'Voice'; the subsequent (unsuccessful) referendum was to become a central fight of Labor's first term. Albanese also reiterated his mantra of 'no one left behind' and 'no one held back' under the government he would lead.

Albanese's start in government wasn't quite as dramatic as when Gough Whitlam in 1972 had himself and his deputy Lance Barnard sworn into all portfolios, to act as a duumvirate to make decisions very quickly while the rest of the ministry was sorted. But the new PM had a pressing overseas engagement and needed to put some temporary arrangements in place. Several senior members of the new government, including Albanese and his deputy Richard Marles, Penny Wong, Jim Chalmers and Katy Gallagher, were sworn in on Monday 23 May, with all portfolios covered. Albanese then left for a meeting of the Quad in Tokyo, to confer with the leaders of the United States, India and Japan. US President Joe Biden quipped, 'If you fall asleep while you're here, it's OK'.

The Quad meeting was the first of many prime ministerial international engagements, which would include a visit to war-torn Ukraine and attention on repairing damaged relationships in the Pacific. But it would be the gradual thawing of Australia–China relations, driven by a change in Chinese diplomacy as well as the change of our government, that would be probably the most significant foreign policy development for Australia over the term. By 2025 China had removed some $20 billion worth of restrictions on Australian imports that it had imposed in the latter Coalition period. If stabilising the China relationship was the term's major international relations success, an unanticipated foreign conflict where Australia had no direct influence – the Israel–Hamas war – would test Australia's social cohesion, and cohesion within the government, with a Muslim cabinet minister, Ed Husic, speaking out strongly and a Muslim senator, Fatima Payman, defecting to the crossbench. On border security, Labor continued the Coalition's tough boat 'turn back' policy, sending a resolute message to potential people smugglers.

In the government's first days Treasurer Jim Chalmers, in an important symbolic gesture, announced he had used his power as interim Home Affairs Minister to allow the Sri Lankan Tamil Murugappan family, the centre of a long-running battle to resist deportation by the Morrison Government, to return home to Biloela in Queensland.

Promotion of gender equality on all fronts was to be a theme of the new government. When Albanese unveiled his ministry, ten of his 23-member cabinet were women, a record. Over the term, a number of key economic appointments, including governor of the Reserve Bank and chair of the Productivity Commission, went to women.

The government quickly made good on its election commitment – which had been controversial in the campaign – on wages. With inflation at more than 5 per cent, it advocated in a submission that the Fair Work Commission ensure 'the real wages of Australia's low paid workers do not go backwards'. The commission's decision awarded an increase marginally above the inflation rate.

Also quickly, the government submitted a new, enhanced target for reducing emissions under the Paris climate agreement, committing Australia to a 43 per cent reduction on 2005 levels by 2030. This target, which the government legislated, was considerably more ambitious than the earlier target of a 26–28 per cent reduction set under Prime Minister Tony Abbott.

Before it reached its first anniversary, the government had an electoral triumph, when it won a by-election in the Victorian Liberal seat of Aston. This had been triggered by the resignation of Alan Tudge, a former Liberal minister. It was the first time in more than a century a government had taken a seat from an Opposition. Labor achieved a two-party swing of more than 6 per cent.

Tilting the industrial playing field and managing the economy

Like Bob Hawke (and Kevin Rudd), Albanese called a national summit early in the term (September 1–2), although the 'jobs and skills summit' was less elaborate than the 1983 national economic summit. In his pre-summit speech Albanese said he wanted to mark 'the beginning of a new culture of co-operation'. He sought 'a renewed understanding – between unions and industry and small business and government and community groups – that building a strong, fairer and more productive economy is our shared responsibility and our common interest'. Fundamentally, the summit was about advancing the government's industrial relations agenda. Workplace Relations Minister Tony Burke announced during the meeting that the government would bring in legislation to facilitate multi-employer bargaining and other industrial relations measures. The summit established the government's 'labour' credentials and made it plain that it would deliver substantially to its union base. By the end of the year it had pushed through a first tranche of industrial relations reforms.

The summit also saw a government commitment to increase migration (though by late in the term it was acting to bring down ballooning net overseas migration), and put pressure on business to improve its performance on gender. A Women's Economic Equality Taskforce, chaired by Sam Mostyn (subsequently appointed governor-general) was to report on 'the best ways to improve women's economic equality and security'.

As the government's first budget approached, a struggle emerged between Albanese and Treasurer Jim Chalmers over the former government's stage 3 tax cuts, which were skewed to higher income earners. In Opposition Labor, driven by politics, had promised to deliver stage 3 as it stood. But Chalmers now argued for recalibrating the cuts to spread them more equitably. The PM allowed his treasurer to test the mood but then decided he must keep his earlier promise. It was not until early 2024, in the run-up to the by-election for the Victorian Labor seat of Dunkley, that Chalmers got his wish.

Chalmers' inaugural Budget, on 25 October 2022, focused on delivering on election promises, including more TAFE and university places, measures for women, and an aged care package. The government kept spending tight, in a Budget brought down against a background of rising interest rates. But the Budget had alarming news that would only get worse, estimating energy prices would soar. In the campaign, Labor had promised a $275 reduction in yearly household power bills by 2025. It was a promise that quickly became unachievable, and would dog the government. By the time of its 2023 Budget the government was handing out credits to help with power bills.

During the term, Chalmers delivered four Budgets. In his second, he was able to announce a surplus, the first in 15 years, and that was followed by another in his third. Chalmers's 2025 Budget was prepared as one that might or might not be delivered, depending on the election timing. When Cyclone Alfred appeared, the election was pushed from April to May and the campaign was launched off the back of the March 25 Budget.

The term was marked by major economic challenges. The first interest rate hike had come under the Morrison Government; it was followed by a dozen more under Labor, with the initial fall only in February 2025. Inflation rose to a peak of 7.8 per cent at the end of 2022. Although recession was avoided, a per capita recession ran for seven quarters, in 2023 and 2024, meaning deteriorating living standards. Late in the term, Treasurer Chalmers could argue things were turning a corner. But economic growth was low, real wage rises were minimal and, with the advent of the Trump administration's unpredictable tariffs, unveiled shortly before the election, the outlook was laden with risks.

The Voice blows government off course

In mid-2022 Albanese attended the Garma Festival in Arnhem Land, where he announced draft wording for the referendum to be put to Australian voters the following year. The Prime Minister said, 'All Australians have the chance to own this change, to be proud of it, to be counted and heard on the right side of history'. The referendum increasingly dominated the political agenda through the months of 2023. Initially its prospects of being carried appeared good; in early February 2023, Newspoll estimated support for the Voice at 60 per cent. But it was always set to be a struggle to clear the hurdle of Australians' reluctance to change the constitution. Only eight of 44 referendum questions had previously been carried. Then the failure to win bipartisan support doomed it. The 'no' side ran a strong campaign – featuring in particular Indigenous Nationals senator Jacinta Nampijinpa Price – that cast the proposal as dividing the country on racial lines, giving First Nations people a right that other Australians did not enjoy, lacking detail and presenting unforeseeable consequences. The October 2023 result turned around the initial support, with 60.06 per cent voting 'no'.

The defeat was a major setback for Albanese, who seemed thrown off balance by it. It also had flow-on implications for an unrelated issue. The government had hoped to run a referendum for a republic in its second term, and had an Assistant Minister for the Republic. But after the Voice's defeat, Albanese made it clear that it had killed off the prospect of a vote on a republic, and later the assistant minister post was scrapped. Talking to Sky News before the election in 2025 Albanese said, 'There'll be no referendums in the next term, if I'm elected Prime Minister on Saturday'.

Cost-of-living crisis

In February 2023, as the Voice debate was ramping up, Labor's national secretary Paul Erickson told Caucus: 'Our core task is to demonstrate we understand the pressure households are under and are taking practical action to provide relief'. It was a message the government did not absorb quickly or fully enough.

Several issues interlinked in the cost-of-living crisis: high inflation, with an increasing number of households struggling with grocery bills and energy costs; the long-neglected problem of declining housing affordability and shortages of properties to buy or rent; and a large post-Covid net immigration intake.

In August 2023 the federal and state governments reached an agreement for 1.2 million homes to be built over five years. But multiple obstacles slowed the start and put the target out of reach. They included problems getting legislation through the Senate, planning hurdles at state and local government level, and difficulties in the building industry, including shortages of tradespeople.

In November the official cash rate hit 4.35 per cent; it would remain there until early 2025. Young people and those in early middle age despaired of ever being able to get into the housing market, given the supply and financing barriers they faced. The Greens elevated the issue of the rental shortage.

Immigration became a contentious and partisan debate. While many argued its contribution to the pressures on housing and community services was overstated, the government recognised its level was unsustainable. In late 2023 it announced that within two years it would halve the intake (from more than 500000 in the previous financial year). In particular, overseas students (and the universities which had come to rely on them for much of their revenue) would feel the brunt of the push to reduce numbers.

The transition to a clean energy economy threw up challenges on various fronts. From the vantage point of most households, it was the cost of energy, which the government sought to partially address with emergency price caps on new wholesale gas sales as well as its subsidies for bills. The transition also produced a backlash from farmers and local communities against wind farms and spreading transmission lines. The government expanded its underwriting scheme to encourage more investment in the transition. But the partisan divide on energy issues denied the full certainty investors wanted.

The government's early enthusiasm to boost Australia's 2030 emissions reduction target had, by 2025, with an election looming, turned into caution when it came to announcing a proposed 2035 target. Rather than being out early with its target, it delayed considering the matter until after the election.

Albanese was deeply committed to industry policy and in April 2024 the 'Future Made in Australia' initiative was announced: this would provide incentives for resource processing and local manufacturing. The new industry policy was a fit for Labor ideology, the views of unions and other groups, and international trends emphasising sovereign capability.

Reforms to change the game

Throughout the term, critics from the left in particular wanted the Labor Government to do more, be more radical and forward-thinking. Albanese was naturally cautious: he did not want to exceed the government's mandate, take voters by surprise, or break promises. To an extent, people's assessment of whether the government did or did not do enough will depend on the observer's viewpoint. However, his government did undertake, or commit to, some landmark reforms. These included bringing in caps on political donations and spending, and a plan to restrict the access of minors to social media accounts.

Labor had long been committed to comprehensive reform on the role of money in elections. It was particularly exercised by the huge spend by billionaire Clive Palmer, which reached $117 million at the 2022 election (and yielded him only a single Senate seat). The pros and cons of caps on donations and expenditure had become even more contested with the growth of independents and the arrival of the 'teals', who received financial support from the Climate 200 fund. Critics feared if caps were too stringent, they would limit the ability of new players to break into the system. Eventually, right at the end of the term, the government and the Opposition finalised a deal. Special Minister of State Don Farrell, who had carriage of the legislation, would always prefer the Coalition as a partner to the deal. That gave the new regime, which would take effect during the following term, the best chance of surviving later changes of government. One thing the government did not pursue was its truth in political advertising measure, which was part of the package but regarded as doomed from the start.

The proposed ban on under-16s having access to social media accounts is a reform of a very different ilk. It came out of growing international as well as local concern about the destructive effects of social media on young people. The South Australian Labor Government planned its own ban. With pressure growing on the issue, Albanese opted for action, even before there was evidence from an age verification trial. The ban passed parliament in late 2024, with uncertainty around how effective it would be and the tech companies' longer-term reaction. Set to start a year on, it was groundbreaking internationally.

One reform the government was unable to land in the term was the introduction of a new environment protection agency – an updated watchdog to regulate and approve developments. This was already a scaled-back part of a more ambitious environmental agenda; it then fell victim to pressure from the Western Australian Labor Government (which faced an election in early 2025), the difficulties of a Senate deal, and tensions between Albanese and his Environment Minister Tanya Plibersek. In the end it was deferred to a second term, and a new environment minister.

On social policy, Albanese abandoned proposed legislation on religious discrimination when he could not get bipartisan support.

An area where hopes for full-blooded reform fell victim to the strength of vested interests was gambling advertising. Despite a strong cross-party report from a committee headed by Labor MP Peta Murphy (who died in office in December 2023), the actions of the government, lobbied hard by media and gambling stakeholders, were limited.

Regaining momentum in the final quarter

In January 2025, polling looked bad for Labor. Newspoll had the Coalition ahead on a two-party-preferred basis at 51–49 per cent. Albanese's net approval rating was minus 21, while Opposition Leader Peter Dutton was at minus 10. As preferred PM, Albanese had a small 44 per cent to 41 per cent lead. More than half the voters were tipping a change of government.

Even if everything had gone well, and been done correctly, an outright Coalition win was always against the odds, given the net gain of 18 seats that would be needed. But speculation that Labor could likely be forced into a minority government, with all the consequences that would bring, seemed reasonable on the basis of general polling. The degree to which campaigns matter is often contestable, but the 2025 one was certainly significant.

Albanese started the year's campaigning early, while the Opposition was slow to get moving. The government, which already had some major announcements out, rolled out more. It put Medicare at the heart of its pitch, building on the fact that health has always been a positive issue for Labor. The government was assisted by the Coalition's strategic mistake of holding back policies (and its failure to undertake sufficient in-depth policy work). The Opposition also opened itself to a scare campaign by promising big spending cuts, with little detail, and its advocacy of nuclear power was replete with political downsides. Then it had serious missteps during the campaign itself, especially on the working-from-home issue, plus a failure to put forward a blueprint for the future. By contrast Albanese avoided mistakes, and presented as the safe option, especially given the new US administration of Donald Trump made the future generally look more uncertain and hence the idea of a switch to Dutton a risk. In addition, Labor managed to paint Dutton as Trump-lite.

As polling day drew near, a consensus emerged that the Opposition had run what many believed the worst federal campaign in memory. In the final weeks, but also in the months and years before, the Coalition leadership's flawed judgments and performance, and Dutton's inability to connect with voters, had handed many advantages to the government. Even so, election night brought a shock, with the extent of the Labor win surprising nearly all observers and even government members. After the count was finished, the returned government would have 94 seats in the 150-member House of Representatives, with the Opposition reduced to 43, and a crossbench of 13. It would be the first election since 1966 in which the government had not lost a lower house seat. In the Senate the Greens (who lost three of their four lower house seats, including that of Leader Adam Bandt) would have the sole balance of power. That meant the government would have to negotiate only with them over legislation the Coalition refused to support.

Table 0.1: 2025 Election Results

Party	Votes percentage	Vote change from 2022	Seats won in 2025	Seat change from 2022
Labor	34.56	+1.98	94	+17
Liberal–National Coalition	31.82	-3.88	43	-15
Greens	12.20	-0.05	1	-3
Others	21.42	+1.95	12	0

SOURCE Australian Electoral Commission

Safe hands in uncertain times

Albanese prided himself on running a traditional Cabinet-style government, and letting individual ministers get on with their jobs. To an extent this was true, but also over-simplified.

The first-term Albanese Government did not seem to have the degree of robust internal debates that marked the Hawke Government. This may have been a product of the personnel involved, but also the times and the lesser degree of ambition. Mostly, the Albanese Government was not pushing into uncharted reform areas comparable to that earlier administration.

Certainly the 2022–25 Caucus was relatively quiet and tame. The Prime Minister put a high score on the maintenance of discipline at all levels of his government.

One feature of Federal Cabinet government these days is that much work is undertaken not in the full Cabinet but in smaller Cabinet committees, notably the expenditure review committee and the national security committee.

Albanese took a lesson from the faults of Kevin Rudd's style, where the prime minister's office micromanaged ministers excessively. But he did keep a keen personal eye on some issues, given their political sensitivity – one was the push for controls on gambling advertising, where he was cautious.

A generally stand-back approach by the Prime Minister had its advantages but could also lead to lack of focus, drift and a failure to nip problems in the bud before they became wildfires. Examples include the row over more access for Qatar Airways, the handling of a High Court decision that opened the way for the release of immigration detainees, many of them with serious criminal records, and the antisemitism issue arising from the Gaza war.

When it came to the government's communications, however, the Albanese office kept a tight hold, and for the most part, centralised and tracked ministerial appearances. Each morning the Canberra press gallery received a WhatsApp message on which ministers would be appearing in the media and elsewhere that day. The Prime Minister gave press conferences most days. The preoccupation, if not obsession, with the media reflected the 24-hour news cycle. Albanese was frequently on FM radio, in light, jokey exchanges; he also increasingly did podcasts (in 2025, there were 20 in the run-up to the election) which were becoming more politically significant, as were influencers on the social media scene (some of whom were invited to the 2025 budget lockup).

Albanese had considerable confidence in his own political skills, which at times made him difficult to advise. Politically, he had seen it all. He had been a factional heavyweight of the Left and a key figure in the fraught Rudd–Gillard–Rudd years. He was a long-term political survivor who had been around longer (after Joel Fitzgibbon left before the 2022 election) than anyone else in the Labor Caucus. His default position was that he could solve problems himself. As he said, 'I feel like I've been underestimated all my life'. With the election approaching, however, and the polling looking grim, he appears to have been more open to advice about how to improve his own and the government's performance.

As Paul Strangio wrote shortly before polling day, for much of the three years Albanese was 'derided as a plodder'. Indeed, even his colleagues, or some of them, were privately unimpressed with what they thought was a lacklustre performance for much of the term. But his strengths were his ability to run a basically competent government, which avoided scandals, and to keep his team united and focused. In the public's mind, he was not an inspiring or charismatic leader but he was the traditional safe pair of hands, especially in increasingly disturbing times.

PART I
PARTIES AND PARLIAMENT

CHAPTER 1

A CAUTIOUS FIRST TERM: THE LABOR PARTY IN GOVERNMENT

BRENDAN McCAFFRIE

The Albanese Government came to office in challenging times. Globally, few governments have answers to the seemingly intractable problems of climate change, economic declines caused by the Covid-19 pandemic and international conflicts, and populations that are polarised and dissatisfied with the way their governments and politics operate. In this context few governments remain popular for long. In addition, many long-established major political parties are struggling with a long-term decline in support. These challenges to major parties globally applied to the Australian Labor Party under Prime Minister Anthony Albanese, which in its first term met significant challenges with modest tinkering rather than major reform.

Labor's 2022 election victory came with a narrow majority. Labor supporters responded to the victory with more relief than jubilation after an error-prone campaign. The result had been curious, with Labor winning despite its lowest primary vote since 1934, and becoming the first Australian Opposition to win government despite a declining primary vote. Rather than sweeping to power with an ambitious agenda for reform, in response to Labor's 2019 failure, Albanese had taken a comparatively restrained suite of policies to the 2022 election.

The government did not begin from a position of strength. With fragile electoral support, a struggling economy, global uncertainty about how to proceed on major policy challenges, and a desire to differentiate itself from the scandal-prone Morrison Government, the Albanese Government was characterised by a circumspect approach. It seemingly preferred to achieve quiet competence than to remake the country with a comprehensive Labor vision.

Small changes rather than bold reform

Historically, Labor governments have seen themselves as transformative. Labor Party histories emphasise the significant reforms leading to the postwar reconstruction by the Curtin and Chifley governments, the sweeping social reforms of the Whitlam Government, and the economic liberalisation of the Hawke and Keating years. However, the most frequent criticism of Labor under Albanese was that it was too cautious and restrained in its policy approach (Grattan, 2025).

As Manwaring and Foley have argued (2025: 2), the Albanese Government's careful approach reflected a contradictory desire to renew the nation's infrastructure, to lead on renewable energy and climate change mitigation, and to boost real wages during a period of high inflation, all while remaining overtly fiscally responsible. For the past 30 years, one of the predominant orthodoxies in Australian political debates has been that lower debt and deficit is the key measure of good economic management. This fiscal responsibility was politically important given long-running (though no longer accurate) arguments from the Coalition parties that Labor governments produce higher taxes, higher deficits, and higher national debt. With ambitions to be a reforming government while spending little, it is unsurprising that the result was broad in scope but modest in effect.

Some held Labor's relatively small-target Opposition strategy responsible for this approach. But Albanese advocated a number of major reforms in Opposition, and the Labor Government acted upon many of them. Early in its term, the Albanese Government introduced the National Anti-Corruption Commission, increased the minimum wage, made adjustments to childcare funding, committed to reduce carbon emissions by 43 per cent on 2005 levels, and implemented the Aged Care Royal Commission recommendations, but provided no core vision for Australia's future (Strangio, 2024).

Many of these policy changes addressed small parts of a bigger problem, or were incremental. For instance, the adjustments to childcare support announced in 2022 raised the maximum amount of financial support available to low earners, and made the drop-off in support as incomes rose more gradual. The 2024 report of the Australian Competition and Consumer Commission (ACCC) found that these changes reduced out-of-pocket costs for parents, but with rapidly rising fees consistently outpacing inflation, for most families the improvement vanished quickly. These were not the only changes in this policy area, but with an ambitious goal of universal high-quality childcare, the government left implementing the structural changes to boost childcare availability by funding new centres until after the 2025 election. Major reform takes time, and an incremental strategy is sensible when additional staff and additional places at newly constructed early learning centres are required. Changes to the childcare sector may be significant once fully implemented but, at the end of Labor's first term, have had limited effect.

In economic policy the government appeared timid. Its actions did not match its ambition. This was most obvious against most Australians' greatest challenge: the rising cost of living driven by high inflation. While in Opposition, Albanese noted the centrality of the inflation problem, and the need to look beyond monetary policy to address it. However, the government was inclined to maintain the status quo, offering short-term rebates on electricity services and relying on the Reserve Bank's adjustment of interest rates, rather than adopting structural changes, or new approaches to fiscal and economic policy.

Similarly, in 2023 Treasurer Jim Chalmers argued in an essay in *The Monthly* that Australia should stop allowing poorly designed markets to determine outcomes, and should instead create well-designed markets through collaboration among business, labour and government. However, these ambitious ideas were not enacted (Manwaring and Foley, 2025: 14).

Labor's budgets showed little attempt at economic reform, focusing heavily on fiscal discipline in an effort to control inflation, while making modest adjustments in areas like childcare, costs of medicine, and welfare payments to support lower income Australians (Manwaring and Foley, 2025: 8). Minor changes in income tax in the 2025 Budget were viewed as an attempt to win votes rather than a reform.

The biggest reform the Albanese Government attempted in its first term was the ultimately failed referendum to create a Voice to Parliament for First Nations people. While the Voice had the potential to change the relationship between First Nations people and the Australian Government, the Albanese Government failed to campaign effectively for it. Referenda are difficult to win in Australia because they need both a majority of votes nationally, and a majority of votes in a majority of states (four out of six). With the Opposition campaigning against the Voice, Albanese and the Yes Campaign struggled to convince people of the merits of an institutional model that somehow both lacked detail and appeared complicated.

The challenge was compounded as for some Australians who were struggling financially, the referendum felt like a distraction (Evans and Grattan, 2024: 9). Fighting against the Voice gave Opposition Leader Peter Dutton a cause to galvanise most of his party behind. He never appeared more comfortable than when fighting for conservative cultural values, and the Voice became a flashpoint in the ongoing culture wars between progressive and conservative Australia, and between the Coalition and Labor.

The Voice had been the first policy Albanese mentioned in his victory speech at the 2022 election. The failure of the referendum felt almost as if the government had lost an election, and its agenda had an enormous hole in it.

Overwhelmingly, the Labor Party in Albanese's first term was, like many of its centre-left contemporaries around the world, a party of technocratic improvements, rather than of bold vision. Advocates for the party can point to improvements in a range of policy areas. However, the first Albanese Government will not be remembered as a big reform government in the mould of Curtin, Whitlam or Hawke, but as a party juggling competing demands while struggling to find a way to explain what the Labor approach to the challenges of the day were.

A more united caucus

Albanese began as Prime Minister keen to pursue a collectivist, consensus governing mode within Cabinet, within the Labor Party Caucus, and for the nation more broadly (Hitch, 2022). The approach was central to Albánese's character, and it differentiated him from both his immediate predecessor, Scott Morrison, who admitted to being 'a bit of a bulldozer', and from previous Labor Prime Minister Kevin Rudd's comparatively presidential, leader-focused style. Within the party Albanese generally had significant respect and there were few overt tensions, despite some consternation that the 2022 election victory was not larger, and that the campaign had not been smoother (Bramston, 2022).

The Labor Caucus was relatively quiet and willing to follow Cabinet's direction. However, one policy issue stood out as more contentious. In opposition Labor had promised to retain the stage 3 tax cuts, legislated by the Morrison Government and due to take effect two years into the Albanese Government's term. This promise avoided giving the Morrison Government the advantage of offering lower taxes during an election campaign.

Stage 3 tax cuts were controversial for Labor because they had been designed to favour wealthier Australians earning up to $200 000, and because they would flatten income taxation by abolishing the 37 per cent tax bracket for those earning over $120 000, retaining a 30 per cent rate for those earning between $45 000 and $200 000. Though few in Caucus felt the cuts as legislated were good policy, some preferred the government to maintain its promise, while others were open to abandoning or overhauling the cuts. While the Caucus debate was robust and ultimately led to change, it was largely of the Cabinet's making, with Chalmers opening it publicly in response to pressure from outside the parliamentary party (Grattan, 2022). The government remodelled the tax cut, giving less relief to higher earners, but cutting taxes for more people. The outcome was broadly politically successful, both within Caucus and beyond.

Labor senator Fatima Payman's decision to cross the floor and support a Greens motion that the Senate recognise the state of Palestine created a moment of Caucus unrest. Payman, a practising Muslim and strong supporter of Palestine, breached Labor Party rules by crossing the floor to support the motion. She should normally have been expelled from the party, and when the Prime Minister only temporarily suspended her from Caucus, many in the party were upset both with Payman and Albanese. Voting collectively is a core tenet of the Australian Labor Party, and many members had in the past voted in ways that were inconsistent with their personal beliefs, so had little sympathy for Payman. Foreign Affairs Minister Penny Wong was publicly critical, as was fellow Muslim Labor MP Anne Aly, and Payman felt that she was being treated with hostility by some colleagues. After she stated that she would cross the floor again if a similar vote was moved, the

Labor Party leadership opted to suspend Payman from Caucus meetings until she recommitted to respecting Caucus rules. She left the party to sit on the crossbench.

These Caucus disagreements were rare, and while in electoral and media management terms the relative lack of turmoil was a significant advantage for the Albanese Government, the party may have lost a source of creative tension, with Caucus arguably too willing to agree with the Cabinet and party leadership and rarely playing a major role in improving policy. This included relative acquiescence on the Albanese Government's agreement to continue the AUKUS nuclear submarine project with the UK and US, at an enormous financial cost. Historically, the Labor Party would have contained strong voices opposed to working too closely with the US, but as Strangio (2024) noted, most of these critical voices appear to have migrated to the Greens. Both major parties are now opposed on two flanks (by minor parties such as the Greens on one, and by the opposing major party on the other), and the ideas within the party come from a narrower base.

Albanese's rare party leadership security

The parliamentary leadership of the party worked relatively harmoniously. Albanese's first cabinet was notable for its near gender-parity, with a record 10 women among the 23 cabinet ministers. Also notable was the apparent demotion of Tanya Plibersek, who became Minister for the Environment and Water, rather than Minister for Education, the shadow portfolio she had held throughout the previous two parliamentary terms. She had also been Shadow Minister for Women, a government post given to Katy Gallagher. When there had been minor tension over the Labor leadership ahead of the 2022 election, Plibersek was reportedly positioning herself to challenge Albanese (Murphy and Karp, 2021), though she later denied ever doing so. A logical conclusion was that Albanese was sidelining her.

Despite internal concern that Labor appeared not to be in an election-winning position in public polling at various times, there were no obvious threats to Albanese's leadership. The combination of the 2013 institutional change that requires 75 per cent of the Caucus to support a leadership challenge and a party membership vote, and the unpopularity of challenges against sitting Labor prime ministers during its last period of government, have discouraged challenges. Most of the government's senior ministers lived through the leadership struggles of the Rudd–Gillard–Rudd years and had seen the political costs of that infighting. Furthermore, while the first Albanese Government sometimes struggled, even during its worst polling period many expected it to be re-elected as a minority government.

Compared with other recent Australian governments, the Albanese Government appeared collegial. Albanese did not share some recent prime ministers' propensity to take charge of everything, allowing ministers authority in their own spheres (Strangio, 2024). This first term saw no major blunders or scandals that might create a flashpoint in Albanese's leadership. While the loss of the Voice referendum was a disappointment that dented Albanese's reputation as a campaigner, it was followed less than six months later by the Dunkley by-election. Labor held what was a potentially vulnerable seat, helping to bolster Albanese's electoral reputation.

Unlike the Rudd and Gillard Labor governments, Albanese's ministry did not leak against the Prime Minister, and even as Linda Burney and Brendan O'Connor departed Cabinet ahead of their parliamentary retirements, they did so amiably and with no hint of controversy. The Albanese Government was largely competent and even boring compared to recent predecessors, and a leadership challenge never felt likely.

Winning but weakening? Labor's continuing organisational decline

The Labor Party faces many threats to its ongoing competitiveness. Election fundraising is a perennial challenge. Undeniably, Labor is a big spender at election time, but even in the 2022 election,[1] when it was expected to win, Labor was unable to raise and spend as much money as the Coalition.

Labor's heavy reliance on trade unions for its election funds has become a concern as the population has become less unionised. While businesses and individuals also donate large sums to Labor, the vast majority of large donations still come from unions.

Compared with the mid-20th century, Labor membership numbers have declined considerably from roughly 270 000 ALP members (about 7 per cent of enrolled voters) in the 1930s and 1940s (Parkin and Warhurst, 2000: 28) to 60 085 (0.37 per cent of enrolled voters) in 2020 (Davies, 2020). From the outside, the party organisation appears relatively hollow. Whereas once the Labor Party organisation and members had considerable influence over the party platform and policy direction, National Conferences are now highly scripted, and the policy direction is determined by the parliamentary leadership. The membership now has a 50 per cent vote in party leadership contests, but in the 12 years since this institutional change, it has been used once, and the party membership was essentially overruled by the parliamentary caucus vote on that occasion.

In the mid-to-late 20th century, the major parties had a near duopoly on voters, and only a small proportion of voters would ever change from one party to another. Today neither Labor nor the Coalition can depend on lifetime voters. The decline in people always voting for the same party is striking, with the Australian Election Study showing a high of 72 per cent of respondents always voting for the same party in 1967, down to 37 per cent by 2022 (Cameron and McAllister, 2022: 22). While a large 2025 election victory no doubt gives Labor cause to celebrate, nothing we have witnessed over the past term suggests that this long-term trend of declining party support is about to change. The 2025 election has shown that significant independents and minor parties are likely to be an enduring feature in both houses of parliament. Resultingly, the extent to which major parties are an institutionalised feature of Australian politics is on the decline. Labor and the Coalition parties are now more vulnerable in electoral terms than they have been since early in their lifetimes.

The new electoral reality presents a challenge for Labor. Long ago, the Labor Party moved away from its old base of manual labourers, as the economy changed and the relative size of that group shrank. Its current status as a party of educated, city-based, progressive voters will continue to be challenged by the Greens on its left, and by independents, many of whom are more willing to push expansive social and climate agendas, while Labor is forced to compromise as a party of government seeking to appeal to all voters.

Staying relevant

The 2025 election result may temporarily obscure the reality that the Labor Party is progressively becoming smaller and narrower as an electoral party, an organisation and a policymaking entity. With other progressive parties and independents rising, Labor's base of ideas and supporters is less certain. Accordingly, the ideas that the Albanese Government pursued in its first term largely maintained the existing paradigm. Potentially, once a two- or three-term Albanese Government is assessed, its reform legacy will appear stronger, but its first term has been cautious, with the central aim appearing to be the pursuit of technical competence. While this is important, it is rarely enough to maintain the support of a population for long, and a general weariness with the Albanese Government ahead of the 2025 election campaign was evident. The eventual landslide victory was less about the population's excitement for three more years of Albanese Labor than a rejection of the Opposition, which campaigned poorly, and seemed unready for government.

Australia's economic context encouraged the government's narrow agenda, particularly as Labor maintained a focus on fiscal restraint, reinforced by the need to tame inflation. Rhetorically, the Albanese Government wanted to be a government of reform, but on almost every important issue the party pursued incrementalism or produced underwhelming actions. Albanese's quiet calm and competence could be interpreted as a lack of energy, contributing to the sense that this was a government of modest achievements.

The list of major challenges facing Australia is significant and is unlikely to be addressed effectively with modest tinkering. The Labor Party needs to define clearly what a Labor agenda in these times is, and to enact it with greater vigour. While the Coalition parties are suffering after a poor 2025 election, Labor's relatively low primary vote means that it cannot afford much of a swing against it before its electoral fortunes reverse and questions about the goals of the party appear urgent. Labor's future is no longer guaranteed, but the second Albanese term provides significant opportunities for Labor to act and to define itself as a continually relevant major political party.

References

Australian Competition and Consumer Commission, *Childcare Inquiry: Final Report*, Canberra, 2023.

Bramston, T, 'Hard lessons of Gillard, Rudd not forgotten', *Australian*, 31 May 2022.

Cameron, S, and McAllister, I, *Trends in Australian Political Opinion: Results from the Australian Election Study 1987–2022*, Australian National University, Canberra, 2022.

Chalmers, J, 'Capitalism after the crises', *The Monthly*, February 2023.

Davies, A, 'Party hardly: Why Australia's big political parties are struggling to compete with grassroots campaigns', *Guardian*, 13 December 2020.

Evans, M, and Grattan, M, 'The Voice to Parliament and the silent majority', *AQ: Australian Quarterly*, vol. 95, no. 1, 2024, pp. 4–11.

Grattan, M, 'Jim Chalmers plays the tease as he pushes to change stage 3 tax cuts', *The Conversation*, 6 October 2022.

— 'Second-term Albanese will face policy pressure, devastated Liberals have only bad options', *The Conversation*, 4 May 2025.

Hitch, G, 'Anthony Albanese promises to lead more inclusive government in first speech to caucus', *ABC News*, 31 May 2022.

Manwaring, R, and Foley, E, 'A "new economic model" in Australia? The political economy of the Australian Labor Party', *Commonwealth & Comparative Politics*, vol. 63, no. 2, 2025.

Milner, C, 'Demoting Plibersek may bite Labor', *Australian*, 10 June 2022.

Murphy, K, and Karp, P, 'Joel Fitzgibbon calls for changes to Labor's leader selection rules as Albanese finalises reshuffle', *Guardian*, 28 January 2021.

Parkin, A, and Warhurst, J, 'The Labor Party: Image, history and structure', in Warhurst, J, and Parkin, A (eds), *The Machine: Labor Confronts the Future*, Allen & Unwin, Sydney, 2000, pp. 21–48.

Strangio, P, 'Is grown-up government enough?' *Inside Story*, 3 September 2024.

CHAPTER 2

THE OPPOSITION: PETER DUTTON'S SUBURBAN STRATEGY

JOSH SUNMAN AND MARIJA TAFLAGA

The 2022 election saw the Coalition decisively defeated after three terms in office. Following Morrison's exit, Peter Dutton emerged as the Opposition leader after an uncontested ballot. Dutton brought a distinctive approach to his leadership, choosing to appeal to voters in the Australian suburbs, and seeking to combine the Coalition's traditional hold on rural and regional seats with potential gains in traditional Labor heartland in the outer suburbs of capital cities.

On policy, Dutton largely stuck to his preferred policy areas of national security, defence and immigration. There was limited economic policy development, with the Coalition relying on its issue ownership and existing credibility on economic management. However, the Opposition did take risks throughout the term, arguing for the construction of state-built and -owned nuclear power stations, and opposing the Indigenous Voice referendum at a time when it enjoyed 60 per cent support amongst Australians. Arguably, the Coalition over-interpreted the electorate's reaction to both choices to their detriment at the 2025 poll, where the Albanese Government decisively defeated the Coalition. Both Coalition parties went backwards: the Liberal Party of Australia (LPA) was almost ejected from the cities, and the Nationals faced co-ordinated challenges from independents and failed to win back their seat lost to a defector during the 47th Parliament.

The Coalition remained largely unified in the aftermath of its historic 2022 defeat, however its strategic direction throughout its term in Opposition contributed to the scale of its 2025 defeat, which precipitated only the third breaking of the Coalition agreement since the formation of the Liberal Party in 1944.

Aftermath of defeat and 'new' strategy

On 21 May 2022, the Liberal Party suffered its worst defeat since the party's first electoral outing in 1946, holding only 42 seats in the House of Representatives. By contrast, the Nationals held on to all their seats, but the results confirmed that the party is confined to rural areas. The loss of 19 seats on the back of a 5.7 per cent two-party-preferred swing disproportionately affected the moderate/left wing of the Liberal party. The seats lost were concentrated in New South Wales, Victoria and Western Australia, many of which the party (or its antecedents) had held since Federation. The moderate wing lost much of its future talent pool, including leadership aspirant Josh Frydenberg, to teal independent Monique Ryan in Kooyong. The National Party, by contrast, held all of its seats, confirming its status as a rural party, relatively insulated from electoral trends and holding off spirited challenges from community independents.

The 2022 defeat also marked the ascendancy of the Queensland Liberal–National Party (LNP) within the Coalition party room – and a northward power shift. The LNP collectively held 23 seats – approximately a third of the Coalition's lower house seats. Dutton, a conservative Queenslander, ascending to the leadership uncontested, exemplified this power shift – with no viable moderate challenger emerging. Dutton was the first Liberal Party leader from Queensland and the first not from New South Wales since Alexander Downer in 1994.

From the outset, Dutton began shaping his pitch to the suburbs, effectively conceding well-heeled and traditionally 'blue ribbon' seats in urban areas. Dutton framed himself as coming from a working-class background and being dedicated to community service, emphasising working at a butcher shop after school and his service in the police force. He also noted a traditionally Liberal background in small business, as well as his personal story of saving for and buying a home at 19. Implicit here is a selective valorisation of public service – with military and police service being framed as important contributions to public life, whilst other public institutions such as the bureaucracy are denigrated as 'elite' and detached from citizens' needs.

Dutton pledged that his Liberal Party would not 'be Labor-lite', and would 'propose strong policy to make the lives of Australians better and to provide more security to them' – promising a bold agenda and a strong contrast with the Albanese Government. Lifted from obscurity by Judith Brett's 1992 book, the 'forgotten people' evoked by founding Liberal Party leader Robert Menzies has become a foundational reference for Liberal leaders. Where Menzies used the phrase to refer to people caught between the self-sufficient upper classes yet not captured by the Labor Party's focus on organised labour and the blue-collar 'working class', Dutton invoked the phrase to refer to what he saw as possible Liberal Party supporters amongst voters who had traditionally aligned with the Labor Party (Brett, 1992).

As such, Dutton committed the party to a strategy which saw it forgo attempting to win back voters in 'blue ribbon' electorates – Menzies' 'moral middle class' – instead focusing on aspirational voters in the outer suburbs who had traditionally backed Labor. This represents something of a realignment, with the Coalition forgoing traditional socially liberal voters and seeking gains with less economically secure 'working class' voters. There was little dissent in the Coalition party room against this strategy, as moderates who had traditionally held and contested the Liberal Party's urban electorates had, largely, been wiped out in 2022. From the vantage point of the 2025 result, the party traded a contested, well-developed policy agenda for unity behind the leader, party strategy and a thin policy program.

Reviewing the recent defeat

The party commissioned former federal director Brian Loughnane and sitting senator Jane Hume to conduct a review into the 2022 defeat. Their remit included reviewing the 'long-term challenge for the Party presented by Independents running in, and winning, seats' and the party's 'electoral performance among different voter segments and candidate selection processes'. The review authors expressed alarm at the party's retreat from metropolitan Australia, noting that the 'only demographic class where the Liberal Party and National Party have a stronghold is in rural electorates' and warned – in contradiction to Dutton's stated strategy focused on regional and outer suburban electorates – that 'no party that is seeking to form government has a pathway to a majority solely through rural and regional electorates'. Yet this warning went largely unheeded in the Coalition party room.

Beyond the electorates' fatigue – both from the pandemic and the Coalition's longevity in office – Loughnane and Hume identified an 'inability' of several state divisions to 'meet their responsibilities', such as the disastrous failure to organise pre-selections in New South Wales. Elsewhere, factional infighting and intense conflicts over the 'culture wars' paralysed the Victorian division, the South Australian division had been ousted decisively after a single term in office and the Western Australian division was left moribund after successive landslide defeats at the state level. Finally, 'scandal, disunity and instability', in addition to 'allegations of the poor treatment of, and attitude toward, women within the Government and the Party, and by associated figures' were listed as major contributing factors in the 2022 defeat (Loughnane and Hume, 2022).

It was revealed in August 2022 that Scott Morrison had been secretly sworn into five ministerial portfolios. In the case of Health, the then Minister Greg Hunt was aware, but the remaining portfolio holders – Treasury, Science and Resources, Home Affairs, and Energy and Industry – were not. The Opposition also had to contend with the continued fallout from the Robodebt Royal Commission, and the human cost of maladministration. Likewise, details surrounding the Brittany Higgins scandal continued to emerge as legal proceedings carried on. This scandal, which exacerbated the Coalition's 'woman problem', combined with the emergence of the 'multiple ministries' scandal ensuring the legacy of the Coalition's previous term in office remained tarnished (Benson and Chambers, 2022).

Despite organisational challenges and holdover scandals, Dutton successfully maintained unity within the Liberal Party across the term at the federal level, and did so in spite of state-level organisational problems in Western Australia, New South Wales and Victoria. Whilst two Liberal representatives (Ian Goodenough and Russell Broadbent) and one LNP senator (Gerard Rennick) defected during the life of the parliament, these were the result of adverse preselections for those candidates, and not ideological division. Even potentially contentious issues, such as the Voice, had minimal disaffection, as noted below.

By-election defeats

The Aston by-election, on 1 April 2023, represented a humiliating defeat for the Liberal Party. It was only the second time since Federation that an Opposition lost a seat in a by-election to an incumbent government (after Kalgoorlie in 1920). Labor's Mary Doyle won the seat on a 6.38 per cent two-party preferred swing. Governments typically go backwards in by-elections, with the average swing -3.5 per cent since 1983.

Table 2.1: 2023 Aston by-election

Candidate	No. of votes	Vote %	Swing %
Owen Miller (Fusion)	2637	2.89	+ 2.89
Roshena Campbell (Liberal)	35 680	39.07	- 3.98
Angelica Di Camillo (Greens)	9256	10.14	- 1.94
Mary Doyle (Labor)	37 318	40.87	+ 8.32
Maya Tesa (Independent)	6426	7.04	+ 7.04
Two-party preferred			
Roshena Campbell (Liberal)	42 042	46.43	-6.38
Mary Doyle (Labor)	48 915	53.57	+6.38

The by-election came at an unfortunate time for the Opposition, as the Labor Party was riding high in the nationwide opinion polls, leading 56–44 per cent two-party preferred. The resignation of Alan Tudge (LPA) precipitated the poll. Tudge ostensibly resigned due to family pressures, but the scandal-plagued MP had been under sustained political pressure over both the scandal surrounding the 'Robodebt' scheme and for his own extramarital affair with his former advisor (Benson, 2023). Whilst Aston had at times been highly marginal, it had been held by the Liberals continuously since 1990 (AEC, 2023).

Dutton attributed the defeat to the Albanese Government's honeymoon period in the polls, and problems with the Victorian division, including ongoing battles over Moira Deeming's exile from the party, and subsequent legal battles. Following the result, he reaffirmed the need 'in Victoria and NSW ... to rebuild our organisational structure because at the moment neither is campaign ready'. He added that the party needed to rebuild its policy and brand credibility. Aston proved a decisive test case for the Liberal Party's fortunes in the 2025 election, with both the national figures reflected in contemporaneous polling, and the eventual 53.4–46.6 per cent result in Aston, reflecting the same dire picture for the Liberal Party nationwide that the by-election had telegraphed.

Whilst a less dramatic defeat, the Coalition also failed to win the marginal Labor seat of Dunkley in outer south-eastern Melbourne at a by-election. Whilst the Coalition candidate Nathan Conroy recorded a 3.6 per cent two-party preferred swing, Jodie Belyea retained the seat for Labor with 52.7 per cent of the two-party preferred vote. Belyea retained the seat in the 2025 election with a margin of 7.1 per cent – making the case that perhaps Dunkley represented an early indicator of Dutton's outer suburban appeals falling flat.

The Voice to Parliament

The Voice to Parliament referendum, held on 14 October 2023, resulted in a decisive defeat. A large majority (60 per cent) of voters nationwide voted 'No', and only one jurisdiction (the Australian Capital Territory) recorded a majority 'Yes' vote. It is an adage of Australian politics that referenda are difficult to pass, with only eight out of 45 succeeding. A commonly advanced explanation for referendum failure is a lack of bipartisan support. That is, one of the two major political actors – Labor or the Coalition – decline to support a particular referendum (Goot, 2024). Following this it is plausible to argue that the Voice referendum was doomed to fail when the Coalition opted to oppose it.

Goot, however, builds upon the data compiled by Biddle and colleagues to argue that party preferences were not a statistically significant predictor of support for either the 'Yes' or 'No' options in the referendum. This is particularly the case in the contemporary political context – where attachments to establishment parties are at an all-time low, and where a third of voters are looking to independent and minor party alternatives. It is impossible to quantify precisely the impact of the Coalition's 'No' position but it nonetheless marked a significant turning point in the 2022–25 political cycle (Goot, 2025 and Biddle et al., 2023).

On 5 April 2023, Dutton announced the Liberals' decision to oppose the Voice, arguing:

> The Liberal Party resolved today to say yes to constitutional recognition for Indigenous Australians, yes to a local and regional body so we can get practical outcomes for Indigenous People on the ground, but there was a resounding no to the Prime Minister's Canberra Voice. It should be very clear to Australians by now that the Prime Minister is dividing our country, and the Liberal Party seeks to unite our country.

Dutton's tone was both partisan and, arguably, populist by labelling the voice proposal the 'Canberra Voice' and a divisive and elitist institution championed by Albanese. It also points to an alternative: constitutional recognition and a mixture of local and regional bodies, purportedly to address better the concerns of Indigenous communities 'on the ground'. Optimistically this could be taken as a commitment from the Liberals to implementing effective grassroots input from Indigenous communities. However, this ignores the deep embeddedness of Indigenous communities in the design of the Uluru Statement and overall referendum proposal.

The Liberals' final position on the Voice mirrored the one the Nationals had announced in December 2022. However, even amongst the Nationals, this position was not unanimous, with the Member for Calare, Andrew Gee, resigning from the party to sit on the crossbench over his 'fundamental disagreement' with the party's position (Karp, 2022). The Liberals also faced some internal dissent, with moderate federal MPs Bridget Archer and Julian Leeser (who resigned from the Shadow Indigenous Affairs portfolio) as well as NSW senator Andrew Bragg advocating publicly for the Voice. Most damaging for the party was the loss of Ken Wyatt, who quit the party. Wyatt, the former Minister for Indigenous Australians in the Morrison

Government, stated that despite still holding core Liberal values, he no longer supported 'what the Liberals had become' in rejecting the Voice proposal (Sakkal and Thompson, 2023).

Overall, the Voice referendum can be judged as a tactical success for the Dutton Opposition, with the Liberal position on the Voice helping to frustrate the government's agenda – a key performance metric for any Opposition. However, this short-term tactical success failed to translate electorally. The Liberal Party arguably adopted a hubristic posture following the referendum. After all, the Prime Minister had been repudiated and the party's position on the Voice endorsed by the electorate – particularly in traditionally Labor seats. However, this proved a pyrrhic victory for the Opposition, clouding their electoral judgment and perhaps contributing to a lack of effort in policy development.

A lack of policy development

Oppositions need to do more than merely oppose and critique government proposals; they need to present themselves as a 'government in waiting' – ready with policy alternatives which speak to the electorate's real concerns. While the Dutton Opposition saw success in opposing the Voice proposal, it failed to develop a convincing and coherent set of policies through the 2022–25 period in Opposition. Oppositions are often forced into responsive policymaking as governments typically dominate the political and media agenda. However, this does not mean Oppositions are without agency – they have choices about how they respond and develop policy, ranging from pure opposition to constructive dialogue, or establishing their own detailed programs for government. Grattan (2019) and Prasser (2023) both cite the example of Bill Shorten in 2019 as an example of where an Opposition brought forward a detailed policy agenda, with proposals to unwind generous tax concessions on negatively geared properties and franked share dividends – ultimately to its detriment in the 2019 election.

Rather than advancing a detailed program for government, Dutton announced a single 'Big Picture' energy proposal – the introduction of nuclear energy into the Australian power grid. The plan centred around the government-funded construction of seven nuclear power plants on land formerly occupied by coal-fired power stations. With the policy announced well in advance of the 2025 election, it was revealing that the Coalition only released its modelling in December 2024. This policy was something of an ideological mismatch for the Liberals: highly interventionist in a largely private sector, centring around government ownership of key energy assets, and overriding concerns of state governments. Traditionally the Liberals have favoured decentralisation, and market control of power supply and sources (Brett, 2024). Cheered on by supportive media commentators, the Coalition failed to develop adequately the details of this policy proposal and understand its potential negative reception by key components of the electorate. Perhaps overlearning the lesson of Labor's loss in 2019, the lack of detail surrounding such a large proposal presented the Albanese Government with its own prime target in the 2025 campaign. It ruthlessly employed the slogan 'He Cuts – You Pay' along with a $600 billion cost projection, tying together fears of cuts to services with the large projected cost of the nuclear program.

A potentially thorny issue for the incoming Albanese Government was the proposed stage 3 tax cuts, which the Morrison Government had legislated in 2018 (Martin, 2023). These tax changes were part of a three-stage package. Stages one and two had relatively even benefits across all tax brackets, but the legislated stage 3 offered disproportionate benefit to the highest income earners and had the potential to distort the progressive nature of Australian income taxation. Labor had committed in Opposition to supporting the stage 3 cuts, seeking to neutralise potential Liberal attacks on taxation which had hampered Shorten in 2019. Labor eventually ceded to calls for the stage 3 cuts to be mitigated, offering a more proportional cut across income brackets than was initially legislated. The Dutton Opposition reluctantly supported these cuts, as they did not want to block tax cuts to low and especially middle income earners, but still reiterated the government's broken promise to implement the stage 3 cuts in full.

Tax reasserted itself in the policy debate following the March 2025 Budget. Treasurer Jim Chalmers announced what he labelled 'modest … top up' tax cuts affecting the lowest tax bracket. In his budget reply, Dutton labelled this measure 'insulting' and a 'cruel hoax', pledging that the Liberals would oppose and repeal the cuts. Instead, Dutton argued for the provision of 'immediate cost-of-living relief', including halving the fuel excise for 12 months. Opposing this tax cut put the Liberals in a strange ideological and campaign position. The Liberals tend to 'own' economic issues – such as government debt and lower taxes. That is, voters tend to associate the Liberals as being the most credible on this set of issues. Instead of 'owning' a low tax agenda, the Liberal party went to the 2025 election promising higher taxes and a suite of 'sugar hit' cost-of-living policies, exemplified by the fuel excise pledge.

The forgotten party?

Coalition unity is the singular success of the Dutton Opposition. However, success on this front corresponded with the Liberals' failure to develop ideologically coherent and credible policies to appeal to urban and suburban electorates necessary to form government. By prioritising unity and narrowing their appeal to an increasingly conservative and regional–rural base, the Coalition advanced a divisive and ideologically incongruent nuclear proposal. On other policy areas it failed to undertake sufficient manifesto development. Remarkably, it became wedged on tax policy and went to the election offering a swathe of ad hoc cost-of-living proposals and a tax increase to a cynical electorate. In the wake of defeat, the Liberal Party faces an uphill struggle to rebuild its organisational capacity and institutional talent. This is a necessary step towards developing coherent and effective policy and political appeals to urban and suburban Australia. The difficulties for the Liberals are compounded by policy disagreements with their Coalition partner, the Nationals, exemplified by the brief rupture in the Coalition in the aftermath of the 2025 election. Failure to rebuild its organisation may leave the Coalition as something of a 'forgotten party', consigned to Opposition for years to come.

References

Australian Electoral Commission, 'Aston, Vic', 2023, <https://results.aec.gov.au/28791/Website/HouseDivisionPage-28791-197.htm>.

Benson, S, 'Voters turn away from Anthony Albanese and Peter Dutton: Newspoll', *Australian*, 23 April 2023.

Benson, S, and Chambers, G, 'Scott Morrison's secret Covid moves to protect power', *Australian*, 12 August 2022.

Biddle, N, Gray, M, McAllister, I, and Qvortrup, M, 'Detailed analysis of the 2023 Voice to Parliament Referendum and related social and political attitudes', ANU Centre for Social Research and Methods, 2023.

Brett, J, *Robert Menzies' Forgotten People*, MacMillan, Sydney, 1992.

— 'With its nuclear energy policy, Peter Dutton seems to have forgotten the Liberal Party's core beliefs', *The Conversation*, 2 July 2024.

Goot, M, 'Without "bipartisanship" have referendums to change the Australian constitution ever succeeded? An unnoticed success, several near-misses, and the struggle to explain why referendums fail', *Australian Journal of Politics and History*, vol. 71, no. 1, 2025, pp. 73–105.

Grattan, M, 'Labor in Opposition: When the Favourite Loses', in Evans, M, Grattan, M, and McAffrie, B (eds), *From Turnbull to Morrison: Understanding the Trust Divide*, Melbourne University Press, Melbourne, 2019.

Karp, P, 'Nationals MP Andrew Gee quits party citing its opposition to Indigenous voice', *Guardian*, 23 December 2022.

Loughnane, B, and Hume, J, *Review of the 2022 Federal Election*, Liberal Party of Australia, 2022.

Prasser, S, 'What should oppositions do?', *Australasian Parliamentary Review*, vol. 38, no. 2, 2023, pp. 208–30.

Sakkal, P, and Thompson, A, 'The decision was tough: Former Indigenous minister Ken Wyatt quits Liberals in Voice protest', *Sydney Morning Herald*, 6 April 2023.

CHAPTER 3

THE LARGEST CROSSBENCH IN A CENTURY: MINORS, MICROS AND INDEPENDENTS

TOM KING AND JOHN HAWKINS

The first Albanese Government faced the largest crossbench (in both houses) since the Coalition formed around a century ago. And it was more diffuse than earlier crossbenches. Rather than being dominated by one or two parties such as the Democratic Labor Party, Australian Democrats or the Greens, there were a large number of minor and micro-parties and independents. The government had a stable, if small, majority in the House but had to assemble various combinations to pass legislation through the Senate.

Growth of the crossbench

Support for the two traditional major party groups has eroded steadily over the past couple of decades. In 2022 as many voters supported neither major party as supported either. This translated into a growing crossbench.

As at March 2025 the Albanese Government faced a crossbench of 19 in the House of Representatives comprising:

- Four Greens: their leader Adam Bandt, first elected in 2010, joined by three Queensland members Stephen Bates, Max Chandler-Mather and Elizabeth Watson-Brown, newly elected in 2022;
- Bob Katter representing Katter's Australian Party (first elected as a National MP in 1993, turned independent in 2001 and formed Katter's Australian Party in 2011);

Figure 3.1.

Primary votes (%)

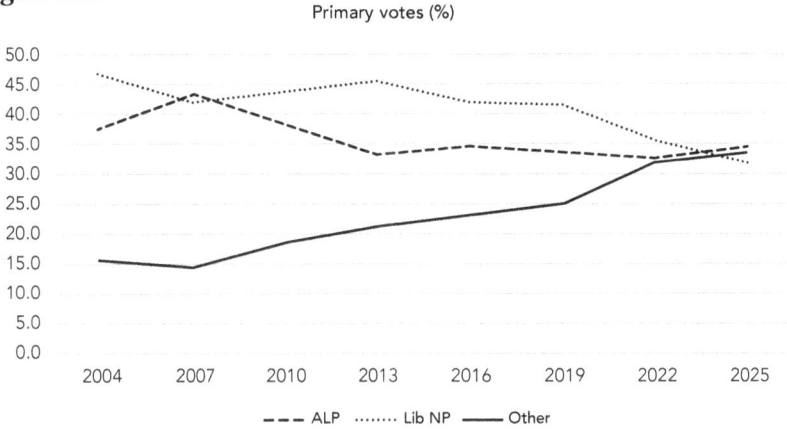

- Rebekha Sharkie representing the Centre Alliance (first elected as a Nick Xenophon Team member in 2016);
- Andrew Wilkie, an independent member since 2010;
- Seven 'teal' independent members: Kate Chaney, Zoe Daniel, Monique Ryan, Sophie Scamps, Allegra Spender, Zali Steggall and Kylea Tink; all but Zali Steggall were newly elected in 2022;
- Two 'community-based' independent members: Helen Haines, first elected in 2019, and Dai Le in 2022; and
- Three former Coalition members: Russell Broadbent, Andrew Gee and Ian Goodenough.

The Senate crossbench was similarly diverse:

- Eleven Greens;
- Two senators from Pauline Hanson's One Nation: Pauline Hanson and Malcolm Roberts;
- Jacqui Lambie of the Jacqui Lambie Network;
- Ralph Babet of the United Australia Party;
- Fatima Payman of Australia's Voice;
- Gerard Rennick of People First;
- David Pocock (the first ACT senator from outside the major parties); and

- Three other independents: Lidia Thorpe, Tammy Tyrell and David Van.

Notably, five of these senators had been originally elected for parties to which they no longer belonged – senators Rennick and Van were originally Liberals, Thorpe a Green, Payman from Labor and Tyrell from the Jacqui Lambie Network.

The 'teals'

The seven 'teals' gained this name, the Australian 'word of the year' for 2022, as their policies were a mix of economically liberal blue and environmental green. The first 'teal', Zali Steggall, had adopted it as her campaign colour in her successful 2019 campaign.[1]

Among features they had in common were: their gender, success in established careers rather than being political party cadres, support for climate action, concern about respect for women, and support for integrity and greater transparency in politics (specifically a federal anti-corruption commission). All held affluent inner suburban seats formerly held by the Liberals. All received some funding from Climate 200, but this group was not involved in selecting them or establishing their policies, merely directing funding to candidates it identified as sharing its basic values and who appeared to have sufficient community support to have a realistic chance of winning (Holmes à Court, 2022). Some commentators have suggested that the teals could have been Liberal members had the party not drifted to the climate-sceptic right and had it more actively tried to promote women into its parliamentary ranks.

Some critics tried to describe the teals as a party, but they are more a collective noun. The teals had no leader, whip, secretariat or common platform of policies. While the seven teals often met to discuss matters of mutual interest over dinner on Monday evenings of sitting weeks, they did not caucus. They voted differently, for example, on the industrial relations bill (10 November 2022) and on workplace gender equality targets (6 February 2025).

The teals more often voted with the government and Greens than with the Opposition when the House divided. But this is a misleading picture. Most motions in the House were passed 'on the voices' without a division. A large number of the divisions were on amendments to climate legislation put by the various teals, so it would be more accurate to say the government was voting with the teals. An examination of voting records suggests Spender was the most 'right-leaning' teal and Ryan and Daniel the most 'left-leaning'.

As Monique Ryan said in her first speech, 'every one of my votes will be a conscience vote'. Unlike Liberal or Labor members, they did not have to mask their own preferences and vote for a party line. Historian Frank Bongiorno (2022: 9), however, commented that, in one sense, the teals were closer to being a mass party than are the Liberals as they involved a larger number of active supporters in their electorates.

The teals benefited in 2022 from mustering an enthusiastic team of supporters. They also benefited from the ineptness of the Liberal campaign. In Warringah, the Liberals had the chance to preselect a moderate candidate more in touch with the electorate than was former member Tony Abbott. They instead chose a candidate widely regarded as divisive on gender and other issues. The Liberal campaign also suffered from arrogance and a sense of entitlement. Liberals often referred to teals 'stealing' their seats and votes (and sometimes the media adopted the same terminology). The teals benefited from many voters' increasing disdain for what they saw as a two-party duopoly akin to Coles and Woolworths, which political scientists Richard Katz and Peter Mair (1995) had dubbed political 'cartelisation'.

As former Liberal prime minister Malcom Turnbull (2023: 9) has reflected, the Liberal Party in 2022 'was seen as socially conservative, homophobic, misogynistic, reluctant to act on climate and, especially under Scott Morrison, profoundly untrustworthy'. As political commentator Michelle Grattan (2022) put it, some potential teal voters 'would find Morrison's ultra-blokey style uncongenial and alienating'. Even one of the Liberal Party's own MPs, Julia Banks (2021: 117), called it a boys' club. It is notable that all seven teals elected in 2022 were women, while six of the Liberals they replaced were men.

As the campaign progressed, the Liberals' attempts to staunch the loss of votes to the teals showed an increasing degree of desperation. Allegra

Spender, a businesswoman with degrees from Cambridge and the University of London, who had worked in the UK Treasury, was disparaged by Liberals as the 'superficial daughter of a fashion designer'. Former Liberal prime minister John Howard called the teals 'anti-Liberal groupies'.

The Labor Party successfully exercised discipline over its numbers, backed by the threat of expulsion for any member 'crossing the floor'. Notwithstanding occasional reports of grumbling, no members crossed the floor or defected in the lower house. So the teals did not get a chance to exercise a decisive vote on any bills.

Both House and Senate cross-benchers could refer matters to committees. They could use speeches and their resources to give more prominence to issues. For example, Allegra Spender commissioned a 'green paper' on tax reform.

Other 'community-focused' independents

There were also other 'voice of … ' independents, such as Helen Haines, who campaigned mainly on improving representation of, and services to, their local area and were typically selected by a group of concerned citizens. They pride themselves on listening to the communities that selected them as candidates, whether through 'town hall meetings' or 'kitchen table conversations' or online (Hendriks and Reid, 2023; and Johnson, 2025). Other independent members such as Dai Le also emphasised their role as representing the interests of their electorates. Rebekha Sharkie placed herself as a middle voice between the two major parties, as exemplified by the name of her micro-party (formerly the Nick Xenophon Team): the Centre Alliance. Andrew Wilkie was best known for his strong stances on gambling reform, climate change and foreign policy.

As independent Tony Windsor (2015, p. 28) observed, electing a crossbencher, or even going close to electing one, can mean an electorate is no longer 'taken for granted'.

This increased emphasis on local candidates has implications for the major parties. After former NSW premier and deputy senate leader Kristina

Keneally lost what had been regarded as a safe Labor seat to Dai Le, they are likely to be reluctant, at least for a while, to 'parachute in' high flyers to areas where they have no links.

The Greens

The Greens have been a longstanding fixture on the Senate crossbench. Adam Bandt had held his House seat of Melbourne since 2010. What was novel following the 2022 election was that he was joined by three colleagues, all from inner Brisbane seats.

During the first term of the Albanese Government, the Greens sought to broaden their brand. They promoted themselves as the party for renters, advocated (with a giant toothbrush) the incorporation of dental coverage into Medicare and were strongly critical of Israel's actions in Gaza. The high-profile Max Chandler-Mather spoke at a CFMEU rally. While all this may have attracted some voters, it possibly alienated some longstanding supporters who had been attracted to the Greens' emphasis on protecting the environment and threatened species and their calls for stronger action on climate change under earlier leaders such as Bob Brown and Christine Milne.

The main impact the Greens had on legislation was delaying some housing initiatives. They achieved $3 billion in additional funding for public and community housing, but in hindsight probably held out too long and many voters likely viewed them as too stubborn or even obstructionist.

The Greens' national primary vote in the House was unchanged at the 2025 election but its distribution was less helpful for them. They lost three of their four seats there, including that of their leader Adam Bandt. They retained their 11 senators at the election (but one, Dorinda Cox, later defected to Labor) and now have sole rather than shared balance of power in the upper house. Their new leader is Larissa Waters, an environmental lawyer, seen as a capable moderate.

How the independents won in 2022

As we discuss further in our 2025 paper 'The psephology of the Teal independents', crossbenchers in the House need to do three things to be elected. First, they need to drag the sitting party's primary vote far enough below 50 per cent. Second, they need to get ahead of the other major party, either on primaries or after preferences. Third, they need to get a substantial proportion of the non-sitting major party's preferences.

In 2022 no crossbenchers won a majority of primary votes and many were placed second (or in one case third). Preferences therefore play a crucial role. The teals are placed in the middle of the political spectrum. In political scientist Alan Siaroff's (2003) terminology, they are a 'hinge' group rather than a 'wing' group. This puts them in a position to pick up preferences from whichever major party they can outpoll on primary votes. By contrast, One Nation is at the right-wing end so would pick up few Labor preferences while the Greens are on the left wing so struggle to pick up Liberal preferences. Tactical voting by supporters of the major party who believe that their party cannot win the seat, but a crossbencher might, also plays a role.

In the Senate the Greens won a senator in each state. Other crossbencher candidates were usually competing for the sixth, final, seat in each state. Clive Palmer's United Australia Party won a seat in Victoria and the Jacqui Lambie Network banner won a seat in Tasmania. For the first time, the ACT did not split one Labor/one Liberal with independent David Pocock replacing the Liberal.

Life on the crossbench

The crossbenchers face a heavy workload. While major party MPs just follow instructions from their whips, crossbenchers have to assess the merits of legislation before deciding their stance.

For the first time two crossbenchers (Andrew Wilkie and Rebekha Sharkie) were appointed to the Speaker's Panel, and so played a role in guiding proceedings on the floor of the House. New sessional orders gave the crossbench priority for three questions during Question Time and guaranteed them opportunities to play a prominent role in other debates. They used the latter to initiate debates on diverse matters of public importance such as immigration detention, the cost of living, climate change and eating disorders. In the first half of the parliamentary term 150 crossbench amendments were agreed to.[2]

The teals were strategic about their committee work, generally keeping to areas of most concern to their constituents. Zali Steggall served on the climate change committee; Zoe Daniel on communications and the arts, employment and social media committees; Allegra Spender on economics and migration; Monique Ryan on health and the NDIS; Kate Chaney on social policy and NDIS; and Kylea Tink on human rights and the library. None were on more than three committees and none were chairs nor deputies.

Senator Pocock's achievements included the establishment of the Economic Inclusion Advisory Committee. This makes suggestions to the government on measures to include in the budget.

Crossbench members drew attention to issues affecting some disadvantaged groups in the community, such as Senator Lambie on military veterans, Andrew Wilkie on problem gamblers and the Greens on health.

Looking forward

The House crossbench shrank after the 2025 election. (For a few days in May it looked to be larger, with the Nationals joining it.) Only one Coalition defector, Andrew Gee, held their seat. As noted above, the Greens lost three seats.

One teal seat was lost before the election, when a redistribution abolished North Sydney. An additional teal was elected in Bradfield, which had absorbed some of North Sydney. One teal, Zoe Daniel, lost her seat, to Tim Wilson, the Liberal MP she had defeated in 2022. There was a 'sophomore surge' in the majority of the teal seats, but it was only small.

There were also many near misses, especially when teal candidates who had run in 2022 stood again in 2025. There are now three Coalition and three Labor seats where a swing of less than 3 per cent would hand it to a crossbench candidate.

Table 3.1: Votes (%) of selected independent candidates (winner in bold)

		Primary vote			Two-candidate preferred (swing)
		Before/estimated after redistribution			
		2019	2022	2025	2025
Zali Steggall	Warringah (NSW)	43	**45** / 40	**40**	**61** (+1)
Kate Chaney	Curtin (WA)	..	29 / 30	**32**	53 (+2)
Sophie Scamps	Mackellar (NSW)	..	38 / 39	**38**	56 (+4)
Allegra Spender	Wentworth (NSW)	..	36 / 36	**36**	58 (+9)
Zoe Daniel	Goldstein (Vic)	..	**34** / 34	31	50 (-2)
Monique Ryan	Kooyong (Vic)	..	**40** / 39	**34**	**51** (-2)
Nicolette Boele	Bradfield (NSW)		21 / 23	**27**	**50** (+3)
Alex Dyson	Wannon (Vic)	..	19 / 19	31	47 (+0)
Jessie Price	Bean (ACT)	..	..	26	50 (n.a.)
Kate Hulett	Fremantle (WA)	..	..	23	49 (n.a.)
Caz Heise	Cowper (NSW)	..	26 / 26	29	47 (-0)
Dai Le	Fowler (NSW)	..	**30** / 29	**33**	53 (+1)
Helen Haines	Indi (Vic)	32	**41** / 41	**42**	59 (-0)
Andrew Wilkie	Clark (Tas)	**50**	**46** / 46	**49**	70 (-0)

SOURCES Australian Electoral Commission; estimates from Antony Green

The unexpected landslide to Labor in the House in 2025 means the crossbench there will not be decisive in this parliament. But after the 2028 or 2031 election, crossbenchers may well hold the balance of power. Some may guarantee 'supply and confidence' to one of the major parties. But the passage of individual pieces of legislation may require the government to make a convincing case for it.

Note: Thanks to Antony Green for estimates of the effect of the redistributions and Josh Black, Linda Botterill, Michelle Grattan, John Halligan, Chris Wallace, Mary Walsh and Larissa Waters for helpful comments.

References

Banks, J, *Power Play: Breaking Through Bias, Barriers and Boys' Clubs*, Hardie Grant, Melbourne, 2021.

Berger, M, 'Beyond the bench: Crossbench influence on a contemporary House of Representatives', *Australasian Parliamentary Review*, vol. 39, no. 2, 2024, pp. 27–39.

Bongiorno, F, 'Politics by other means', *Australian Book Review*, no. 442, May 2022.

Grattan, M, 'Could going too negative on "teals" do Liberals more harm than good?', *The Conversation*, 24 April 2022.

Hawkins, J, and King, T, 'The psephology of the teal independents', updated version of paper presented to University of Canberra seminar, 2025.

Hendriks, C, and Reid, R, 'The rise and impact of Australia's movement for Community Independents', in Gauja, A, Sawer, M, and Sheppard, J (eds), *Watershed: The 2022 Australian Federal Election*, ANU Press, Canberra, 2023, pp. 279–304.

Holmes à Court, S, *The Big Teal*, Monash University Publishing, Melbourne, 2022.

Johnson, A, 'Doing politics differently: Safeguarding Australian democracy', in Chang, A, and Grundy, A (eds), *What's the Big Idea?*, Australia Institute Press, Canberra, 2025, pp. 107–10.

Katz, R, and Mair, P, 'Changing models of party organization and party democracy: the emergence of the cartel party', *Party Politics*, vol. 1, no. 1, 1995, pp. 5–28.

Sawer, M, 'Wearing your politics on your sleeve: The role of political colours in social movements', *Social Movement Studies*, vol. 6, no. 1, 2007, pp. 39–56.

Siaroff, A, 'Two-and-a-half party systems and the comparative role of the half', *Party Politics*, vol. 9, no. 3, 2003, pp. 267–90.

Turnbull, M, 'The Libs are all right', *The Monthly*, May 2023, pp. 8–10.

Windsor, T, *Windsor's Way*, Melbourne University Press, Melbourne, 2015.

PART II
PUBLIC INSTITUTIONS

CHAPTER 4

REFORMING THE AUSTRALIAN PUBLIC SERVICE: HIGHER CAPACITY, GREATER INTEGRITY

JOHN HALLIGAN

The Australian public service (APS) enjoyed a heyday during the Albanese Government's first term because it implemented and sustained a carefully designed reform program. This was by comparison with the previous Morrison Government, which represented a nadir for public governance and administration. The APS reform program has been both expansive and systematically pursued, engaging a spectrum of public servants in developing and implementing it. The program is claimed to be the most significant since the first Hawke Government, and in some respects, it exceeds that in breadth, schematic planning and implementation.

The inheritance from the previous government was fundamental in shaping the Albanese Government's early agenda. Rectifying unique governance failures was challenging for political and public service leaders. It was an ambitious reform program with a myriad of elements, so here I have focused on encapsulating and evaluating the most salient.

A public service exposed to malfeasance

As I have explored elsewhere (Halligan, 2023; 2024), under the Morrison Coalition Government (2019–2022), the public sector was traumatised by politicisation, externalisation, integrity issues, accountability deficits and corrupt practices. The prime minister was central in orchestrating partisan governance. The depth of questionable practices was indicated by their penetrating down the system, facilitated by political actors and compliant public servants. Systematic overt pork barrelling, appointment biases and other acts serving partisan interests increased dramatically. Their magnitude and scope indicated a governing style committed to partisanship and practices that lacked the tenets of good public governance (Halligan, 2024).

The Robodebt fiasco exemplified government dysfunction. The government knowingly acted unlawfully, negligently and secretly, and refused responsibility for the scheme's failure. After years of citizen and expert protestations and public inquiries, the government announced in 2020 that it would repay 470 000 invalid debts (Dawson, 2023; Morton, 2024).

There were other issues too, notably the government's behaviour towards the institution of the public service as exemplified by its reliance on external labour hire and consultants, and its rejection of the Independent Review of the Australian Public Service's recommendations (Thodey report, 2019; Halligan and Evans, 2024).

Albanese Government's reform agenda

The Albanese Government's challenge was how to address these issues and its own policy agenda with a public sector reform program that spanned the public service and the institutions of governance. It would be assisted by its commitment to strengthening capability and integrity and to rebalancing relationships between the public service and the political executive.

Much of the agenda derived from the Thodey report (2019),[1] the 'bedrock' for the reform agenda with 40 recommendations regarded as relevant, systematically applied and reported on (APS Reform, 2023a). The Labor Government's program was also an extension of the Thodey report because of the continuity of key participants, Glyn Davis, head of the Department of the Prime Minister and Cabinet, and Gordon De Brouwer, Australian Public Service Commissioner. There was a need to 'reshape traditions that fall on hard times' (Davis, 2021). As the consequences of institutional decay continued to emerge, rebuilding and refining the foundational elements of Australia's government became an imperative.

The Albanese Government had an unrivalled opportunity to drive a comprehensive reform program because core governance institutions needed renewal, basic principles and values reaffirmed, and the public service reformed. A plethora of audits, reviews, and taskforces investigated issues and means for moving forward. The overdue rebalancing of roles and relationships within the system (Halligan, 2020; 2024) was now apparent in official statements about rebuilding capability and strengthening institutional independence. The Minister for the Public Service provided constant political leadership, an ultimate goal being 'to rebuild the culture of frank and fearless advice, integrity and stewardship'. A merit and integrity-based framework for appointing and managing the performance of senior public servants formed the centrepiece of the program (Gallagher, 2023). Developing the APS culture through top-down leadership became an imperative, including augmenting the APS Commissioner's responsibilities.

The reform program was implemented using a staged roadmap, with dimensions reflecting international experience and benchmarking. The phases of the APS reform program were based on four priorities: an APS that 'embodies integrity in all it does', 'puts people and business at the centre of policy and services', 'is a model employer and 'has the capability to do the job well (Gallagher, 2023). For the second phase, the priorities were also expressed as: 'bolster integrity through legislative amendments and non-legislative initiatives', 'build an outwardly-engaged APS' and 'strengthen capability' An elaborate reform performance framework covers the pillars, 'outcomes',[2] indicators, performance measures and metrics (APSC, 2024a).

The government mobilised an extensive cast of senior officials and a range of agencies to investigate, make decisions and provide oversight. The core apparatus for reform has three governance levels: agency delivery, oversight units for the reform program and program management, and the decision makers: the minister, the secretary's board (and subcommittees), and the APSC commissioner and executive board (APSC, 2024a, Figure 4).

They envisaged three phases of progress: establishing the foundations, embedding the reforms and continuous improvement. The first entailed developing the program logic, designing delivery and implementation architecture, launching initiatives, and developing a transformation strategy. Twelve departments and central agencies led on process initiatives. Several were introduced at an early stage; for example, the National Anti-Corruption Commission, an employment audit, an in-house consulting service, and annual reporting on APS reform (APS Reform, 2023b, 2024a; Australian Government, 2023).

Two of the priorities are summarised here. The one centred on people and business for policy and services has two 'outcomes'. The first is that the APS delivers human-centred policy and service and covers a range of briefings, surveys partnerships and ensures quality engagement. The second is that the APS must have 'effective relationships and partnerships with First Nations peoples'.

The 'model employer' priority has three desired 'outcomes'. The first is the APS 'employee value proposition is attractive' with various actions and plans for improving service conditions. The second is the APS sets the standard for equity inclusion and diversity. The third is setting standards and producing results supported by metrics for First Nations employment and cultural competency (APSC, 2024c).

Reforming to embody integrity

A core reform priority is that 'the APS embodies integrity in everything it does' with two 'outcomes'. The first outcome is 'public sector employees act with and champion integrity' with initiatives including 'pro-integrity systems and culture' and an integrity maturity model; however, the most concrete results do not apply directly to employees, but senior staff. The completed initiatives focus on 'strengthening integrity across the public sector', and cover a range of actions that do not directly affect employees. Specific measures included a taskforce on integrity systems, the Public Governance, Performance and Accountability Fraud and Corruption Rule, strengthening the APS Commissioner's 'own motion' powers to undertake inquiries into employees, and protections for whistleblowers (APSC, 2024a: 13–4).

The second 'outcome' is identifying employees as 'stewards of the public service' with three completed initiatives for supporting employees. The most directly relevant was installing stewardship as an APS value; the others were increasing the Secretaries Board's transparency and producing an annual ministerial statement on reform progress (APSC, 2024a: 15).

In the post-election era ministers paid greater attention to integrity and to mitigating corrupt practices. Early government initiatives included establishing a corruption and integrity commission in 2023 comparable to state bodies (see chapter 5 of this volume); initiating a Royal Commission into Robodebt; and a review of grants administration and processes, and issues concerning responsible government.

The issues arising from Robodebt were the main contributor to the malaise of the public service. The Royal Commission on the scheme produced 57 recommendations. The Royal Commissioner (RC, 2023: iii) was aghast about:

> how little thought was given to how it would affect welfare
> recipients and the lengths to which public servants were prepared
> to go to oblige ministers on a quest for savings. Truly dismaying was
> the revelation of dishonesty and collusion to prevent the Scheme's
> lack of legal foundation coming to light [and] the ineffectiveness
> of … institutional checks and balances.

The ramifications of the Royal Commission's report continued to reverberate because of the impact Robodebt had on the standing and integrity of the public service. A report to the Royal Commission indicated systemic issues and how agencies departed from the principle of and legislation for the public service (Podger, 2023a). The public service continued to be traumatised by the repercussions from the ongoing integrity questions raised by the Commission, unprecedented issues with public service leaders, and revelations about corrupt practices and accountability deficits under past governments (Halligan, 2024). Robodebt was officially declared to be an unprecedented failure in policy design and implementation, and 'the worst failure of public administration in history'. The government implemented many of the Royal Commission's recommendations, including legislation for stronger scrutiny of agencies, while progressing responses to others (Gallagher, 2024a; APSC, 2024a). A Robodebt Centralised Code of Conduct Inquiry Taskforce reported that 12 officials, including two named departmental secretaries, were found to have breached the code of conduct (APSC, 2024d). The decision not to name the other public servants attracted public debate and contributed to the public service malaise.

A further symptom of institutional decline was the behaviour of the Home Affairs Department secretary, Michael Pezzullo, whose actions were unparalleled for a secretary in modern times. He was asked to stand aside pending an investigation of revelations about using his position to influence policy and governance beyond his role and contravening standards, and then removed for breaching the government code of conduct. Concern was expressed about whether his behaviour reflected a 'systemic problem of APS leaders failing to meet their responsibilities' (Podger, 2023b).

The reform process brought about some landmark changes: the establishment of a National Anti-Corruption Commission and a new system of administrative review (Attorney-General's Department, 2023), and integrity was supported through the Open Government Partnership and a review of the code of conduct (APSC, 2024a).

Under the second phase of reform (Gallagher, 2023), a focus was a merit and integrity-based framework for appointing and performance managing senior public servants, including secretaries. Developing the APS culture through top-down leadership became an imperative. The APS Commissioner acquired augmented responsibilities for initiating inquiries into breaches of the Code of Conduct.

A centrepiece was that the APS reduced its reliance on external consultants and contractors by strengthening internal capability and introducing an in-house consulting capacity, Australian Government Consulting, and an APS Strategic Commissioning Framework (Australian Government, 2023) that precludes the outsourcing of core functions.

Improving the capabilities of the APS

This major aspect of the reform program has centred on the inherited condition of the APS, plus the use of ongoing programs and fresh initiatives. The 'outcome' is that 'the APS continuously improves its capabilities' and the initiatives span capability reviews, an evaluation culture and funding to reinvest in capability. There are also those that pertain directly to the diminished APS: an employment audit and in-house consulting. The results cover a workforce plan, a strategic commissioning framework, 'leadership at all levels', specialised capabilities and, vaguely, 'developing great policy'.

The smaller government programs of Coalition governments meant that agencies were abolished and consolidated, and government activities were reviewed for contestability. Public service staff numbers were reduced, and staffing ceilings introduced, along with a commitment to holding average staffing at the 2006–07 level. Spending on labour contractors and consultants increased greatly while spending on Australian public service wages and salaries was flat (Thodey, 2019: 186). Externalising public service work registered a huge impact. By 2021–22 over 37 per cent of staff were not directly employed public servants. The external labour workforce in 2022 comprised outsourced service providers (52 per cent), contractors (33.7), labour hire (12.5) and consultants (1.8) (Australian Government, 2023; Podger and Halligan, 2023).

The implosion of the consultancy industry in 2023 provided evidence of questionable practices that affected public governance. Consultancy companies had long presided over much of the public sector as an integral part of the operations of government. Scrutiny by the Albanese Government and Parliament clearly exposed the main issues: details on the scale of the para-public service, questions about the costs of relying on consultants at the expense of developing internal capabilities, and issues concerning conflicts of interest and inconceivable violations of trust (SFPARC, 2024). The latter question led to the downfall of PricewaterhouseCoopers, which used privileged access to confidential tax information to benefit their multinational clients,[3] and had broader ramifications.

The government was highly committed to reducing dependence on external actors. Its response was to increase ongoing public sector positions, reduce the reliance on outsourcing and external consultants and abolish the staffing cap. An in-house consulting capability, Australian Government Consulting, was established to reduce excessive reliance on external advice. The objectives were 'to provide a new source of high-quality management consulting services', which could support government priorities at a lower cost than external sources, while strengthening internal APS capabilities. A key tool for doing so is a strategic commissioning framework based on the precept that employees undertake core APS work and that the institution enhances its skills and organisational capabilities. Spending on consultants was reduced by $624 million for 2023–24 (APSC, 2025).

The revival of and commitment to the capability review program was another indication of normalisation, particularly with a legislative basis from 2024 that required a quinquennial review for agencies, and the tabling of the reports in Parliament (APSC, 2025a). Eight agency reviews were completed in this term of government and two were in process. It is unclear whether a meta-review of the program will validate the template in the future.

Other innovative actions to strengthen organisational capability included the Capability Reinvestment Fund, which invested in innovative projects typically involving multiple agencies, usually led by a central agency (APSC, 2024c).

The Australian development of professions within the APS began in 2019 (long after the United Kingdom: Craft and Halligan, 2020) to increase employees' capability in specific areas and to address gaps. Heads of streams were to provide leadership and stewardship. The Albanese Government inherited three professions – data, digital and HR. Other foreshadowed streams (legal, economics and policy) were dropped, and the concept has been weakly utilised compared to the UK, which refined the profession model to encompass four types and 31 professions.[4]

Policy capability has been problematic in Australia for over a decade. Analysis of capability review reports (2011–2015) indicated that departments were weak on policy development, strategy, research and analysis, policy implementation, stakeholder engagement and evaluation (Halligan, 2020). Despite recommendations to enhance policy capability, the APS did not formalise an agenda until it created a policy hub. However, Prime Minister Morrison rejected the policy development role because he believed the public service had to focus on implementation and delivery (Halligan, 2023).[5] The Albanese Government has not reactivated a policy capacity profession, even though recent capability reviews have reported strategic policy as a field requiring development. The approach was to provide learning resources and workshops through the APS Academy, and an Australian Government Futures Primer to enhance strategic foresight capability (APSC, 2024a: 21).

Enhancing the APS Professions has been confined to Complex Project Management and Procurement, Contract Management and Evaluation (which the Thodey report, 2019: 223, had recommended to ensure programs and policies were evaluated systematically. The Department of Finance had been developing a central evaluation function by building expertise and practices culminating in the creation of the Australian Centre for Evaluation in Treasury (see chapter 6, this volume). The centre's survey of the state of evaluation documented its mixed condition (ACE, 2025).

Ensuring digital transformation is here to stay

The Thodey (2019) reform agenda regarded digital as a core component which would require incorporating digital transformation and public administration. Much of the governance and operating principles for digital governance had been installed by the time of the Albanese Government. The imperative was to embed and extend this through digital mainstreaming and architecture and whole-of-government practices.

The Digital Transformation Agency (DTA) is an agency within the Finance portfolio responsible for supporting the digital transformation of government services. Its mission is to 'provide strategic and policy leadership and expert investment advice and oversight to drive government digital transformation that delivers benefits to all Australians'. Strategic objectives include co-delivery of the Data and Digital Government Strategy and Implementation Plan; leadership in policy design, strategy, advice and whole-of-government architecture; and overseeing the 'whole-of-government digital and ICT investment portfolio' (DTA, 2025).

Highlights have been implementing the Data and Digital Strategic plan and enhancing DTA architecture for supporting departments. From 2025, digital experience policy-based benchmarks apply for the performance of digital services and supporting agencies to design and deliver improved experiences in the digital service ecosystem.[6]

Australia has recorded commendable scores for its digital performance compared to other countries. According to the OECD Digital Government Index for 2023, Australia was ranked fifth overall. Of the six dimensions to the index, Australia performs exceptionally well with four (noting that indicators do not necessarily represent actual impacts but design, building blocks and capacities): Digital by design (rank: 1st). Government as a platform (5th), User-driven (4th) and Proactiveness (5th). Of the two remaining rankings, Data-driven is 8th, and Open by default is 23rd (OECD, 2024). The Blavatnick Index of Public Administration's (2024) 'digital services theme' ranked Australia 41. According to Adobe's Digital Government Index, Australia ranked second in 2024, and the myGov website was ranked first internationally (out of 102 government websites) (Adobe, 2024). This followed the reintroduction of a life events approach (pioneered by Centrelink: Halligan, 2008), for myGov and the Services Australia website.

Performance reporting framework

The contributions of independent agencies to good governance need to be recognised; here I touch on just one example. The Australian National Audit Office played a pivotal role in exposing the misallocation of grants under the Morrison Government and is notable for its endeavours to improve performance reporting. Sustained processes over the past decade to enhance performance reporting have ultimately achieved considerable success in reducing minimal compliance. Following a major review in 2018 of the *Public Governance Performance and Accountability Act 2013*, which found progress was poor and inadequate compliance too prevalent, the pressure on departments and agencies intensified through the use of performance statement audits, designed to improve transparency and the quality of performance reporting, incentives for imbedding a performance culture, and ultimately accountability to parliament and the public. These audits focused on selective departments and agencies from 2019 to 2024, with the number of audits increasing over time and defaulting practices publicly documented by the Auditor General. The audits addressed improving performance reporting and making use of the performance framework internally for strategic planning, management and driving business improvement. The overall position was still mixed, but substantial overall improvement in performance reporting was evident (ANAO, 2024; van Dooren, Bouckaert and Halligan, 2025).

Institutional development
Strengthening government administration

There was an immediate need to confront the aggrandisement of prime ministerial power which occurred when Morrison appointed himself to the portfolios of five of his ministers without advising parliament, relevant departments, the public, or even the minister. The Solicitor-General's advice was that 'an unpublicised appointment to administer a department … undermines … the relationship between the Ministry and the public service'. Further, the ability of parliament and the public to determine 'which Ministers have been appointed to administer which departments is critical to the proper functioning of responsible government, because [they] determine the matters for which a Minister is legally and politically responsible' (2022, secs 44, 48). The report of the Bell inquiry (2022) recommended how to prevent these issues arising again, which the government accepted.

The *Public Service Amendment Act 2024* clarified ministerial responsibilities by limiting minister power to direct agency heads on employment questions (APSC 2024a: 14).

Patronage in appointments to government agencies

The Senate Legal and Constitutional Affairs References Committee reported on the performance and integrity of the administrative review system, and the selection process for the Administrative Appeals Tribunal (AAT). The then Attorney-General's revised protocol for appointments allowed the government to decide on the appointments rather than adhere to those recommended by the AAT (SLCARC 2022, 40–44). The committee reported a lack of transparency with AAT appointments, concerns about the risk of patronage, and disquiet about the trend in appointments. The proportion of AAT political appointees was low under Prime Minister Howard but rose greatly under subsequent Coalition governments. Politicised appointments were also apparent with other tribunals. The stacking of public boards with political appointments was rife, with prestigious positions being rewards for party loyalists. The range of diplomatic positions awarded to politicians also increased (Wood et al., 2022; Halligan, 2025).

Issues with administrative review were publicly scrutinised and reformed (Attorney-General's Department, 2023). The subsequent Albanese

Government reverted to a more mainstream approach to appointments, although patronage appointments still occurred (for example, envoys) and ministerial advisers increased (Halligan, 2025).

Senior public service

Departmental secretaries have usually been professional public servants, but top positions have also been subject to politicisation in two respects, providing opportunities for patronage appointments. The propensity of Coalition prime ministers to sack departmental secretaries, often for unclear reasons, was notable during the past two decades. There have also been issues with heads of central agencies where the career paths of appointees have been overly partisan, and the merit basis questioned. Two of the most egregious derelictions of responsibilities involved departmental secretaries who received preferment by the government of the day (Halligan, 2024).

The head of the public service in Australia has traditionally changed when there is a new government, and most of the appointees have not been overly contentious. Following the modern Australian convention (and despite Thodey report recommendations: 2019), Prime Minister Albanese chose the head of the Department of the Prime Minister and Cabinet.[7] Although his appointment was from outside the public service, his credentials were exemplary, including membership of the Thodey Review. But his predecessor was regarded as a political fixer (Halligan, 2024). According to Podger (2025b), Minister Gallagher reneged on her 2023 promise to reform appointment (and termination) processes for secretaries and the Public Service Commissioner by failing to create an incentive system that achieves 'an appropriate balance between responsiveness and independence', akin to the processes under the Hawke Government.

The APS has also needed to rebuild foundational elements of governance, which has exposed limitations. Unintended consequences arose in the short term because of disruptive inheritances, and missteps, but it will require the medium to long term to clarify how effectively the reforms resonate, and whether they will endure if politicisation occurs again.

The goal of rebuilding the culture, integrity and stewardship (Gallagher, 2023) subsequently focused on stewardship as a panacea in amendments to the Public Service Act, and constraints on ministers directing secretaries on staff employment. However, the idea that public servants have become 'guardians of the public interest' because stewardship has been made a core value (Gallagher, 2024b) is fanciful when it does not involve the relationship with the political executive.

The lengthy and contested processes on integrity issues encouraged public debates about transparency, such as freedom of information and whistleblowing, not all of which have been resolved in the public mind. A comprehensive institutional vision has not been fully articulated, and at least one telling review has not been acted upon. The public release of a Review of Public Sector Board Appointments Processes was expected late 2023, but it was still with the government in 2025.[8] Where do governments draw the line for their integrity?

Further reform was promised, but questions remained about the nature of change and the level of attention given to embedding reforms; an institutional vision and roadmap emerged piecemeal; and pivotal reviews were not acted upon in a timely way.

How is the public service to be insulated in a way that reinforces institutional governance? The main reason reform implementation has failed in Australia has been pendulum swings in government. The Albanese Government has placed a huge emphasis on integrity, but this matters little if a backsliding government takes office (and the government provided a precedent by not disclosing its review of appointments). There are also questions about its poor record in responding to freedom of information requests (CPI, 2025).

The reform process has widely engaged senior staff but is heavily top-down with reform governance descending from the Minister for the Public Service, the Secretaries Board and the APSC (APSC, 2024a: 26). Only passing reference, and without explicit elaboration, is made to the need for reform to be bottom-up as well in order to realise 'whole-of-program outcomes' (APS, 2024a: 6). There are however constant stipulations about applying values (stewardship) and integrity in everything.

While surveys indicate that the service is perceived to be operating in a superior way (which could be expected given the low ebb it had reached), anecdotal indications suggest that public servants perceive a gap between leaders and the led or what has been previously reported in Australia as 'vertical solitude' (Jabes et al., 1992), with poor communication down the line about reform agendas and how they apply to their agencies.

Some departments neglected to counsel staff about Robodebt issues because they did not consider them relevant to their agencies. Casey and Maley (2025: 21) analysed Freedom of Information data from over 100 agencies to examine public service leaders' communications with staff after the Royal Commission report was released. Their analysis was based on the premise that 'if leaders do not communicate about lessons, then no lessons can be learnt'. They report that 'only 29 agencies engaged with the underlying cultural issues ... Some of these leaders responded with genuine introspection and engaged with the challenge to public servants' sense of identity ... only four of the 16 departments directly addressed the problem of over-responsiveness' (p. 32).

Australia's international standing in public service

This has been the most comprehensive reform program of the past 40 years, judged by the breadth of measures and their sustained implementation. It has been engineered in a way that provides an international model, but there are limitations. Understanding of it can sometimes be obscured by self-congratulations, while ignoring areas of weakness, and ambiguous evidence or contrary indicators.

The Blavatnik Index is used by the APSC to herald 'Australia as an international leader in APS reform' (APSC 2024a, 8) and Glyn Davis (2025), the former DPMC secretary, notes that Australia is ranked eighth for 'overall effectiveness of its national public service'. Of the four 'domains' of the Index (each with four components), Australia scores well on Strategy and Leadership at seventh place (with Strategic Capacity, at fifth place, the best component). For the Public Policy Domain that evaluates 'core public administration functions', the rank is 15th with the policymaking component being seventh. Australia's rank for the National Delivery Domain is ninth with the 'system oversight' component (third) being the best overall result. For other components Australia's lowest ranks are tax administration at 41, and crisis and risk management at 49. The index is advanced as a tool for country learning. Much depends on the sources used to produce composite indicators.

Australia's international ranking for the corruption perceptions index was back in the top ten in 2024 with a score of 77 (having dropped to a low of 73 in 2016 following a 2012 peak of 85) (Transparency International Australia, 2025).[9]

According to the OECD (2024, 8), the figure for high or moderately high trust in the federal government was 46 per cent in 2023, above the OECD average, and an increase from 2021.

APSC (2024b: 3) surveys report that overall trust in the APS has 'remained steady' while trust in specific services is stable.

How do we envision a system of innumerable moving parts?

The Albanese Government has addressed acute problems with the public service. Despite debates about the pace of change and the handling of some issues, it has a strong record of achievement in its APS reforms. A more balanced executive branch with firmer checks and balances, and improved transparency and accountability, has become apparent. A second term is needed to progress long-term improvements to the public service as envisaged by the government's agenda and to substantiate their value and institutionalisation. A discussion paper, supported in principle by 28 mainly mandarins, advances areas where the reforms have been tardy or desirable options have not been picked up (Podger, 2024).

The official claim that this is the most significant reform program in 40 years (APSC, 2025) needs to be followed up by a more reflective judgment about the condition of the public service that goes beyond a barrage of accomplishments of varying levels. The performance framework does recognise that 'deep-dive research is required after three to five years, but this is confined to 'the lived experience of people and businesses affected by APS reform outcomes' (APSC, 2024a: 29). Another model was the Task Force on Management Improvement (1992), which provided a mature analysis of a decade of management reform under the Hawke Government, except a more expansive review would be required to encompass the complexities of this enormous reform program.

References

Adobe, Digital Government Index for Australia, 3rd ed., <2024.https://business.adobe.
    com/content/dam/dx/au/en/resources/reports/16568122_anz_fy24q4_dx_aemf_
    thirdparty_gdpi_report_and_kit_au_fa(1).pdf>.
APS Reform, Thodey Review Progress Report, November 2023a,
    <https://www.apsreform.gov.au/resources/reports/thodey-review-progress-report-
    november-2023>.
— Australian Public Service Reform: Annual Progress Report 2023, 2023b.
    Australian Public Service Commission, Trust and Satisfaction in Australian
    Democracy: 2023 National Survey, Canberra, 2023.
— Australian Public Service Reform: Annual Progress Report 2024, 2024a.
— Trust in Australian Public Services: 2024 Annual Report, 2024b.
— State of the Service Report 2023–24, Canberra, 2024c.
— Capability Review Program, 2025, <https://www.apsc.gov.au/initiatives-and-programs/
    workforce-information/research-analysis-and-publications/capability-review-
    program>.
— APS Reform Branch, Laying the Foundations for Enduring Change. Outcomes and
    Emerging Impacts from the First 2 years of the APS Reform Agenda. Evaluation
    snapshot, March 2025, <https://www.apsreform.gov.au/sites/default/files/resource/
    download/2025_0320%20APS%20Reform%20Evaluation%20Snapshot_accessible_0.
    pdf>.
Attorney-General's Department, Administrative Review Reform: Issues Paper, 2023,
    <https://consultations.ag.gov.au/legal-system/administrative-review-reform-issues-
    paper/user_uploads/public-issues-paper-new-system-federal-administrative-review.pdf>.
Australian Centre for Evaluation, State of Evaluation in the Australian Government 2025,
    Treasury, 2025, <https://evaluation.treasury.gov.au/publications/state-evaluation-
    australian-government-2025>.
Australian Government, The Australian Government's report on the Audit of Employment,
    2023, <https://www.finance.gov.au/sites/default/files/2023-05/Audit%20of%20
    Employment%20-%20Report_1.pdf>.
Australian National Audit Office, Audits of the Annual Performance Statements of
    Australian Government Entities – 2022–23, 12 February 2024, <https://www.anao.
    gov.au/work/performance-statements-audit/audits-of-the-annual-performance-
    statements-of-australian-government-entities-2022-23>.
Bell, V, Report of the Inquiry into the Appointment of the Former Prime Minister to
    Administer Multiple Departments, 25 November 2022.
Blavatnik School of Government, Blavatnik Index of Public Administration 2024,
    University of Oxford, Oxford, 2024, <https://www.bsg.ox.ac.uk/sites/default/
    files/2024-12/Blavatnik-Index-Report-2024.pdf>.
Casey, D, and Maley, M, 'Robodebt and the limits of learning: exploring meaning-making
    after a crisis', Journal of European Public Policy, 2025, <https://doi.org/10.1080/1350176
    3.2025.2513651>.
Centre for Public Integrity, 'Still shrouded in secrecy', Briefing Paper, 2025, <https://
    publicintegrity.org.au/wp-content/uploads/2025/07/Still-Shrouded-in-Secrecy-2.pdf>.
Craft, J, and Halligan, J, Advising Governments in the Westminster Tradition: Policy Advisory
    Systems in Australia, Britain, Canada and New Zealand, Cambridge University Press,
    Cambridge, 2020.

Davis, G, 'The first task is to find the right answer … Public service and the decline of capability', Jim Carlton Annual Integrity Lecture, Melbourne Law School, Melbourne University, 7 May 2021, <https://www.accountabilityrt.org/the-first-task-is-to-find-the-right-answer-public-service-and-the-decline-of-capability/>.

— 'Valedictory', National Press Club, Institute of Public Administration Australia, 2025.

Dawson, E, 'Robodebts and roller coasters: Social (in)security in the 48th Parliament', in McCaffrie, B, Grattan, M, and Wallace, C (eds), *The Morrison Government: Governing through crisis, 2019–2022*, UNSW Press, Sydney, 2023, pp. 128–41.

Department of the Prime Minister and Cabinet, *Cabinet Handbook*, 15th ed., Canberra, 2022.

Digital Transformation Agency, 'About us', <https://www.dta.gov.au/about-us>.

Gallagher, K, 'Annual statement on APS Reform', Speech, 2 November 2023, <https://ministers.pmc.gov.au/gallagher/2023/annual-statement-aps-reform>.

— 'Update on Robodebt royal commission reforms', 7 November 2024a, <https://ministers.pmc.gov.au/gallagher/2024/update-robodebt-royal-commission-reforms>.

— 'Annual statement on APS Reform', Speech, 5 December 2024b, <https://ministers.pmc.gov.au/gallagher/2024/annual-statement-aps-reform>.

Halligan, J, *The Centrelink Experiment: Innovation in Service Delivery*, ANU Press, Canberra, 2008.

— *Reforming Public Management and Governance: Impact and Lessons from Anglophone Countries*, Edward Elgar, Cheltenham, UK, 2020.

— Public administrative reform in Australia', in Goldfinch, S (ed.), *International Handbook of Public Administration Reform*, Edward Elgar, Cheltenham, UK, 2023, pp. 390–410.

— 'The Coalition and the institutions of government (2013–2022)', in Prasser, S (ed.), *Tragedy Without Triumph: The Coalition in Office 2013–2022*, Connor Court, Brisbane, 2024, pp. 65–95.

— 'Politicization and political patronage in Australia', in Peters, B, Knox, C, Panizza, F, Ramos, C, and Staroňová, K (eds), *Handbook of Politicization and Political Patronage*, Edward Elgar, Cheltenham, UK, 2025, pp. 413–29.

Halligan, J, and Evans, M, 'The Australian public service', in Evans, M, Dunleavy, P, and Phillimore, J (eds), *Australia's Evolving Democracy: A New Democratic Audit*, LSE Press, London, 2024.

Jabes, J, Jans, N, Frazer-Jans, J, and Zussman, D, 'Managing in the Canadian and Australian public sectors: A comparative study of the vertical solitude', *International Review of Administrative Sciences*, vol. 58, no. 1, 1992, pp. 5–21.

Morton, R, *Mean Streak*, 4th Estate, 2024.

National Anti-Corruption Commission, 'Commonwealth Integrity Survey: Highlights Report: Overall results', 2024.

OECD, '2023 OECD Digital Government Index: Results and key findings', *OECD Public Governance Policy Papers*, no. 44, OECD Publishing, Paris, 2024.

OECD, *Drivers of Trust in Public Institutions in Australia*, OECD Publishing, Paris, 2025.

Podger, A, *Report to the Royal Commission into the Robodebt Scheme*, 2023a, <https://robodebt.royalcommission.gov.au/ publications/andrew-podger-ao-report-robodebt-royal-commission>.

— 'The Pezzullo Affair shows it's time to clarify the APS values and responsibilities', *Mandarin*, 6 October 2023b.

— 'Further reform of the Australian Public Service', Discussion Paper, ANU Centre for Social Research and Methods, July 2024.

Podger, A, and Halligan, J, 'Australian Public Service capability', in Podger, A, Chan, H, Su, T, and Wanna, J (eds), *Dilemmas in Public Management in Greater China and Australia*, ANU Press, Canberra, 2023.

Royal Commission into the Robodebt Scheme, Report, Canberra, 2023.

Senate Finance and Public Administration References Committee (SFPARC), *Management and Assurance of Integrity by Consulting Services: Final Report*, Canberra, 2024.

Senate Legal and Constitutional Affairs References Committee (SLCARC), *The Performance and Integrity of Australia's Administrative Review System*, Canberra, 2022.

Solicitor-General, Opinion, 'In the matter of the validity of the appointment of Mr Morrison to administer the Department of Industry, Science, Energy and Resources', Department of the Prime Minister and Cabinet, 2022.

Task Force on Management Improvement, *The Australian Public Service Reformed: An Evaluation of a Decade of Management Reform*, Australian Government Publishing Service, Canberra, 1992.

Thodey report, *Independent Review of the Australian Public Service, Our Public Service, Our Future*, 2019, <https://pmc.gov.au/sites/default/files/publications/independent-review-aps.pdf>.

Transparency International Australia, 'Australia turns the corner in corruption fight', 11 February 2025, <https://transparency.org.au/australia-turns-the-corner-in-corruption-fight/>.

van Dooren, W, Boukaert, G, and Halligan, J, *Performance Management in the Public Sector*, 3rd ed., Routledge, Oxford, 2025.

Wood, D, Griffiths, K, Stobart, A, and Emslie, O, 'New politics: A better process for public appointments', *Grattan Institute Reports*, no. 2022–09, July 2022.

CHAPTER 5

A DISAPPOINTING START: THE NATIONAL ANTI-CORRUPTION COMMISSION

GEOFFREY WATSON SC

Before the National Anti-Corruption Commission (NACC)[1] was established in 2023, I, along with others, raised concerns that certain of its statutory features, such as the condition that public hearings be held only in 'exceptional circumstances',[2] might hamper its ability to achieve its objectives under the *NACC Act 2022*. These include the 'detection of corrupt conduct', a term that covers a wide range of conduct by public officials.[3]

Yet two years into its existence, the NACC has proven disappointing, not because the scope of its legal powers are limited, but because the probity of its own decision-making in relation to the Robodebt referrals has been questionable, as has the nature of its public activities more generally.

The number of complaints individuals have made regarding the NACC's initial decision regarding the Robodebt referrals – some 900[4] – suggests that the NACC has fallen short of the trust many placed in it. This is a deeply regrettable development, particularly for those who championed its creation. Over time, that trust can no doubt be regained, but doing so will require a serious reckoning with what exactly has gone awry.

In my view, the early years of the NACC raise fundamental questions about whether it possesses the necessary understanding of its jurisdiction, and the ability to hold itself to the ethical standards it is tasked with protecting, and that it requires to occupy a trusted role in ensuring integrity in Australian governance. These are matters that go beyond procedure or structure and can only be addressed at the level of its leadership.

The Robodebt scandal
Royal Commission referrals

The most prominent chapter of the NACC's brief institutional history commenced in early July 2023, when it received corruption referrals from the Royal Commission into Robodebt. The referrals asked the NACC to examine the conduct of six public officials for their possible engagement in corrupt conduct. Five of the six were public servants; the sixth was rumoured to be a prominent former politician.[5]

There is no need to discuss the details of the awful scheme known as Robodebt (Morton, 2024). It was unlawful and those applying the scheme knew it. Worse, it ruined lives. Three men are known to have committed suicide; two other possible instances have been identified; the real figure would be higher. No peacetime administrative failure has been worse.

Given the gravity of the failure, and the NACC's mandate, many expected it to act upon the referrals without hesitation. The public interest could not be greater, and Australians were entitled to know, one way or the other, whether corruption was involved. The referrals were welcomed as a timely opportunity for the NACC to conduct a highly significant investigation in the early days of its operation.

But the NACC took a different view: in a media statement published in June 2024, it announced that it would not be commencing a corruption investigation on the basis of the referrals.[6] Its conclusion – that an investigation would not 'add value in the public interest'[7] – was supported by at least three considerations, which Commissioner Brereton and Deputy Commissioner Rose reiterated in their oral evidence to the Joint Parliamentary Oversight Committee that November.[8]

The first was a lack of utility. Given that it was 'unlikely to obtain significant new evidence', the NACC considered that conducting a corruption investigation would only 'duplicate work' that had 'already been fully explored' in the Royal Commission[9] – a view that is difficult to reconcile with the implicit request for further examination requested by way of the referrals.

The second reason reflected a concern for the six persons referred – the NACC was worried about 'the oppression in subjecting individuals to repeated investigations'.[10] While perhaps an understandable concern, its relevance to the decision at hand remains unclear, particularly given the procedural fairness provisions accorded to subjects of investigation under the NACC Act, and especially when assessed in light of the mismanaged conflict that was ultimately found to have marred the decision.

Third, the NACC observed that because it could not 'grant a remedy', 'impose a sanction', nor 'make any recommendation that could not have been made by the Robodebt Royal Commission', any investigation it undertook could not provide 'any individual remedy or redress' to victims or their families.[11] Deputy Commissioner Rose later raised its inability to impose a 'punishment' or 'fine'.[12]

The NACC's statement ended by disclosing that the NACC Commissioner had delegated its decision to a deputy commissioner, 'in order to avoid any possible perception of a conflict of interest'.[13] The conflict in question was relatively well known. Among those criticised in the Royal Commission report was Ms Kathryn Campbell, the former secretary of the Department of Social Services, who was a former military colleague of the inaugural NACC Commissioner, Paul Brereton AM RFD SC.

The outcry prompted by this decision of the NACC was immediate and sustained. Not only had politicians and bureaucrats repeatedly dismissed the concerns of the public regarding Robodebt; the new integrity agency now also informed the public that Australia's most egregious instance of public administrative failure did not merit a corruption investigation.

Inspector finds misconduct

Following a flood of complaints about the decision, the statutory inspector of the NACC, Gail Furness SC, opened an investigation, seeking advice from the retired Federal Court judge, Alan Robertson SC.[14] In October 2024, Inspector Furness provided her report, finding that Commissioner Brereton breached the rules of natural justice. Rather than removing himself, his involvement in the NACC's decision-making process was 'comprehensive', and he had even participated in formulating the reasons for the decision and in rewriting the media statement. The way in which he mismanaged his conflict of interest was found to have constituted 'officer misconduct' under the NACC Act.[15] In a remarkable turn of events, the first finding of misconduct associated with the NACC was thereby made against its own commissioner.

In a further blow, the inspector found that the media statement released by the NACC was 'misleading'.[16] The assertion that the Australian Public Service (as distinct from the NACC) had 'remedial power' and could grant a remedy or impose a sanction was simply not correct. In any event, one of the six subjects of referral was not a public servant.

Addressing these errors required engaging an outsider – 'an eminent independent person' – to review the decision of the NACC. For reasons that remain unknown to the public, the retired High Court judge, Geoffrey Nettle AC KC, was appointed for this purpose in December 2024.[17] Mr Nettle, who was effectively tasked with re-making the decision of NACC in its place, reversed it, deciding that it should indeed pursue an investigation.[18]

As a result, the corruption investigation into Australia's most serious integrity failing has been significantly delayed, due to findings of institutional misconduct by its flagship integrity agency.

What jurisdiction?

These early missteps of the NACC seem to rest, at least partly, on its conception of its jurisdiction. Its leadership has taken a cautious approach to defining that jurisdiction, influenced to some extent by a hyper-alertness to the threat of litigation. A general overview of the rationale for the existence and jurisdictional bounds of anti-corruption institutions like the NACC may help to place these matters in context.

Anti-corruption bodies

Anti-corruption bodies are in place across all Australian jurisdictions.[19] Though they sit in the executive branch of government, they, for obvious reasons, must always be independent of the government and the legislature. Their operations are restricted to examining the conduct of public officials or governmental or quasi-governmental agencies – although the jurisdiction can extend to the private sector when it intersects with the public sector.

There are two principal reasons why anti-corruption bodies like the NACC are needed. The first and foremost is to improve or restore public trust in our governmental institutions; when that trust erodes, civil society collapses. The second is that public sector corruption is complex and well beyond the capacity of ordinary policing: this is why we give integrity agencies exceptional investigative powers which we would never entrust to the police.[20]

The extent and definition of its jurisdiction was a hotly debated issue when the NACC was being designed. Prior to its establishment, responsibility for investigating corruption within the Australian public sector sat with the Australian Commission for Law Enforcement Integrity (ACLEI) – a body whose narrow remit precluded investigations into public sector corruption of many kinds.[21] In replacing the ACLEI, the NACC was given a statutory duty to investigate potentially corrupt conduct and ample powers to so.

The NACC investigates and exposes corrupt conduct in the public sector – that is the reason for its existence. Accordingly, an effective NACC brings its findings to public attention through its reporting function. In some instances it can go further and find that particular conduct was 'corrupt conduct'. It is by these means that the NACC reassures the public that something is being done to keep government honest, bring bad actors and bad systems to account, and deter aspiring crooks.

Importantly, the NACC has neither policing nor quasi-judicial functions. It cannot find someone guilty of something; it cannot impose a penalty – and that is so even where it finds an individual committed corrupt conduct. This is not an oversight but a deliberate design feature, consistent with the doctrine of the separation of powers.

How jurisdictions are understood within the NACC

The reasons NACC has given for not pursuing the Robodebt referrals, canvassed above, provide some indication of how its leadership understands its jurisdiction. Each reason is questionable, but the third theme, regarding its remedial limitations, is perhaps the most troubling.

To some extent, it is simply not accurate. The NACC can offer more than the Royal Commission – a statutory finding of corrupt conduct. And while such a finding admittedly does not constitute an individual remedy in the strict legal sense, the NACC seems to have misjudged the potential value of such a finding for victims, their families, and the wider public. The NACC's reasons also suggest a misunderstanding of the means by which it was designed to fulfil its function – public reporting on corruption, not punishment through fines. Such a misunderstanding, should it persist, would have serious implications for the work of the NACC in the future. If its inability to administer punishment is relevant to determining whether an investigation can commence, many worthwhile investigations could be foregone on that basis.

Beyond the reasons pertaining to the decision itself, the NACC has indicated an overall hesitation to assume control over its jurisdiction. Deputy Commissioner Rose gave oral evidence of 'serious concerns' held within the NACC that it might not meet the threshold for a finding of corrupt conduct.[22] In my view, this concern is unwarranted: at that stage, the NACC was merely deciding if it should open an investigation – whether it would find corrupt conduct could only occur later. In written materials, Commissioner Brereton expressed his concern that a finding of corrupt conduct 'would likely be the subject of a legal challenge'.[23] Realistically, those sorts of challenges will not go away – answering challenges to its findings and jurisdiction is part of the everyday work of an anti-corruption agency. If too much weight is given to the prospect of legal challenge, the risk is that otherwise compelling investigations will not be pursued.

What conflict?

The inability of the NACC Commissioner to properly manage his conflict of interest raises, like the substance of the decision, significant concerns. After all, recognising and managing conflicts of interest are the bread and butter of governmental integrity work. Potential conflicts arise on a daily basis. Federal public officials need authoritative guidance and, in that event, it is the NACC from which such advice should be obtained.

Commissioner Brereton should never have participated in assessing the referral. He should not have shared his reasons for withdrawing and simply excused himself on personal grounds. Instead, he identified the person with whom he had his connexion and alerted his colleagues that the person was one he knew well. He then remained in the room during each aspect of the assessment except the moment when the actual decision was made.[24] Such an approach is inadequate: the head of an organisation repeatedly says that the person is one with whom he has a close association, then steps out. The pressure on the underlings is clear. The opinion of the eminent judge, Alan Robertson, that natural justice was denied is clearly correct.[25]

In his oral evidence to the Joint Committee, Commissioner Brereton stated several times that legal friends had informed him that Mr Robertson was wrong,[26] which is contrary to the views of many other lawyers. There seems to be little prospect of a change in approach. During his oral evidence to the Joint Committee, Commissioner Brereton was pressed about what had been learned from this. He maintained his opposition to the conclusions reached, repeatedly stating that he did not agree with Mr Robertson's view.[27]

A conflict will almost certainly arise again. One focus of the NACC will likely be the Department of Defence – expensive military procurement contracts are an attractive lure for corruption. Commissioner Brereton remains a major general in the ADF Reserve and continues to have close personal and professional contact with military figures. His decision, announced in October 2025, to refrain altogether from considering any referrals which involve the interests of the ADF or Defence, regardless of any perceived conflict of interest they might involve, is to be welcomed –notwithstanding the very real questions one might raise about its rationale.

What else?

While the decision of the NACC regarding the Robodebt referrals and all that has flowed from it have garnered much attention, it is also worth considering what it has achieved.

The year 2025 has been a particularly noteworthy one for the NACC, making its first corruption finding and securing its first conviction. The finding of 'corrupt conduct' involved a senior public official at the Department of Home Affairs, who had improperly used her position to influence a recruitment process in favour of a family member.[28] The conviction, the first to result from an investigation initiated by the NACC, involved an official at Western Sydney Airport, who had solicited a bribe for influencing a contract procurement process.[29]

Any instances of the NACC performing its functions are, of course, welcomed. But in my view, the relatively minor nature of these matters jars with the public perception of more serious corruption issues requiring attention. After all, the creation of a NACC received strong support before the 2022 election. The public wants an effective federal integrity agency. This is particularly so given the absence of any public inquiries or hearings, and the surprising decision of the NACC to conceal the identity of the corrupt Home Affairs official.

Even ardent supporters of the NACC would agree that its public output has, as yet, been disappointing. What can explain this? There are two interrelated reasons. The first relates to the narrow approach the NACC took to its own jurisdiction, as discussed above. The second is the absence of a sufficiently dynamic leadership, a factor which has arguably contributed to the jurisdictional approach.

This is not to question the personal qualities and experience of Commissioner Brereton – he is of utmost personal integrity, an exceptional lawyer, a respected former judge, and a long-term military leader. I am yet to be convinced that a military background provides the right skillset for the head of an agency dedicated to the promotion of transparency in collaborative decision-making.[30] This consideration may inform the appointment of future commissioners.

What needs to be done?

I have had firsthand experience of the critical role played by the leadership in organisations like the NACC. Dynamic, fearless, independent, even aggressive – these are the desirable characteristics of an effective integrity agency.

If the NACC is to develop into a useful contributor to public sector integrity, change will need to come from above. For the NACC to fulfil its promise, its leadership must learn from its early missteps. At the very least, its recent decision regarding Defence and ADF referrals gives us some reason to hold out hope.

Note: The author praises the indispensable assistance of Mahalia McDaniel, a senior researcher at the Centre for Public Integrity.

Reference

Morton, R, *Mean Streak*, 4th Estate, 2024.

CHAPTER 6

ARE BEHAVIOURAL CHANGE INITIATIVES WORKING? EVALUATING THE PROGRAMS SO FAR

UWE DULLECK, JOHN HAWKINS AND REBEKAH RUSSELL-BENNETT

We are currently seeing calls, not just from libertarians, for governments to be less prescriptive and avoid banning or compelling behaviours under threats of fines. Additionally, many call for 'evidence-based policy' (Gade, 2024). This refers to evaluating policies for their effectiveness before introducing or maintaining them – particularly where human behaviour is not as predictable as assumed by rational choice (economic theory). This approach has been explored and popularised in Ezra Klein and Derek Thompson's recent book *Abundance*, which argues that progressive parties need to avoid regulations imposed to achieve one goal inadvertently making it harder to achieve other goals (Hawkins, 2025).

Two relatively new Australian government agencies are committed to these ideas. One is the Behavioural Economics Team of the Australian Government (BETA), which the Turnbull Government established within the Department of the Prime Minister and Cabinet (DPMC) in 2016. The other is the Australian Centre for Evaluation (ACE), which the Albanese Government established within Treasury. Both are underutilised and could contribute more to effective government policy. This chapter describes the agencies and discusses their potential and constraints on their roles.

The idea behind BETA: Behavioural economics

Behavioural economics seeks to combine insights from economics with insights from psychology. It is often focused on documenting deviations from what classical economists regard as rational behaviour. Daniel Kahneman (2012), one of the leaders in the field, gives an introduction.

His collaborator Richard Thaler applied the concepts to policy design, developing the idea of a 'nudge' in the eponymous book co-authored with Cass Sunstein. A 'nudge' refers to a policy that does not change the options people have available but encourages them to take decisions 'in a way that will make the choosers better off, as judged by themselves'. A successful nudge leads to the decision a person would have taken 'if they had paid full attention and possessed complete information, unlimited cognitive abilities and complete self-control' (Thaler and Sunstein, 2008: 5–6). To be a nudge, the intervention must be easy and people must be able to override it easily. Putting fruit at eye level in the supermarket to encourage healthier eating counts as a nudge as people can still seek out a less healthy option. Banning junk food does not.

The role of BETA

The *Nudge* book was an intellectual success (with over 30 000 citations) and a publishing success (with over 2 million sales) (Mills, 2023). But it was also a policy success. It inspired governments to set up agencies, which became colloquially known as 'nudge units' (Shah, 2024). The first, and probably still the best-known, was the Behavioural Insight Team (BIT) founded in 2010 in the UK (Halpern, 2016). Former UK prime minister David Cameron placed it within the Cabinet Office. BIT developed the 'EAST' framework, which refers to nudge initiatives which make desirable behaviours Easy, Attractive, Social and Timely.

Inspired by the UK example, BETA was established in 2016. It was and remains hosted in DPMC. The National Commission of Audit set up by the Abbott Government had suggested an agency along these lines in 2014 to examine the efficiency of the Commonwealth Government. The agency's acronym carries the double meaning of both a 'beta' test (that is, a trial) and a 'better' approach (Ball, 2023).

This was not, however, the first time the Australian Government drew on insights from behavioural economics. Australia was leading the way in this field with respect to work done to increase tax compliance, where the

ATO used behaviourally informed approaches in the 1980s and applied econometric methods to evaluate their effectiveness (Verhorn and Brondolo, 1999; Torgler, 2007). More recently, the increase in superannuation contributions reflected a view that workers had 'present bias' and would reach retirement regretting they had not built up more savings (Ball, Hiscox and Oliver, 2017). The policy response was a mix of compulsory contributions and encouraging voluntary contributions.

The government hoped, however, that setting up a specific agency would lead to making better use of behavioural insights. Drawing on the UK experience, BETA started with small and quick projects such as work with the Australian Energy Market Regulator to provide better information (BETA, 2018).

BETA's remit is to develop and test potential 'nudges' to influence behaviour in ways that make the actors themselves, and/or the broader community, better off, and then test which ones will work best. In BETA's (2025) website, it sets out its objectives as:

1   Conduct research to better understand how people interact with programs and policy issues.
2   Design and rigorously test policy solutions informed by behavioural science.
3   Translate our research and expertise into practical advice on how to improve policies and programs.
4   Uplift APS capability and support application of behavioural science to public policy in the APS.

BETA's activities under the Albanese Government

Under the Albanese Government, BETA has been involved in projects aimed at supporting reductions in the cost of living (covering shifting between bank accounts, home energy upgrades, and foreign exchange transactions) and meeting the net zero greenhouse gas emissions target (electric vehicle take-up). It also studied the impact of a new entitlement for ten days of paid family and domestic violence leave; and another addressing the problem of improving retention in the NDIS workforce. A list is available at BETA's website.

It is perhaps surprising that BETA did not conduct more cost-of-living projects to test different approaches that could help consumers manage or save money. These could include cooling-off periods (addressing impulse spending), uptake of financial assistance, reducing food waste, affordable meal options, affordable domestic tourism and use of national parks.

BETA has undertaken 49 published projects partnering with federal government departments since 2016, with 11 projects commenced after the Albanese Government came to power in May 2022. While the number of projects under the Albanese Government (average of four projects per year) seems fewer than under previous governments (average of six), this may be due to delays in publishing results. Furthermore, there has been a shift towards a more programmatic approach to employing BETA's capacity. Instead of looking at very detailed projects like how to provide fact sheets to consumers to help them make better choices of electricity providers, the priorities have shifted to larger programs of research including understanding what drives the energy-saving behaviours of low-income households, and general investigations of how to address cost-of-living pressures (BETA, 2024).

Another possible reason for this decline is the establishment of the Australian Centre for Evaluation (see below), which shares the focus on randomised control trials and hired some of BETA's staff. Fewer staff, but also a richer library of studies published and a more mature field of (applied) research available in journals and other organisations, potentially explains why an increasing number of projects remain unpublished with 21 projects undertaken in 2024 (DPMC, 2024: 51) but only four published on the BETA website. As BETA (2025) states on its website, its focus was always not only to inform policy development but also to build capacity in the public sector, and publications of current research may be less urgent now that the evidence base has been built.

One measure of success for BETA is the number of departments partnering with it, including Treasury; Climate Change, Energy and the Environment; Employment and Workplace Relations; Health; Social Services; and Industry, Science and Resources as well as other public agencies including ACCC, Asbestos and Silica Safety and Eradication Agency, Australian Public Service Commission, Safe Work Australia and the National Mental Health Commission. While this breadth indicates the wide relevance of behavioural economics as a policy tool across government, the limited number of projects indicates opportunities for further contribution. In particular, BETA could bring together behavioural research that behavioural economics groups in other departments are doing.

While BETA's staff are public servants, in some ways it functions like a consultancy. Many of the staff are seconded from other departments (Ball, 2023). The most common qualifications are in economics and psychology but there are also staff trained in law, sociology and international development. There may be some division between the perspectives of the more 'academic' and 'specialist' staff and the more 'generalist' policy-oriented 'public servants' (Ball, 2023).

BETA also provides several training programs for public servants. They have also hosted annual conferences, known as 'BI Connect'. Over a thousand people participated in 2024 (BETA, 2025).

Issues facing BETA

BETA has operated for nine years and under three different governments. But some departments and policy areas are still less engaged with behavioural economic approaches, or only engage within their own departments. This may limit the breadth of research that it can do and reduces cross-department learning. Departments with less responsibility for service delivery, such as Finance, Defence, Foreign Affairs and Trade, or Industry, Science and Resources, may not see the full potential of BETA for their operations.

Behavioural insights can be applied to internal processes as much as to the delivery of services to citizens. Hiscox et al. (2017) and BETA (2024) provide insights relevant to the government's internal operations; that is, they consider the use of behavioural economics to improve the efficiency and effectiveness of government operations.

Funding government services that have an element of the public good, as research always has, is difficult. One of BETA's goals was to build capacity for behavioural analysis within departments. This gives rise to the usual public choice arguments (Wilkins, Phillimore and Gilchrist, 2015). Some departments, such as the Department of Agriculture, Water and the Environment (DAWE), and Energy, have built their own behavioural units, and external consultants also compete with BETA.

A possible concern is that some government departments, for example DAWE, have in recent years closed their behavioural economics units. While this may in some cases reflect the priorities and views of department leadership, it may also reflect that in many cases behavioural economics has become part of the standard policy repertoire.

BETA does not have a separate published budget or annual report. These are included with the rest of DPMC. The only public record of BETA projects is the website. This does not, however, contain all projects it has undertaken. In 2023–24 BETA was given a target of completing 20 projects and completed 21 (DPMC, 2024: 51). Only having four of these projects published on its website means BETA may be underselling the value of the behavioural economics work it is undertaking.

Australian public servants, like their peers in the United Kingdom and New Zealand, have tended to be 'champions of evidence-based policy making' but 'their political masters were generally not' (Halligan and Evans, 2024: 315–316). There are sceptics of BETA's work, or of nudges in general. Some opponents regard behaviourally informed policy as manipulative. This is traditionally seen as a more conservative argument against the use of behavioural economic methods in government. On the other hand, in some policy areas behavioural economics may be seen as being too slow. This is the usual criticism from the progressive side of politics (Thaler and Sunstein, 2008; Halpern, 2016).

The Australian Government's choice to complement the DPMC-based BETA unit with behavioural groups and/or communities of practice in the departments raises the question of whether the benefits to scale and scope from having a centralised agency outweigh the deeper understanding of departmental issues and experiences from a decentralised model.

Martin (2023) expressed concern about the involvement of behavioural economists in the Robodebt fiasco. Frain and Tame (2017) think it was too focused on individuals and paid insufficient attention to inequality.

This belief is contradicted, however, by the BETA projects focused on addressing inequality, such as those addressing mental health-related discrimination in 2021, support for injured workers returning to the workforce in 2022 and paid family and domestic violence leave in 2024.

The Australian Centre for Evaluation

The Australian Centre for Evaluation (ACE) was established within Treasury by the Albanese Government in 2023 (Leigh, 2024). Its $10 million cost over four years is a fraction of the more than $50 million governments previously spent on evaluation reports from private consultants (Leigh, 2023). The desirability of improved evaluation had been raised in the 2019 Thodey Review of the public service (Bogaards, 2023). Andrew Leigh, the assistant minister responsible for ACE, is a former professor of economics who has written a book on randomised control trials (Leigh, 2018).

ACE offers to collaborate with evaluation units and branches within government departments to improve the evaluation of their programs. The difference from BETA is that ACE focuses on evaluating the rollout of new policies. With a focus on improving delivery, or – in case the policy fails – to allow for a faster correction, stopping ineffective policies quickly. ACE provides assistance, resources and networking opportunities. They have a specific strategy to ensure that evaluations of policies and programs affecting Indigenous Australians are culturally appropriate.

In ACE (2025) the centre undertook an assessment which concluded that 'while there are promising signs of increasing evaluation effort across the APS, there is still work to do to achieve consistent and high-quality evaluation practice and a genuine culture of evaluation'.

The agency initiated the Impact Evaluation Practitioners Network and the Commonwealth Evaluation Community of Practice. It also helps with the Paul Ramsey Foundation's Experimental Methods for Social Impact Open Grant Round.

The outlook for BETA and ACE

There is clearly some overlap between BETA and ACE, with both stressing the value of randomised control trials. BETA's focus is more on policy development – a small-scale trial and error process to then inform policy design. ACE aims to roll out new policies in such a way that they can be evaluated using randomised control trial methodology. That both teams are in close contact, and senior personnel in ACE joined from similar roles in BETA, is helpful. Ensuring that this close connection and collaboration prevails will be important to the success and efficiency of both teams. BETA and ACE might be able to co-ordinate their activities better if they were not in separate departments.

There is an issue about whether behavioural insights and randomised control trials are best kept in a central government department or whether the work BETA has done to build capacity in the main service delivery departments has gone far enough, and behavioural insights sufficiently integrated into mainstream economics, to place such activities in individual departments.

A different question to ask is whether a different setup would be more effective. Given that BETA runs on a 'consulting' model – other departments and agencies (but in some cases also private sector organisations) commission projects with BETA – a possible future for BETA would be 'corporatising' it and locating it outside a department. This is the path the UK BIT team took. After being set up as part of the prime minister's office in 2010, in 2014 BIT was converted to a mutual joint venture with a charity, the government and employees as shareholders.

The case for ACE is potentially easier to make. It is still in the building phase and the capacity in individual departments has not been built yet. Furthermore, policy evaluation – even though usually before rollout – is a core function of Treasury. One could see ACE enhancing Treasury's ability to fulfil its role. Corporatising its role could still be considered as there may be advantages in the evaluator having more independence.

References

Australian Centre for Evaluation, *State of Evaluation in the Australian Government 2025*, Australian Treasury, Canberra, February 2025.

Ball, S, *Behavourial Public Policy in Australia: How an idea became practice*, Routledge, Oxford, 2023.

Ball, S, Hiscox, M, and Oliver, T, 'Starting a behavioural insights team: three lessons from the Behavioural Economics Team of the Australian Government', *Journal of Behavioural Economics for Policy*, 2017, 1(S), pp. 21–26.

BETA/Behavioural Economics Team of the Australian Government, 'Saying more with less: Simplifying energy fact sheets', 2018.

BETA, 'BETA in 2024: Behavioural insights with impact', December 2024.

— website, <https://behaviouraleconomics.pmc.gov.au/>, 2025.

Boggards, R, 'Australian Centre for Evaluation: a quick guide', *Parliamentary Library Research Paper*, 7 June 2023.

Department of the Prime Minister and Cabinet, *Annual Report 2023–24*, 2024.

Frain, A, and Tame, R, 'Government behavioural economics "nudge unit" needs a shove in a new direction', *The Conversation*, 4 July 2017.

Gade, C, 'When is it justified to claim that a practice or policy is evidence-based? Reflections on evidence and preferences', *Evidence and Policy*, vol. 20, no. 2, 2024, pp. 244–53.

Halligan, J, and Evans, M, 'The Australian public service', in Evans, M, Dunleavy, P, and Phillimore, J (eds), *Australia's Evolving Democracy: A new democratic audit*, LSE Press, London, 2024.

Halpern, D, *Inside the Nudge Unit*, Penguin, 2016.

Hawkins, J, 'Can a book help the left rebuild the good life? Ezra Klein's *Abundance* is the talk of Washington – and Canberra', *The Conversation*, 6 June 2025.

Hiscox, M, et al. *Going Blind to See More Clearly: Unconscious Bias in Australian Public Service shortlisting processes*, BETA, 2017.

Kahneman, D, *Thinking, Fast and Slow*, Penguin, London, 2012.

Klein, E, and Thompson, D, *Abundance*, Profile, London, 2025.

Leigh, A, *Randomistas: How radical researchers changed our world*, Black Inc, Melbourne, 2018.

— 'Australian Centre for Evaluation to measure what works', media release, 25 May 2023.

— 'Discovering what works: Why rigorous evaluation matters', Speech to Australian Evaluation Showcase, Canberra, 17 June 2024.

Martin, P, 'Behavioural "experts" quietly shaped Robodebt's most devilish details – and their work in government continues', *The Conversation*, 25 July 2023.

Mills, S, 'Nudge theory: What 15 years of research tells us about its promises and politics', *The Conversation*, 7 September 2023.

Shah, Z, 'Why every government needs a Behavioural Insights Unit', London School of Economics, 5 September 2024.

Thaler, R, *Misbehaving: The Making of Behavioural Economics*, Penguin, London, 2016.

Thaler, R, and Sunstein, S, *Nudge*, Penguin, London, 2008.

Torgler, B, *Tax Compliance and Tax Morale: A Theoretical and Empirical Analysis*, Edward Elgar, Cheltenham, UK, 2007.

Vernon, C, and Brondolo, J, 'Organizational options for tax administration', *Bulletin for International Fiscal Documentation*, vol. 53, 1999, pp. 499–512.

Wilkins, P, Phillimore, J, and Gilchrist, D, 'Public sector collaboration: Are we doing it well and could we do it better?', *Australian Journal of Public Administration*, vol. 75, no. 3, 2016.

PART III
POLICY ISSUES

CHAPTER 7

INFLATION, TAX CUTS AND THE COST OF LIVING: ECONOMIC POLICY AND REFORM

JOHN HAWKINS

The Covid-19 pandemic and associated lockdowns ended what had been arguably the longest economic expansion any developed country had ever achieved. But as scientists managed to produce vaccines in months rather than the years initially expected, the recession turned out to be not as severe as initially feared.

The fiscal stimulus and the near-zero interest rates were sensible responses given the available information at the time. But with the benefit of hindsight, they were excessive and contributed to inflationary pressures. These were compounded by (arguably underestimated) supply bottlenecks and then the impact on commodity prices of Russia's invasion of Ukraine.

Inflation, which had been below 1 per cent during 2020, spiked quickly, going over 5 per cent in the March quarter of 2022 and peaking at 7.8 per cent in the December quarter. This surprised almost everyone. In a survey of 24 economists in January 2022, the average forecast for underlying inflation in 2022 was under 3 per cent. The same pattern of unexpected inflation occurred in other comparable countries.

In response, the Reserve Bank, notwithstanding its earlier predictions that it was unlikely to need to start raising interest rates until 2024,[1] started a tightening cycle. The first increase in its cash rate target, from 0.10 per cent to 0.35 per cent, occurred just before the election, in May 2022, and was widely and correctly seen as the first of many to come.

The expansionary fiscal policy adopted to offset some of the contraction in economic activity due to the Covid lockdowns meant that the Morrison Government never achieved the budget surplus about which it had already boasted on souvenir 'back in black' mugs. Instead, Treasurer Chalmers inherited an estimated budget deficit of 3.4 per cent of GDP for 2022–23, among the largest on record, and government debt headed for over $1 trillion. Chalmers described the Albanese Government's economic focus during its first term as 'primarily inflation without forgetting productivity'.

Chalmers's budgets and the cost of living

The 2022 Budget had been brought forward, from May to March, to accommodate the election. This would have meant a gap of 14 months between outgoing Treasurer Frydenberg's last budget and Chalmers's first on the usual timetable. The Albanese Government instead opted for a second budget in 2022, in October, to start implementing their own priorities. Regular budgets followed in May 2023 and May 2024, and the 2025 Budget was brought forward to March.

Between the March quarters of 2022 and 2024, consumer prices rose by 11 per cent while average wages only rose by 8 per cent. This meant the 'cost of living' became the dominant economic issue. It posed a dilemma. On the one hand, the government wanted to do what it could to salve the pain households were feeling. But, on the other hand, giving extra money to households could exacerbate inflation by bolstering demand for goods and services. This required any cost-of-living relief to be limited and well targeted. In some cases, subsidies were paid, which had the direct effect of reducing, if only temporarily, the consumer price index.

In formulating budget measures, the government is advised annually by an Economic Inclusion Advisory Committee it established. But it seemed to place fiscal conservatism ahead of the concerns, such as the inadequacy of JobSeeker payments, the committee had identified.

Unwinding Covid stimulus and support measures meant that government spending actually fell in 2021–22, and only grew modestly in 2022–23, while revenues grew strongly. Budget surpluses were recorded in 2022–23 and 2023–24, the first since before the Global Financial Crisis in 2007–09. (The budget moved into deficit in 2024–25, but a much smaller one than initially expected.) With tax revenue slowing as the Reserve Bank lifted interest rates (firstly removing the extraordinary Covid stimulus and then going

Figure 9.1.

Inflation and unemployment

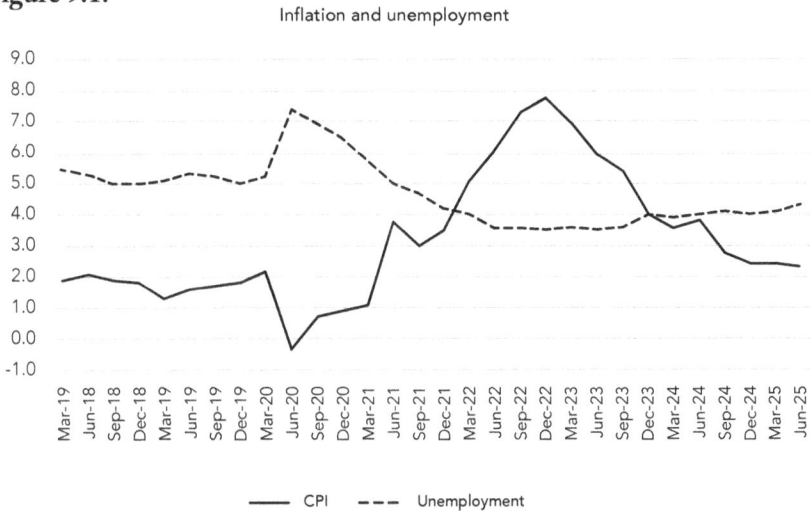

beyond this to dampen emerging inflation) and thereby dampened economic activity, this required spending restraint. There were some cuts and deferrals in discretionary spending. When revenue estimates were upgraded, such as when commodity prices and hence tax payments by mining companies were stronger than expected, these were mainly 'saved' (used to reduce government debt) rather than spent.

The October 2022 Budget included initiatives to render childcare more affordable. It cut medicine costs and provided more university and TAFE places. A National Reconstruction Fund was established. On the revenue side there were measures to improve the integrity of the tax system, including ensuring multinational corporations paid a fairer share.

A Housing Accord set an aspirational target of building one million new homes over five years. A Housing Australia Future Fund was established to provide social housing.

The May 2023 Budget included further measures to reduce the cost of medicines and healthcare. Eligibility for the single parenting payment was extended. The JobSeeker payment was increased by $40 per fortnight in addition to the regular indexation. Commonwealth Rent Assistance was increased. An instant asset write-off was introduced to cut tax paid by small business.

The May 2024 Budget focused even more on the cost of living. Electricity rebates of $300 per household, and $325 for one million small businesses, were introduced. Treasury forecast this would directly reduce headline inflation by around half a percentage point in 2024–25. A further increase in Commonwealth Rent Assistance supported nearly one million households. There were also significant income tax cuts and cuts to student debt. The Albanese Government also announced the Future Made in Australia program aimed at ensuring that Australian industry benefits from the transition to net zero greenhouse gas emissions.

The March 2025 Budget included modest cuts for all income taxpayers. It projected budget deficits out to 2034–35. And this may be optimistic. A number of large and fast-growing spending areas have bipartisan political support. Aged care, childcare, medical benefits and hospitals, defence (notably commitments under the AUKUS agreement), the NDIS and interest on government debt are all projected to grow by more than 5 per cent a year over the next decade. This is faster than the rate at which the nominal economy is forecast to expand (and hence the rate at which tax revenues may grow). This poses a challenge of restraining growth in other areas of spending so it remains below growth in the economy.

Government debt is projected to stabilise at the equivalent of about a third of GDP, not far short of what it reached during Covid, although still lower than in most comparable economies.

Some economists are concerned that government spending is increasing through using funds that are not accounted for in the main measure of the budget balance, the 'underlying cash balance'.[2] Taken too far, this would significantly reduce transparency and accountability.

The stage 3 tax cuts debate

The Turnbull Government announced three stages of tax cuts in 2018 and the Morrison Government modified them in 2019. By the time the Albanese Government was elected, the first two, relatively uncontroversial, stages were essentially in place. The third stage was not due to come into effect until July 2024, so could be amended. But, as part of a 'small target' strategy,

Albanese had committed to maintaining them in the election campaign. Despite misgivings of some colleagues, he then repeated this pledge in the early months of his government.

The Australia Institute consistently opposed the tax cuts, relentlessly pointing out that most of the third stage would go to the top 10 per cent of taxpayers, the bottom fifth of income taxpayers would get nothing, twice as much would go to men as to women, and that the public thought that economic policy should adapt to changing circumstances even if it meant breaking an election promise (Grudnoff, 2024).

Eventually the government changed its mind and announced a broadly revenue-neutral redesign of the stage 3 tax cuts in January 2024. The tax cuts were still slanted towards the rich in dollar terms but now the cuts for middle-income earners are a higher proportion of their taxable income than they are for high-income earners. Every income taxpayer has now got a tax cut, and only the top tenth of taxpayers, those on incomes over $146 486, got tax cuts smaller than originally proposed. There was little sign that the broken promise concerned many voters.

Other tax reform (or lack thereof)

Labor had taken a large number of significant tax reforms to the 2019 election and doing so was seen as a major contributor to their loss. They therefore ran a 'small target' strategy in 2022. Once in government, they introduced few tax initiatives, other than trying to improve compliance with existing rules, notably by multinationals.

In the 2023 Budget the government announced a reduction in tax concessions for the fewer than 0.5 per cent of individuals whose superannuation balance exceeds $3 million, but was unable to get it through the Senate. The proposal would have increased the concessional tax rate from 15 to 30 per cent. There was (often exaggerated) criticism that the $3 million threshold was not indexed and over time could affect more people, and applied to unrealised gains. The government will try again in the new parliament with a modified version.

Employment and the White Paper

The Albanese Government had a good story to tell on employment. Despite tepid growth in GDP, unemployment remained under 4 per cent for most of its term and over a million jobs were created. The proportion of the working-age population with a job reached an all-time high.

In an echo of the wartime Curtin–Chifley Labor governments, the Albanese Government released a white paper on jobs. While the original white paper, reflecting optimism about the potential of Keynesian policies to manage the economy, was called *Full Employment in Australia*, Chalmers's was called *Working Future* (Treasury, 2023).

The paper stated the government's objective as 'sustained and inclusive full employment', which it defined as a situation where 'everyone who wants a job should be able to find one without having to search for too long'; wording later incorporated into the Treasurer and Reserve Bank Board's *Statement on the Conduct of Monetary Policy*. The government did not put a number on the unemployment rate to which this would correspond, arguing that 'a broader range of labour market measures' was needed to measure how close the economy was to full employment (Treasury, 2023).

The white paper commented that to be 'sustained', employment had to be 'consistent with low and stable inflation'. This makes the unemployment rate representing full employment sound much like the 'non-accelerating inflation rate of unemployment' (NAIRU). The Reserve Bank had estimated the NAIRU as around 4.5 per cent (Ellis, 2019) but noted it had declined since 2000. The Reserve Bank, however, is also now paying more attention to a range of other measures of spare capacity in the labour market.

The Inter-Generational Report

The sixth Inter-Generational Report (IGR) was released in August 2023. It projected the budget implications of influences such as population ageing, technology, climate change and the transition to net zero and geopolitical risk over four decades. It suggested the economy will be about 2.5 times its current size by 2063 and the population will have reached 40 million.

The budget, forecast to return to balance around 2034, is projected to then move back into increasing deficits. The five fastest-growing government payments (health, aged care, NDIS, interest on government debt and defence) are projected to increase from a third of government payments now to around a half by 2063. The care and support workforce could need to double.

Another example of the report's conclusions is that the tax system may become more reliant on income tax as increased use of electric vehicles and reduced smoking reduce fuel and tobacco excise revenues. The cost of superannuation concessions will increase, but the greater role of superannuation will enable spending on age pensions to fall as a share of GDP.

A feature of the most recent IGR is a more realistic assumption on annual labour productivity growth, down from 1.5 per cent to 1.2 per cent. This is the average of the past 20 years, although productivity has been much weaker more recently.

'Measuring What Matters'

The government acknowledged that the common emphasis, bordering on obsession, with (mis)using small differences in real GDP to compare differences in wellbeing across regimes or across countries was misplaced. It produced instead a chapter in the Budget papers in October 2022 and a full report in July 2023 on *Measuring What Matters* with a much more comprehensive selection of relevant indicators. Responsibility for the framework was then transferred to the Australian Bureau of Statistics.

The framework reflects that a good society is healthy, secure, sustainable and cohesive in addition to being prosperous. It is in some ways a revival of Treasury's wellbeing framework developed under Ken Henry as Treasury Secretary (Treasury, 2004) but quietly discarded by John Fraser, Abbott's appointment as Secretary. When Chalmers foreshadowed this approach in Opposition, the then Treasurer Josh Frydenberg had mocked him for his 'yoga mat and beads' approach.

The report was criticised because in some cases recent statistics on some concepts it wished to measure were not available; a rather cheap shot, as the writers could only use what was available to them. The government allocated $14.8 million over five years in the 2024 Budget to improve the data by conducting a General Social Survey.

Reforming the Reserve Bank

An important component of cost-of-living pressures, for the third of households with a mortgage, is interest payments. With the mortgage belts in the outer suburbs replete with marginal seats, especially as the election approached, the government became keen to see an interest rate cut, or at least no further increases. This meant that the Reserve Bank board and staff became almost as important an audience for the Treasurer as was the general public.

Chalmers has a mantra of referring to the 'independent Reserve Bank' when discussing its decisions on interest rates. This is both a commendable sign of respect and a means of deflecting blame for its unpopular decisions.

But as well as the short-term policies to placate the bank by not exacerbating inflation, Treasurer Chalmers set up an inquiry into longer-term reform of the bank in July 2022. Such a review had been first suggested by the OECD (2021). By the 2022 election, support for the review was bipartisan.

The report was evolutionary rather than revolutionary (Hawkins, 2023). The review recommended the bank continue with the regime of flexible inflation targeting and maintain the target at 2–3 per cent. They wanted the cash rate target to remain the primary instrument of monetary policy and for it to continue to be set independently of government by a nine-person board, chaired by the governor and including the deputy governor and Treasury secretary. The main change was that they wanted to transfer the board's governance work (such as personnel and premises, auditing and risk management) to a second board so the monetary policy board could concentrate on monetary policy and have appointees with more expertise in that area.

The bank introduced some of the ideas from the review unilaterally, such as moving to eight meetings a year. Others, such as slight changes to the wording around inflation and employment, were incorporated into the

Treasurer and Reserve Bank Board's *Statement on the Conduct of Monetary Policy* in December 2023. The reforms to establish the separate monetary policy board finally passed the Senate, with the support of the crossbench after the Coalition withdrew their support, in November 2024. Implementing the changes fell to Michele Bullock, who was promoted to RBA governor from deputy effective September 2023. Andrew Hauser from the Bank of England (which has long had separate boards) was appointed the new deputy.

Productivity, competition and other reforms

After the appointment of Danielle Wood as the new chair of the Productivity Commission, a Statement of Expectations for it was released in November 2023. In December 2024 the government formally tasked the commission with five inquiries, covering a productivity agenda of creating a more dynamic and resilient economy; building a skilled and adaptable workforce; harnessing data and digital technology; delivering quality care more efficiently; and investing in cheaper, cleaner energy and the net zero transformation.

A National Productivity Fund was established in November 2024 to provide incentives for states to introduce reforms that raise productivity. The government announced an agreement with state and territory governments for a ten-year reform of National Competition Policy.

Another contribution to improving efficiency was the abolition of nearly 500 'nuisance' tariffs, which involved compliance and administrative costs but raised minimal revenue and often applied to products with no Australian competitors, effective from July 2024. A tariff on toasters, for example, raised less than $1000 per year.

The Australian Competition and Consumer Commission (ACCC) was directed to investigate competition in the supermarket industry. A new merger regime to come into effect in 2026 will require all mergers over a set size to be reported to the ACCC for their approval.

A Statement of Expectations was issued for the Future Fund, requiring it to consider the national priorities of increasing the supply of residential housing, supporting the energy transition and delivering improved infrastructure. Its primary focus would remain on maximising returns, with the benchmark remaining at 4–5 per cent over CPI inflation. The government announced it would not start any drawdowns from the fund until at least 2032–33, by which time its assets should have increased to $380 billion.

Under Chalmers's tenure, the addition of two new appointments meant that women now headed all the key economic agencies in his portfolio: Reserve Bank (Michele Bullock), Productivity Commission (Danielle Wood) and the Australian Competition and Consumer Commission (Gina Cass-Gottlieb). Jenny Wilkinson was appointed to head the Department of Finance.

Overall assessment

The Reserve Bank and the government succeeded in returning inflation to the 2–3 per cent target band while keeping unemployment below the 4.5 per cent rate many commentators thought this would require. Treasurer Chalmers has indicated his priority in his second term will switch to improving Australia's weak productivity performance.

Note: Thanks to Craig Applegate, Stephen Bartos, Selwyn Cornish, John Halligan and Mary Walsh for helpful comments.

References

Ellis, L, 'Watching the invisibles', Freebairn lecture in public policy, 12 June 2019.

Eslake, S, 'Fiscal policy under the Albanese Government, 2022–2025' in Prasser, S (ed.) *Promise and Performance: Albanese's First Term*, Connor Court Publishing, Reland Bay, 2025.

Grudnoff, M, 'Polling – stage 3 tax cuts and election promises', Australia Institute Report, January 2024.

Hawkins, J, 'The Reserve Bank review is not revolutionary – and that's a good thing', *Guardian*, 21 April 2023.

Organisation for Economic Cooperation and Development, *OECD Economic Surveys: Australia*, September 2021.

Treasury, *Working Future: the Australian Government's White Paper on Jobs and Opportunities*, 25 September 2023.

— 'Policy advice and Treasury's wellbeing framework', Paper presented to Australian Statistics Advisory Council, 25 May 2004.

CHAPTER 8

AGAINST THE ODDS: INDUSTRY POLICY AND THE ALBANESE GOVERNMENT

ALAN FENNA

In launching the ALP's 2022 election campaign, Anthony Albanese held out the prospect of 'a future where Australia makes things here again, a stronger, more diverse, more self-reliant economy'. This heralded the return of an industry policy activism that had been largely absent since the 1980s and early 1990s. It matured into the 'Future Made in Australia' policy and program announced in early 2024 and legislated later that year.

This new interventionism was consistent with Labor's defining ideological orientations, and something that set it clearly apart from the Coalition parties. However, there was more to the return of industry policy than simply the Left/Right divide. Circumstances had changed, and as with earlier episodes of activism, crisis played an important role. So, in addition, did Labor's need to square the circle on its plans for what would inevitably be a costly shift to a low-carbon economy. And so did the long decline in productivity growth since the beginning of this century.

There are very good reasons to be wary of industry policy interventionism: it is something of a bet against markets, one that assumes an astuteness and competence of government, a governing consensus and sustained commitment. The self-proclaimed ambition of Future Made in Australia was 'to transform Australia into a global leader in manufacturing and innovation' (NRFC, 2024: 5). Given that Australia is very far from being even a respectable contender, let alone a 'global leader' in a world dominated by such industrial powerhouses as China, the United States, Germany, Japan and South Korea, this was ambitious indeed.

Industry policy challenges

'Industry policy' refers to the actions governments take to mould the economy and maximise the development of value-added activities. Those value-added activities have traditionally been the manufacture of goods – though today it has to be recognised that high-end services are just as important. Australia has always been a resource-based economy with its 'comparative advantage' being in primary products (Fenna, 2016). From wool, wheat and gold to coal, gas, bauxite and iron ore, Australia's natural wealth has fuelled economic growth and development for much of the country's history and continues to do so. But that dependence on natural resources also has its vulnerabilities, and, in such a context, industry policy is oriented to diversifying the economy away from agriculture and resources to manufactured goods (Phillimore and Leong, 2017). This can be done by fostering industries that supply inputs for the agriculture and resource sectors ('backward linkages'); by fostering the local processing of the outputs of those sectors prior to export ('forward linkages'); or by fostering industry independent of agriculture and resources. In the latter case, that can be either for the home market or for export.

Import tariffs that provide domestic manufacturers with some protection from overseas competition were historically the main instrument of industry policy in Australia, operating from colonial times through to the 1990s (Fenna, 2012, 2016). Other instruments include government procurement policies that privilege local firms; tax advantages that make investment deductible, particularly investment in research and development (R&D); direct grants or subsidies; public enterprise; and infrastructure provision.

The secular decline of Australian manufacturing

Manufacturing's contribution to the Australian economy peaked in 1960 at just under 30 per cent of GDP and has been declining ever since. Most emblematic was the Australian car industry, created and maintained by public policy, never internationally competitive. Its demise was inevitable as the tariffs came down, but the industry lingered on until October 2017, when the last Holden came off the assembly line. By the time the Albanese Government was elected in May 2022, manufacturing's share of output had fallen to 5.8 per cent of GDP from 14.9 per cent in 1990. In one international league table of 146 economies, while Australia ranks as the eighth richest economy *per capita*, it has fallen to 102nd in terms of economic complexity (Growth Lab, 2025). As a consequence, Australia has the lowest level of 'manufacturing self-sufficiency' in the entire OECD (Stanford, 2020: 62). Manufacturing's share of exports had fallen less – to 6.3 per cent from 12 per cent – but that is not surprising given that with its very broad and inclusive definition, 'manufacturing' encompasses simply transformed manufactures (STMs) for export, such as aluminium, where Australia retains a comparative advantage, as well as elaborately transformed manufactures (ETMs). Meanwhile, total spending on research and development – a crucial investment in future competitiveness – has been steadily declining: down from 2 per cent of GDP in 2013–14 to 1.7 per cent in 2021–22, with less than half of that being by the private sector (ABS, 2023).

With deindustrialisation and globalisation, Australia had become 'a hungry importer of other nations' high-end knowledge-intensive manufactures' (AITI, 2021). When the Covid-19 pandemic struck in 2020 and international supply chains were disrupted, the vulnerabilities consequent upon that dependence became a serious concern (PC, 2021).

Arresting the slide?
Was there a way forward for the Australian economy in this regard? A Labor-dominated February 2022 Senate Committee report on manufacturing recommended, among other things: establishment of a 'Manufacturing Industry Fund' to subsidise private sector investment; changes to the superannuation regime 'to increase the level of Australian superannuation fund investment in Australian manufacturing industries'; preferencing Australian suppliers in public procurement by both levels of government; and, in amongst these measures, 'take steps to improve the diversity of workers in manufacturing industry' (SSCE, 2022). Liberal members dissented, *inter alia*, from the emphasis on 'a government driven interventionist approach', notably as reflected in the first two of the proposals above.

In theory, such efforts to revive Australian manufacturing could dovetail nicely with the incoming government's commitment to decarbonisation and renewable energy. This connexion had been highlighted by prominent public policy economist Ross Garnaut (2019), who spruiked Australia's enormous potential to become a renewable energy 'superpower'. Encouraging thoughts that government could engineer a turnaround in Australia's manufacturing fortunes was the revival of intellectual enthusiasm for active industry policy internationally (for example, Baquie et al., 2025; Mazzucato, 2013; Juhász, Lane and Rodrik, 2024; Robson, 2023).

Implementing Labor's promises

The government's first budget, delivered in late 2022, highlighted its plans for 'A Future Made in Australia'. The centrepiece would be a '$15 billion National Reconstruction Fund' that 'will help finance projects that expand our industrial base, diversify our economy, create sustainable, well-paid jobs, and grow our regional centres' (Chalmers, 2022). The *National Reconstruction Fund Corporation Act 2023* and associated legislation was passed early the following year and the corporation established as a statutory Commonwealth body in September (ANAO, 2025). 'The pandemic highlighted the importance of an agile advanced manufacturing capability that can pivot to produce critical products, and meet our needs at a time when we need them most', declared the sponsoring minister (Husic, 2022). As flagged above, this program was designed to be dual purpose: economic and environmental, with the latter focused on helping meet the emissions-reduction targets legislated under the *Climate Change Act 2022* soon after the government took office. The question of reinvigorating Australian manufacturing was also referred by the minister to the House of Representatives Standing Committee on Industry, Science and Resources (HSCISR, 2023).

The unfolding industry policy program was of course supported by the relevant unions, such as the AMWU. Business also favoured greater government commitment in this area, but, also predictably, in the form of less interventionist measures: ensuring smooth approvals processes; investment in common user facilities; R&D support; and contribution to workforce training (for example, MCA, 2023).

Betting on …

In 2023, the government identified the 'critical technologies' it had selected for support:

- Advanced manufacturing and materials technologies
- Artificial intelligence (AI) technologies
- Advanced information and communication technologies
- Quantum technologies
- Autonomous systems, robotics, positioning, timing and sensing
- Biotechnologies
- Clean energy generation and storage technologies (DISR, 2023b).

The overarching framework for this policy was the *Future Made in Australia Act 2024*, which after difficulty getting through the Senate, where it was introduced at the beginning of September, was eventually passed at the end of November. The Act laid out a 'National Interest Framework' that would govern investment decisions.

Building on comparative advantage

In the 2024 Budget, the government announced the Future Made in Australia Innovation Fund: $1.5 billion in grant funding to be administered by the Australian Renewable Energy Agency (ARENA) to subsidise 'green metals', clean energy manufacturing and low-carbon liquid fuels. At the same time, though, Australia's steel industry needed a more conventional industry policy rescue package to keep it afloat, with the Commonwealth and South Australian governments stumping up $2.4 billion in early 2025 to rescue the Whyalla Steelworks (Husic, 2025a). Steel was not the only metal receiving support, with the government committing $2 billion in production credits to support transition of Australia's large and very electricity-intensive aluminium smelting industry to renewable power.

In 2024, the government presented its national hydrogen strategy, involving a selection of facilitating measures aimed at making 'Australia a global hydrogen leader' (DECCEEW, 2024). The government's Clean Energy Finance Corporation was tasked with providing the investment necessary for 'kickstarting the green hydrogen economy' (CEFC, 2024).

In early 2025, the government injected $2 billion to recapitalise the Clean Energy Finance Corporation.

More reflective of the traditional concern with maximising the benefits of Australia's comparative advantage in natural resources through local processing (forward linkages), though, was the government's 'critical minerals production tax credit' scheme. This was introduced to promote exploitation of the suddenly much-sought-after rare earths and other minerals so important to cutting-edge technology (DISR, 2023a). It responded to the US Government's Inflation Reduction Act of mid-2022, which introduced a system of tax credits to promote the US domestic critical minerals industry. Any such boost to American industry put Australian rare earth miners at a disadvantage, and their main industry organisation, the Association of Mining and Exploration Companies, lobbied for Australia to adopt a similar arrangement (Mandala, 2023). While the industry's peak body, the Minerals Council of Australia, was initially ambivalent about the idea, it eventually came on side and in mid-February 2025 the *Future Made in Australia (Production Tax Credits and Other Measures) Act 2025* became law. The scheme allows companies to claim a 'tax offset for expenditure incurred in carrying on processing activities at facilities in Australia that substantially transform feedstock containing critical minerals into purer or more refined forms of the critical minerals that are chemically distinct from the feedstock'.

Industry and the government of Western Australia were, however, dismayed by the extent to which the government included elements of its broader agenda of ensuring 'community benefit' and Indigenous consultation into the legislation (Yim and Thompson, 2025). Expert observers had already raised concerns about this insistence on piggybacking separate Labor Party desiderata onto industry policy and thereby potentially compromising the policy's effectiveness (for example, Wood and Reeve, 2024: 13).

Brave new world
While the majority of the Future Made in Australia initiatives quite logically sought to build on the country's comparative advantage in land and resources, its largest single initiative was a bold step into terrain where Australia enjoys no such advantage. In May 2023, the government released its National

Quantum Strategy, a program to promote Australia as a centre for the next stage of information technology, quantum computing (DISR, 2023c). A year later, it announced that 'the Australian and Queensland Governments will invest almost $1 billion into frontier technology company PsiQuantum', a US-based company, on the basis that it would 'build and operate successive generations of its Fault Tolerant Quantum Computer in Brisbane'.

In the same vein as this 'moonshot' investment was the government's announcement of its self-styled 'Solar Sunshot' program, allocating $1 billion for investment to create a local solar panel manufacturing industry (Albanese, 2024). The program was to be administered by ARENA through a combination of capital grants and production credits. This investment was welcomed by sectoral advocates such as the Clean Energy Council, who saw it as providing the 'missing piece of the puzzle' given Australia's enormous demand for solar panels and scope for solar energy generation (Thornton, 2024). Much less supportive was the view of the Albanese Government-appointed head of the Productivity Commission, who noted that Australia benefits greatly from China's ability to produce solar panels so cheaply and that it would be economically perverse to pay over and above to have the pleasure of manufacturing them at home.

Not dissimilar was the government's 2024 National Battery Strategy, committing $500 million to subsidise development of local manufacture (DISR, 2024). Alongside a range of other industries being subsidised, the government announced substantial investment in production of new battery technologies in 2025.

Buying power
Finally, the government recruited another policy instrument, public procurement, to advance its industry policy. Before coming to office, the ALP had announced its intentions to implement a 'Buy Australian Plan' involving 'laws that will lock in key elements of Commonwealth Procurement Rules to actively support local industry in taking advantage of government purchasing opportunities' (Albanese, 2021). The program was established soon after taking office, with a Procurement Capability Branch created with the Department of Finance and rules laid down for what constituted an Australian business for purposes of public procurement.

'Defence is the largest Commonwealth procurement agency' (Defence, 2024: 34). Sheer size, the cutting-edge technologies it deals with, and the strategic importance of domestic supply chains, have always made military spending a focal point of procurement considerations (Ross, 1995). It is, however, particularly challenging for a small country (Markowski, Hall and Wylie, 2010). Australia builds or has built major naval weapons platforms at home – submarines, destroyers, frigates, patrol boats – notwithstanding the inevitable economic inefficiencies because of their perceived industrial value. As an element in the 'buy Australian' component of its industry policy, the Albanese Government released its *Defence Industry Development Strategy* document in 2024, outlining a commitment to strengthening the country's 'sovereign defence industrial base' through facilitation and cultivation of domestic firms (Defence, 2024).

Future of the 'future made in Australia'

Active industry policy made its return with the Albanese Government's Future Made in Australia package, a signature theme of its first term in office. Such an initiative to stem the decline of Australian industry is inherently ambitious – critics would say foolhardy – working very much against the odds. It reflects the intellectual revival of industry policy enthusiasm and the headwinds that Australia and other countries have faced with interruptions to supply chains in what has become a highly interdependent world economy as well as disruptions inflicted by the Trump administration's tariff policies in the United States. Money has been committed; programs and procedures have been established; and various subsidies distributed. To considerable extent it is a 'picking winners' approach of targeted funding for specific firms and industries. This can take various forms: propping up existing firms; encouraging domestic processing of resource exports; promoting import substitution; buying Australia a seat at the table in areas of new technology. Overall, there is a strong whiff of the infant industry argument that with a bit of help, new Australian firms and industries can be launched on their way.

Of outcomes, little can be said at this stage; strategic industry policy is not an investment that will bear fruit in the short term. Only over the medium to long term will it be possible to judge the program's overall success, and for that to occur, it is a program that must be maintained over the medium to long term. It must be embedded in institutions and processes and pursued on a scale sufficient to make a measurable difference. From that point of view, the re-election of the Albanese Government in May 2025 is auspicious. Potential clearly exists to maximise economic benefits from the energy transition, but at the same time there are undeniable risks in policies that threaten to increase the price of the electricity on which processing and manufacturing relies. And then there is the matter of business taxation: cutting corporate tax may well promote the kind of investment required here, but it is not a policy the Labor Party tends to embrace enthusiastically (Sobeck, 2024).

The idea of making Australia a 'global leader in manufacturing and innovation' is clearly preposterous, but more modest gains are possible. That takes sustained political will, which itself generally has certain prerequisites – notably 'a clear and present economic or strategic danger' (Fenna, 2016: 630).

References

ANAO, *Design and Establishment of the National Reconstruction Fund*, Australian National Audit Office, Canberra, 2025.

Australian Bureau of Statistics, *Research and Experimental Development, Businesses, Australia*, Canberra, 2023.

Australian Industrial Transformation Institute, *Manufacturing Transformation: High Value Manufacturing for the 21st Century*, Flinders University of South Australia, 2021.

Albanese, A, 'Labor's Buy Australian Plan to support Australian businesses and jobs in COVID recovery', 9 October 2021.

— Election Campaign Launch Speech, 2022.

— '$1 Billion Solar Sunshot program', 31 August 2024.

Baquie, S, et al., *Industrial Policies: Handle with Care*, International Monetary Fund, March 2025.

Clean Energy Finance Corporation, *Investing in Green Hydrogen*, Canberra, 2024.

Chalmers, J, 'Budget Speech 2022–23', 2022.

Defence, Department of, *Defence Industry Development Strategy*, Canberra, 2024.

Department of Climate Change, Energy, and Environment and Water, *National Hydrogen Strategy 2024*, Canberra, 2024.

Department of Industry, Science and Resources, *Critical Minerals Strategy 2023–2030*, Canberra, 2023a.

— *Critical Technologies Statement*, Canberra, 2023b.

— *National Quantum Stragegy*, Canberra, 2023c.

— *National Battery Strategy: Leading the Charge Towards a Competitive and Diverse Australian Battery Industry*, Canberra, 23 May 2024.

Fenna, A, 'Putting the "Australian Settlement" in perspective', *Labour History*, vol. 102, 2012, pp. 99–118.

— 'Shaping comparative advantage: The evolution of trade and industry policy in Australia', *Australian Journal of Political Science*, vol. 51, no. 4, 2016, pp. 618–35.

Garnaut, R, *Superpower: Australia's Low-Carbon Opportunity*, La Trobe University Press, Melbourne, 2019.

Growth Lab, *Australia*, Harvard University, 2025.

House Standing Committee on Industry Science and Resources, *Developing Advanced Manufacturing in Australia*, Canberra, 2023.

Husic, E, 'Second reading speech', House of Representatives, Canberra, 2022.

Juhász, R, Lane, N and Rodrik, D, 'The New Economics of Industrial Policy', *Annual Review of Economics*, vol. 16, no. 1, 2024, pp. 213–42.

Mandala, *Production Tax Credit for Value-Added Processing of Australia's Critical Minerals*, Association of Mining and Exploration Companies, 2023.

Markowski, S, Hall, P, and Wylie, R (eds), *Defence Procurement and Industry Policy: A Small Country Perspective*, Routledge, Oxford, 2010.

Mazzucato, M, *The Entrepreneurial State: Debunking Public vs Private Sector Myths*, Anthem, London, 2013.

Minerals Council of Australia, *Submission to the House Standing Committee on Industry Science and Resources Inquiry into Developing Advanced Manufacturing in Australia*, 6 April 2023.

National Reconstruction Fund Corporation, *Corporate Plan 24–25*, Canberra, 2024.

Phillimore, J, and Leong, K, 'Economic Diversification in Australia', in *Economic Diversification Policies in Natural Resource Rich Economies*, Mahroum, S, and Al-Saleh, Y (eds), Routledge, Oxford, 2017, pp. 148–74.

Productivity Commission, *Vulnerable Supply Chains*, Melbourne, 2021.

Robson, A, 'Optimal industry policy', CSIRO Innovation for Impact Summit, 2023.

Ross, A, *Armed and Ready: The Industrial Development and Defence of Australia 1900–1945*, Turton and Armstrong, Sydney, 1995.

Senate Standing Committee on Economics, *The Australian Manufacturing Industry*, Canberra, February 2022.

Sobeck, K, 'Suddenly, there's talk about Labor reforming company tax. What did minister Ed Husic say, and what might actually work?' *The Conversation*, 30 May 2024.

Stanford, J, *A Fair Share for Australian Manufacturing: Manufacturing renewal for the post-COVID economy*, Australia Institute, Centre for Future Work, 2020.

Thornton, K, 'Statement on the Federal Government's Solar Sunshot Manufacturing Announcement', Clean Energy Council, 28 March 2024.

Wood, T, and Reeve, A, *How to Forge a Future Made in Australia*, Grattan Institute, 2024.

Yim, N, and Thompson, 'Anthony Albanese stares down critical minerals bureaucracy concerns', *Australian*, 8 January 2025.

CHAPTER 9

INDUSTRIAL RELATIONS POLICY: BALANCING EFFICIENCY WITH FAIRNESS

BRADON ELLEM, CHRIS F WRIGHT, STEPHEN CLIBBORN, RAE COOPER, FRANCES FLANAGAN AND ALEX VEEN

Industrial relations policy reform was central to the Labor Party's victory at the May 2022 election, as it has been in national politics for 30 years. In 1996 and 2005, the Howard Liberal–National Coalition Government radically overhauled the system, but an electoral backlash was core to its defeat at the 2007 election (Wilson and Spies-Butcher, 2011). The Rudd–Gillard Labor Government then introduced the *Fair Work Act 2009*, but neither employer groups nor unions were satisfied with it. Despite pressure from employer groups, the Abbott–Turnbull–Morrison Coalition governments largely shied away from undoing Labor's reform (Cooper, 2016). Nevertheless, as the economy and workplaces changed, policy stasis served business needs (Ellem et al., 2025).

In 2022, Labor pledged to 'get wages moving again' following a long period of stagnation. Labor argued that policymaking had not engaged with this or other labour market problems. A large share of the workforce was engaged on insecure (non-permanent) contracts. Gender inequality at work had received heightened public attention during Covid when the community's reliance on low-paid, undervalued, female-dominated jobs in care and health became obvious. As for collective bargaining – critical for regulating wages and working conditions – employer groups and unions agreed, albeit for different reasons, that the framework had become dysfunctional.

Managing industrial relations is tricky for governments keen to balance employer demands for 'efficiency' with worker demands for 'fairness'. After 30 years of 'efficiency-oriented' industrial relations policies that generally favoured employers, the Albanese Government's changes were largely aimed at making the wage-setting system easier to use for workers and unions whose weakened position had contributed to low wage growth and insecure work (Stanford et al., 2018).

Background and key provisions for reform

Soon after Labor's 2022 election victory, the new Minister for Employment and Workplace Relations, Tony Burke, announced plans to 'boost job security and get wages moving'. He highlighted the government's intention of making 'job security an object of the Fair Work Act, getting a better deal for gig workers, stopping the labour hire rorts that are undermining wages, making wage theft a crime, limiting the use of fixed-term contracts and ensuring a better deal for women' (Burke, 2022).

These plans were further developed at the September 2022 Jobs and Skills Summit where there was broad support for these objectives – seen as necessary for productivity improvement and inclusive growth – from employer, union, government and community sector representatives and academics in attendance (Australian Government, 2022).

At the summit's conclusion, the government announced commitments that later formed the 'Secure Jobs, Better Pay' amendments to the Fair Work Act. These amendments, introduced to parliament in October 2022, were aimed at addressing the above-mentioned problems, notably improving workplace gender equality, strengthening collective bargaining and making jobs more secure. These amendments were passed in December 2022, coming into effect the following year.

The government introduced the second major component of industrial relations reform, the 'Closing Loopholes' amendments to the Fair Work Act, to parliament in September 2023. These amendments, discussed further below, aimed to respond to the impacts of labour market disruption, like the platform economy and business outsourcing. These disruptions had undermined the effectiveness of industrial relations laws and compounded inequality and insecurity.

The Secure Jobs, Better Pay and Closing Loopholes amendments attracted strong support from unions, who believed the new laws provided necessary protections for workers, and strong opposition from employer associations, who asserted they were an impost on businesses. Australian Industry Group CEO Innes Willox said they would 'not create a single job, do nothing to boost productivity, and will stifle innovation' (Yun, 2023). However, the research evidence cited in the Senate reviews of both sets of laws suggested the provisions would address gender inequality, lead to fair and more productive employment arrangements and improve job quality, particularly for workers in female-dominated occupations and sectors (Senate Education and Employment Legislation Committee, 2022, 2024). This evidence helped the government convince the Senate crossbench of the merits of these changes.

Gender equality at work

Since the 1980s, a marked increase in women's participation in the paid workforce has constituted a profound shift. Despite the narrowing of the gap between women's and men's labour force participation, significant gender inequalities in work remain, as evidenced by the enduring gender pay gap, low pay, poor job quality in female-dominated occupations and the major challenges workers face in balancing their work and care responsibilities. The Rudd–Gillard Government's paid parental leave scheme and a right to request flexible working arrangements addressed these problems, but only partially.

Improving wages and job quality in highly feminised sectors was a foremost objective of the 2022 Secure Jobs, Better Pay reforms. Four specific elements are noteworthy. First, the legislation added 'gender equality' to the objectives of the Fair Work Act. This requires the Fair Work Commission to address gender pay inequity and gender-based undervaluation when reviewing minimum wages. Second, it is now easier for the Fair Work Commission to address the undervaluation of jobs in female-dominated sectors. Third, it allowed workers in low-paid, typically female-dominated, sectors to seek to establish and extend collective bargaining agreements covering multiple employers. Finally, a more rigorous process was established for evaluating employees' right to request flexible working arrangements.

This last change is especially significant because this right had previously been framed such that employees were merely allowed to request flexible working arrangements, but employers were not compelled to grant them. Such requests were typically refused on 'reasonable business grounds' with little recourse for employee appeal, resulting in very low uptake of flexible work arrangements. The enhanced right to request requires employers to justify their decisions in response to flexible work arrangements requests in writing, and grants employees the capacity to appeal refusals to the Fair Work Commission (Cooper and Lee, 2024).

Many employees experienced flexible working arrangements, such as working from home, for the first time during the Covid pandemic. This change in practice heightened employee demands and union campaigns for better access to flexible working arrangements.

Other notable changes improved workplace gender equality: amendments making pay secrecy clauses in employment contracts unlawful, strengthening workplace protections for family and domestic violence and sexual harassment victims, and changes to statutory paid parental leave. The last of these extended the duration of paid parental leave from 18 weeks to 26 weeks and encouraged greater use of paid parental leave by non-birthing parents. These changes aimed to make workplaces more responsive to employees with family needs and improve the experience of women in the labour market.

Collective bargaining

Strengthening collective bargaining was central to the Albanese Government's industrial relations policies. It was undoubtedly the most controversial element of the reforms, fiercely resisted by national employer organisations, who claimed it would result in increased industrial action, economic malaise and unemployment. The Business Council of Australia (2022) argued the changes would: 'cripple supply chains, leave supermarket shelves empty, commuters unable to get to work and lives disrupted'.

This reaction was at odds with international research showing that forms of multi-employer bargaining, which the reforms aimed to promote, could lead to better economic and social outcomes compared with the decentralised, enterprise-focused arrangements hitherto operating in Australia (Organisation for Economic Cooperation and Development, 2019).

The government declared at the Jobs and Skills Summit that it would 'make bargaining accessible for all workers and businesses' (Australian Government, 2022). This would help to fulfil its election promise to 'get wages moving again', since average earnings for employees covered by collective agreements were nearly twice those of employees whose wages were set by awards only (Australian Bureau of Statistics, 2023). The proposal to strengthen multi-employer agreements reflected a long-running concern of the union movement. The Australian Council of Trade Unions had proposed shifting the bargaining system from its focus on enterprise-only agreements to one allowing agreements covering multiple employers. It was not only the unions calling for reform. The Governor of the Reserve Bank of Australia had argued that the 'crisis of low pay' was due to 'changes in the nature of work and bargaining arrangements [which] mean that many workers feel like they have less bargaining power than they once did' (Lowe, 2017).

The Secure Jobs, Better Pay reforms aimed to promote multi-employer bargaining through three mechanisms:

- The 'supported bargaining' stream for low-paid, government-funded and mainly female-dominated sectors, such as aged care, disability care and early childhood education.
- The 'cooperative workplaces' stream allowing employers and unions to establish multi-employer agreements voluntarily with the majority support of affected employees.
- A 'single-interest' bargaining stream allowing unions or employers to apply for the creation of multi-employer agreements among enterprises with 'reasonably comparable' operations.

The single-interest stream was the most controversial. The amendments left it to the Fair Work Commission to interpret what 'reasonably comparable' means, but it might include employers in the same industry, region or business structure. Partly in response to employer and crossbench parliamentarian concerns, the government agreed to exclude the construction industry, employers with fewer than 20 employees and employers with an existing enterprise agreement from the multi-employer bargaining laws (Ellem et al., 2025).

The Closing Loopholes reforms included provisions designed to give effect to the new bargaining laws, such as increased protections for union workplace delegates to represent employees during bargaining and in discussions with their employer (Peetz, 2024). The proportion of employees who are members of unions has been in near-continuous decline for the past half-century, falling from 50 per cent in 1980 to 12.5 per cent in 2022. However, union membership density increased slightly to 13.1 per cent in 2024 (see figure 1), to which these changes to union rights may have contributed.

Figure 9.1: Trade union membership by sex, 1980 to 2024, Australia

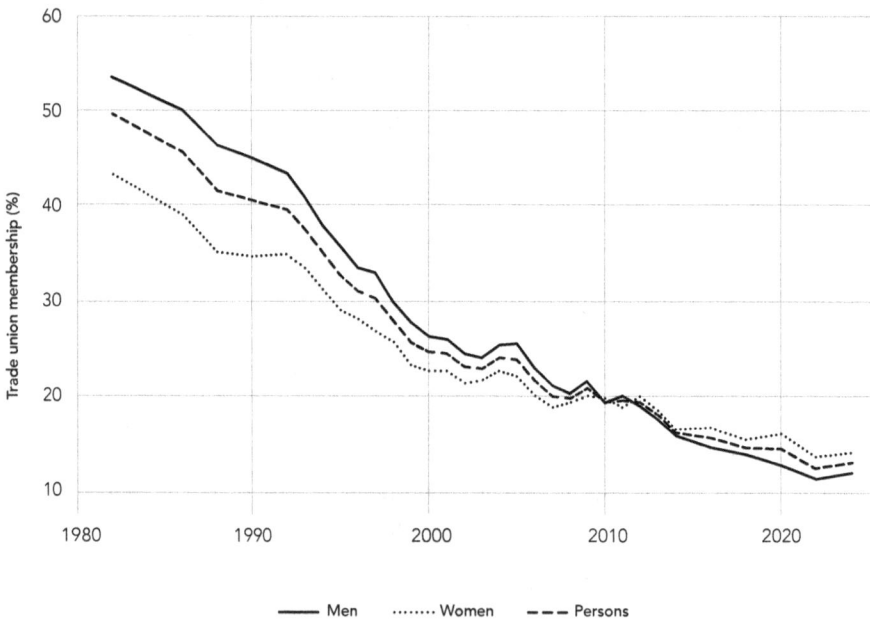

SOURCE Australian Bureau of Statistics (2024)

The Closing Loopholes legislation also empowered the Fair Work Commission to require labour hire employees to be paid in line with a host company's collective agreement through 'same job, same pay' orders. This aimed to stop employers engaging labour hire operators to circumvent an agreement's minimum standards.

Improving worker security

The Secure Jobs, Better Pay and Closing Loopholes amendments to the Fair Work Act aimed to strengthen job and income security. These reforms sought to address underpayment or 'wage theft', introduced minimum standards for contract workers including those in the platform economy, established a 'right to disconnect' and allowed workers on casual or fixed-term contracts to convert to permanent employment more easily.

Underpayment had intensified under the previous Coalition Government. According to Minister Burke, this occurred 'because of loopholes that allow pay and conditions to be undercut. For these workers the minimum standards in awards and enterprise agreements are words on a page, with little relevance to their daily lives'. This disadvantaged not only workers but also compliant employers, because the 'businesses which use these loopholes are able to undercut Australia's best employers in a race to the bottom' (Burke, 2023).

The Albanese Government legislated for stronger penalties, including increased fines for those recklessly, and criminal sanctions for those intentionally, underpaying their employees. The government expanded the Fair Work Ombudsman's enforcement activities and allowed paid union officials to apply to the Fair Work Commission to enter workplaces to inspect company pay records without notice in cases of suspected wage theft. It also changed immigration policies to try to reduce the vulnerabilities of temporary migrant workers.

These reforms were accompanied by protections for workers not previously covered by the Fair Work Act, most obviously those in the platform economy. While previous governments had resisted calls to extend the coverage of the Fair Work Act to these workers, who are legally classified not as 'employees' but as 'contractors', the Albanese Government gave the Fair Work Commission power to set minimum protections for these workers, along with certain contractors in the road transport industry (Workplace Express, 2023). The reforms also created a new unfair contracts jurisdiction, enabling defined contractors across the economy to turn to the Fair Work Commission rather than the more costly court system to seek adjudication.

The government also introduced a 'right to disconnect', following the examples of some other countries, to limit employers from encroaching upon workers' non-work time, a practice which had intensified with the rise of smartphones. This measure, introduced in response to calls from the Greens, whose support Labor relied upon to get the Secure Jobs, Better Pay and Closing Loopholes legislation through the Senate, 'empower[ed] workers to ignore work calls and emails after hours [from their employers], where those demands are unreasonable', according to Greens Senator Barbara Pocock (Marin-Guzman, 2023). The new Australian laws empowered the Fair Work Commission to impose sanctions against employers who 'unreasonably' expect employees to perform unpaid work outside of normal hours (Josserand and Boersma, 2024).

The reforms amended the Fair Work Act's definition of casual employees and arrangements for converting from casual to permanent employment. The new casual employee definition recognised the reality of the employment relationship, a departure from the existing definition, which gave primacy to the express terms of the contract. Limitations were also placed on the use of fixed-term contracts.

Complementary labour market reforms

Industrial relations policy changes were accompanied by complementary labour market and regulatory reforms. These included changes to the power and composition of the Fair Work Commission, the forced administration of the Construction, Forestry and Maritime Employees Union (CFMEU), addressing problems with the regulation of skills and workforce supply, and reforms to industry policy.

The Fair Work Commission and its national predecessor bodies have always been significant actors. For most of the 20th century, the Australian Constitution was read as limiting the power of the executive and legislature to regulate industrial relations. Instead, the Fair Work Commission's predecessors were tasked with this role. Reinterpretations of the Constitution mean the Australian Parliament now has greater direct authority in setting minimum employment standards, but the Fair Work Commission remains vital, setting minimum wages and resolving disputes – increasingly individual disputes (Bray and Macneil, 2023). The Albanese Government's changes enhanced these functions of the Fair Work Commission. It gained new powers to set minimum standards for contract workers (discussed above) and absorbed the functions of the Australian Building and Construction Commission and Registered Organisations Commission.

Following media investigations into the CFMEU's ties with organised crime, the government placed the union's national and divisional branches into forced administration for up to five years (Marin-Guzman, 2024). While the government resisted pressure to deregister the union, this development placed a spotlight on its abolition of the Australian Building and Construction Commission.

The government oversaw changes to workforce policy that complemented its industrial relations reforms. It created a new agency, Jobs and Skills Australia, to co-ordinate different elements of workforce policy across education, training and immigration in collaboration with employer associations and unions. The government commissioned a major independent review of the immigration system to fix the longstanding problem of employers underpaying and mistreating workers on temporary visas (Australian Government, 2022). The review resulted in notable changes, including allowing workers on temporary skilled visas to leave their employer more easily and helping migrant workers to recover underpaid wages (Department of Home Affairs, 2023).

A Future Made in Australia, the Albanese Government's policy aimed at steering Australia towards a lower carbon emissions economy, also complemented its industrial relations policy. It will provide support for workers transitioning from fossil-fuel employment through an Energy Industry Jobs Plan.

A signature achievement?

Industrial relations policy reform was one of the Albanese Government's signature first-term achievements. Labor's 2025 election victory will likely allow the government to take steps to embed its reforms, despite strong opposition from business groups who claimed the changes would lead to economic chaos. However, the previous system had been heavily skewed in employers' favour, and early evidence suggests the Albanese Government's changes have helped to address this without notable negative economic impacts. A major independent review of the Secure Jobs, Better Pay reforms found they were 'operating appropriately and effectively and with minimal unintended consequences' (Bray and Preston, 2025). After a prolonged period of wage stagnation, there has been real wages growth (Peetz, 2025) and the gender wage gap has fallen to historically low levels. The result is an industrial relations system that appears more attuned to balancing businesses' need for efficiency with workers' demands for fairness. The long-term impacts of the reforms remain to be seen and will likely depend on future election outcomes and whether the long-term decline in worker membership of trade unions can be arrested.

References

Australian Bureau of Statistics, 'Employee earnings and hours, Australia', 2023.
— 'Trade union membership', 2024.
Australian Government, *Jobs and Skills Summit – Outcomes*, Canberra, 2022.
Bray, M, and Macneil J, 'Still central: change and continuity in Australia's major industrial tribunal', *Industrial Relations Journal*, vol. 54, no. 4–5, 2023, pp. 359–76.
Bray, M, and Preston, A, *Secure Jobs, Better Pay Review: Draft Report*. Canberra, 2025.
Burke, T, 'New ABS labour force figures', Minister for Employment and Workplace Relations, media release, 16 June 2022.
— 'Second reading speech: Fair Work Legislation Amendment (Closing Loopholes) Bill 2023', 4 September 2023.
Business Council of Australia, 'Australia can't afford workplace relations own goal', media release, 27 October 2022.
Cooper, R, 'Dead, buried, cremated and exhumed? Consensus in industrial relations policy and politics in Australia, 2007–2015', in Hancock, K, and Lansbury, R (eds), *Industrial Relations Reform: Looking to the Future Essays*, Federation Press, Sydney, 2016, pp. 66–84.

Cooper, R, and Lee, T, 'What's IR got to do with it? Building gender equality in the post pandemic future of work', in Rönnmar, M, and Hayter, S (eds), *Making and Breaking Gender Inequalities in Work*, Edward Elgar, Cheltenham, UK, 2024, pp. 116–36.

Department of Home Affairs, *Migration Strategy*, Canberra, 2023.

Ellem, B, et al., *Work and Industrial Relations Policy in Australia*, Bristol University Press, Bristol, 2025.

Josserand, E, and Boersma, M, 'Australia's right to disconnect from work: Beyond rhetoric and towards implementation', *Journal of Industrial Relations*, vol. 66, no. 5, 2024, pp. 703–20.

Lowe, P, 'Some evolving questions. Address to the Australian Business Economists Annual Dinner', 21 November 2017, <https://www.rba.gov.au/speeches/2017/sp-gov-2017-11-21.html>.

Marin-Guzman, D, 'Business fights back against "right to disconnect" from work', *Australian Financial Review*, 21 December 2023.

— 'CFMEU fights back against administration', *Australian Financial Review*, 23 August 2024.

Organisation for Economic Cooperation and Development, *Negotiating Our Way Up: Collective Bargaining in a Changing World of Work*, OECD Publishing, Paris, 2019.

Peetz, D, *Employee Voice and New Rights for Workplace Union Delegates: Impacts on Wages, Productivity, Cooperation and Union Training*, Carmichael Centre, Canberra, 2024.

— *The Curious Incident of Low Wages Growth*, Carmichael Centre, Canberra, 2025.

Senate Education and Employment Legislation Committee, *Fair Work Legislation Amendment (Secure Jobs, Better Pay) Bill 2022 [Provisions]: Inquiry Report*, Canberra, 2022.

— *Fair Work Amendment Bill 2024*, Commonwealth of Australia, Canberra, 2024.

Stanford, J, Hardy, T, and Stewart, A, 'Australia, we have a problem', in Stewart, A, Stanford, J, and Hardy, T (eds), *The Wages Crisis in Australia: What It Is and What to Do About It*, University of Adelaide Press, Adelaide, 2018, pp. 3–20.

Wilson, S, and Spies-Butcher, B, 'When labour makes a difference: union mobilization and the 2007 federal election in Australia', *British Journal of Industrial Relations*, vol. 49, no. 2, 2011, pp. 306–31.

Workplace Express, 'Burke lays out year's IR agenda', *Workplace Express*, 1 February 2023.

Yun, J, 'Why Labor's $1 billion gig work, labour-hire reforms have been shelved', *Sydney Morning Herald*, 8 September 2023.

CHAPTER 10

HOUSING: BETTER LUCK NEXT TERM

BRENDAN COATES

Upon its election in May 2022, the Albanese Government inherited a housing crisis which only worsened over the course of its first term. Sharply rising house prices, despite rapid rises in interest rates, and a spike in rents kept housing affordability squarely on the national agenda.

The first term of the Albanese Government was marked by constant activity on housing. The government made incremental but steady progress on social housing investment and more assistance to renters. But it largely failed to shift the dial on the underlying problem of supply.

A slow-building housing crisis, worsened by the pandemic

Australia's housing problem had been building for decades before the election of the Albanese Government. House prices had grown much faster than incomes across Australia: from about four times median incomes in the early 2000s, to nearly eight times by September 2024, and nearly ten times in Sydney.

Housing had always been most expensive in the two largest capital cities – Sydney and Melbourne – but the pandemic and its aftermath have seen Australia's housing crisis go truly national.

Between March 2020 and September 2025, house prices had spiked across the country. House prices rose by 90 per cent in Perth and 80 per cent in Brisbane and Adelaide, compared to 46 per cent in Sydney and just 20 per cent in Melbourne. The prices of units grew more slowly in each city but there were still price gains in all capitals except Melbourne.

Figure 10.1: House prices have risen significantly post-pandemic, but have since slowed in most cities

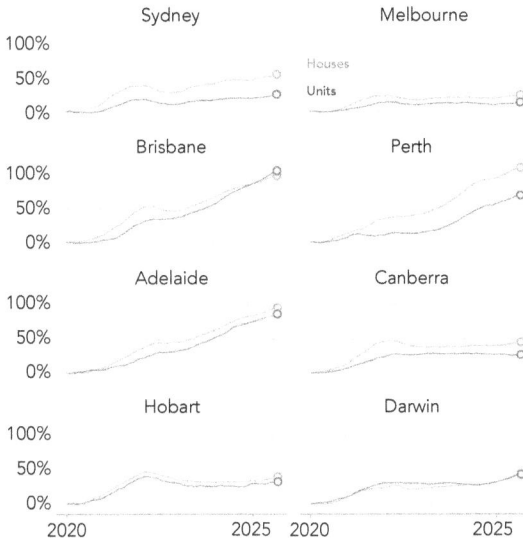

SOURCE Grattan analysis of PropTrack Home Price Index (October 2024)

Figure 10.2: Rents have risen sharply since the pandemic across most of Australia

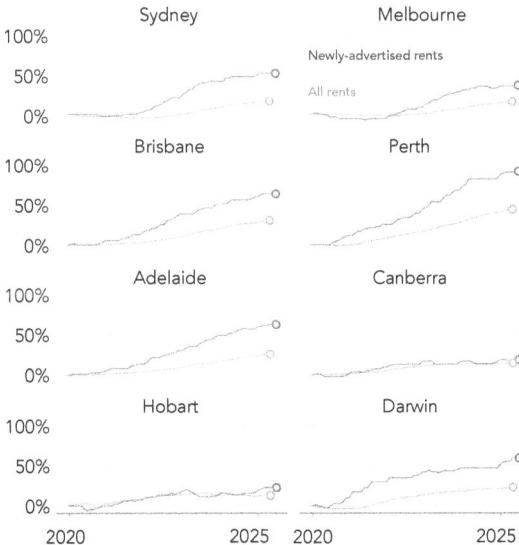

SOURCE Grattan analysis of PropTrack and ABS Consumer Price Index (June 2024)

These price increases occurred despite sharply higher interest rates over the term of parliament. Between May 2022 and November 2023, the Reserve Bank increased interest rates 13 times, lifting the cash rate from 0.1 per cent to 4.35 per cent, before cutting rates in February 2025 to 4.10 per cent. As a result, a first home buyer now needs to spend a larger share of their income to pay the mortgage on a median-priced home than at any time in the past two decades.

Over the first term of the Albanese Government, rental vacancy rates fell to record lows and asking rents (that is for newly advertised properties) rose by roughly 40 per cent in Sydney and Perth, and 30 per cent in Melbourne, Brisbane and Adelaide. Rents paid by all renters – as measured by the consumer price index – rose in line with the spike in inflation, but still have further to rise.

And Australia's stock of social housing had barely grown over the 20 years before the Albanese Government was elected, while the population has increased by one-third (Coates et al., 2025).

Australians demanded more homes

House prices and rents rose sharply in the aftermath of the pandemic because demand for housing rose much faster than our capacity to build more of it.

The pandemic and the ensuing work-from-home revolution spurred a 'race for space', with some people moving out of the family home or share house, or using an extra bedroom as a home office. Despite falls from the pandemic-era peak, the share of people working remotely at least some of the time has stabilised at 30 per cent, up from 10 per cent before Covid.

Migration rebounded

A sharp rebound in migration after the pandemic added further to housing demand. Net overseas migration – the net change in the resident population of Australia due to migration – jumped sharply as migrants returned in

Figure 10.3: Australia's population is about where it would've been if the pre-pandemic trend had continued

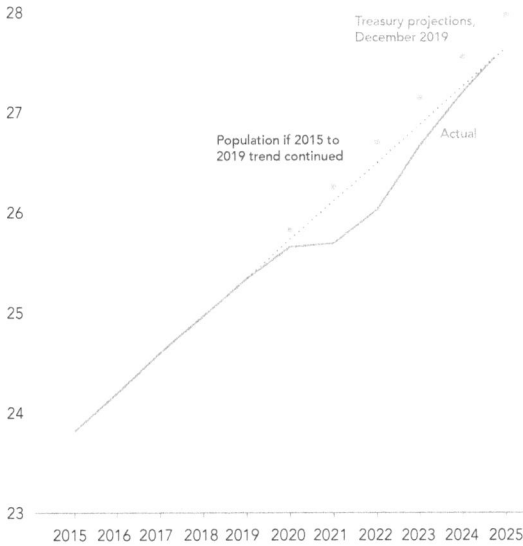

SOURCE Grattan analysis of ABS

record numbers after Australia's international border reopened, while fewer residents than usual left Australia.

After a net outflow of 84 000 migrants in the year to March 2021, net overseas migration rebounded strongly to peak at 555 798 in the 12 months to September 2023, the highest figure on record, before falling to 446 000 over the year to June 2024. That's well above the long-term average of 21 000 per year over the decade to 2019–20.

The Grattan Institute estimates that with every 100 000 extra migrants, rents rise by about 1 per cent. Those higher rents benefit property owners – and boost national income – but they hurt vulnerable Australians already struggling to pay the rent.

Yet Australia's resident population is only now around where it was expected to have been without the disruption of closed borders, based on the pre-Covid trend. Therefore, stronger local demand, rather than migration, has arguably been the bigger driver of rising rents since the pandemic.

A modest set of housing election commitments

The Labor Party went to the 2022 federal election with a modest pitch to build more social housing, and to help first home buyers.

The Housing Australia Future Fund (HAFF), based on a Grattan Institute proposal, is expected to support construction of 20 000 social homes and 10 000 affordable homes over five years. In the 2023 Budget, the Albanese Government committed to a further 10 000 affordable homes, at a cost of $350 million over five years.

The federal Help to Buy shared equity scheme would help first home buyers to purchase a home. The government would provide an equity contribution of up to 40 per cent of the purchase price of a new home, and up to 30 per cent for an existing dwelling, with buyers needing a minimum deposit of only 2 per cent. Just 10 000 places would be offered each year for the first four years, limiting any upward pressure on house prices.

The 2023 Budget announced that build-to-rent housing projects – where new homes are held by institutional investors and rented out, rather than sold off – would benefit from accelerated tax deductions and a lower tax withholding rate for foreign investors in managed investment trusts.

All these policies were a step in the right direction but were delayed by the crossbenchers in the Senate for much of the term of parliament.

Housing election commitments delayed

The 2022 election delivered a Senate broadly sympathetic to the Albanese Government's housing agenda.

But over the first 18 months of the Albanese Government, the Greens made a series of demands in exchange for passing the government's housing legislation, including a national rent freeze for two years, a substantial boost in funding for social and affordable housing, and reforms to negative gearing and the capital gains tax discount.

The Albanese Government largely refused to countenance these demands.

The HAFF only passed the Parliament in September 2023 in exchange for a guarantee that at least $500 million would be spent each year from the

HAFF, and a minimum of 1200 homes would be built in each state and territory across the five-year period. A further $1 billion would also be spent building more homes.

The delay in passing the fund, plus the slow pace in allocating HAFF funding for new homes, meant that only 8246 social and affordable homes, out of a planned 40 000, were contracted to be supplied before caretaker conventions came into effect before the May 2025 election.

The Help to Buy shared equity scheme passed the Parliament in November 2024, one year after the legislation was introduced, but the scheme did not come into effect during the term, because the states each needed to pass their own legislation before it could commence.

More support for vulnerable renters

A key success of housing policy during the term was boosting the maximum rate of Commonwealth Rent Assistance for the 1.3 million households that rely on the payment.

The government raised the maximum rate of Rent Assistance by a total of 27 per cent – over and above inflation – in the 2023 and 2024 budgets. These increases boosted the maximum rate for singles by $44 a fortnight, or $1158 a year. These were the first back-to-back real increases to Commonwealth Rent Assistance in more than 30 years and boosted the incomes of vulnerable renters by a combined $1.35 billion a year.

But even with these increases, Rent Assistance remains inadequate. After accounting for a basic budget of non-housing essentials, a single age pensioner has less than $300 per week to pay for rent – enough to rent just the cheapest 4 per cent of one-bedroom homes in Sydney, 13 per cent in Brisbane, and 14 per cent in Melbourne (Coates et al., 2025).

Working-age welfare recipients, whose primary income support payment is much lower than the Age Pension, can afford to spend even less on rent after covering basic essentials. For example, someone on the single rate of JobSeeker would have only $100 per week left to pay rent after covering an essentials-only budget, less than half the amount needed to share a cheap two-bedroom home in a capital city (Coates et al., 2025).

Australia hasn't built enough homes

Historically, Australia had not built enough housing to meet the needs of Australia's growing population. As of 2021, Australia had just over 400 dwellings per 1000 people, which was among the least housing stock per person in the developed world. Australia is one of only a few countries to see a decline in housing stock relative to the adult population over the 20 years leading into Covid.

Land-use planning rules that constrain development have led to less medium- and high-density housing than Australians actually want. The result is 'missing middles': hectares of prime inner-city land in our biggest cities, close to jobs and transport, with housing rising barely taller than two storeys. The flow-on effect is high prices and rents, and a weaker economy because fewer people can live close to jobs.

Figure 10.4: Australia's housing per adult has gone backwards over the past two decades, change in dwellings per 1000 adults, 2000 to 2020 or closest available

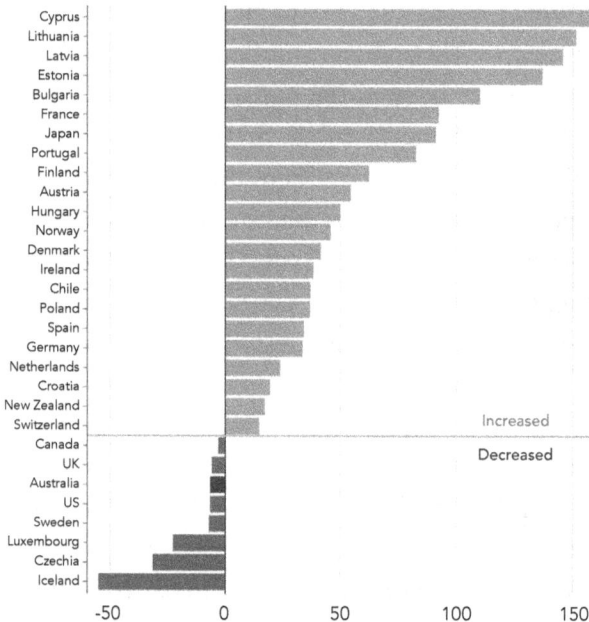

SOURCE OECD Affordable Housing Database, ABS 2021 Census

Housing construction slowed further

But housing construction slowed further in the aftermath of the pandemic, just as demand for housing really took off. New building approvals for housing have fallen substantially over the past decade to just 188 000 in the year to August 2025.

The slow pace of new housing construction over the first term of the Albanese Government reflected three constraints.

First, the cost of construction materials had jumped sharply since the start of the Covid pandemic. The cost of constructing new housing rose by 36 per cent between March 2020 and early 2025.

Second, the cost of labour has jumped, with low unemployment, which remained at or below 4 per cent over the term of parliament and competing demands for construction workers from the public infrastructure boom.

Third, sharply higher interest rates slowed housing approvals, especially for higher-density developments. Researchers at the Reserve Bank estimate that each 1 percentage point rise in real interest rates reduced housing approvals in the following year by 7 per cent (Saunders and Tulip, 2019).

National Cabinet Housing Plan for 1.2 million homes

While much of Australia's debate on housing affordability plays out nationally, the real power to solve it rests with the states. They govern the local councils that assess most development applications, and they largely set building regulations that affect the cost of new housing.

Which is why the National Cabinet agreement to build 1.2 million homes over five years, announced in August 2023, was a major step forward. More importantly, the National Cabinet Plan included $3.5 billion in incentive payments to push the states to get more housing built. Most of that money comes from the New Home Bonus, which will give states and territories $15 000 for every home they build above their state or territory's per capita share of a 1 million-home baseline target over five years.

Federal leadership to co-ordinate state action is worthwhile because improved housing supply in one state spills over into cheaper housing elsewhere. The federal government would also collect three in every five extra tax dollars from the larger economy that would result from any reforms.

But most states are likely to undershoot substantially their per-capita share of the national baseline target of 1 million homes over five years – even if they were to make substantial reforms to get more housing built – because the cyclical conditions that make housing construction difficult are largely beyond their control. The National Housing Supply and Affordability Council expects net new housing supply to total only 938 000 homes over the five years to 2028–29 (National Housing Supply and Affordability Council, 2025).

And the federal government's incentives to push the states to get more housing built are much less effective than they could be. For example, the New Home Bonus will only be paid in arrears at the end of the five-year period, meaning states won't get the money until after 1 July 2029. Yet states will have to wear both the political blowback from reforms and the cost of supporting infrastructure for new housing in the interim.

Ultimately, the poor design of the New Home Bonus meant that the Albanese Government's support for planning reform was largely rhetorical over its first term.

The states stepped up

The biggest steps towards solving the housing crisis in Australia during the first term of the Albanese Government came not at the federal level, but from the states.

The state governments of New South Wales and Victoria have responded to the crisis with bold reforms to planning controls to allow more homes to be built in the established suburbs of Sydney and Melbourne – cities which collectively house two in five Australians. And the Victorian Government has set its own ambitious goal to build 800 000 homes over a decade.

The Victorian Government's Train and Tram Activity Centre Program will permit more housing on scarce inner-city land around 60 transport hubs across Melbourne. The New South Wales Government's Transport Oriented Development program will do the same around 45 precincts across New South Wales, including 37 in Sydney.

The Victorian Government's Townhouse and Low-Rise Code and the New South Wales Government's dual occupancy and Low- and Mid-Rise Housing policies will permit greater density more broadly across Melbourne and Sydney, especially townhouses and low-rise apartments.

And both states have established accelerated approval pathways for major residential developments.

These reforms have the potential to unlock hundreds of thousands of extra homes in the coming decades in areas of both cities with some of the best infrastructure, amenities, and public spaces.

The NSW Productivity Commission estimates that a 10 per cent increase in the housing stock – that is, over and above the level needed to match population growth – would lower housing costs by 25 per cent (NSW Productivity Commission, 2023).

This isn't merely theory. In 2016, Auckland – a city of 1.5 million – rezoned about three-quarters of its suburban area to promote denser housing. Researchers later found that the policy had boosted the housing stock by up to 4 per cent. About three-quarters of the extra housing built was two- and three-storey duplexes and townhouses scattered across the city. That extra housing reduced rents for two- and three-bedroom dwellings by up to 28 per cent, compared to if the rezoning hadn't happened, with the biggest fall in rents among cheaper dwellings (Greenaway-McGreevy, 2024).

In Australia, the rising cost of constructing new housing since the pandemic – especially higher-rise apartments – only increases the urgency of land-use planning reforms. The cost of constructing new housing in Australia has risen by 36 per cent since March 2020. But more housing can be made feasible by allowing greater density where people want to live. And streamlining development approval processes, as the Victorian government's reforms do, can reduce uncertainty and cost, reducing the return on capital that developers require and making more developments feasible.

Public opinion polls suggest these reforms are popular (Smith, 2024). And the political winds appear to be shifting. Millennials and younger generations now make up a larger share of the electorate. And they – more than their parents – seem to understand that housing will only get more affordable in Australia if we build a lot more of it.

2025: A housing election campaign to forget

Given sharp rises in rents and house prices since 2022, housing was always going to be *the* hot topic of the 2025 federal election campaign.

The Albanese Government pledged, if re-elected, to extend the First Home Guarantee scheme, which guarantees 15 per cent of the property's value for first home buyers, allowing people to buy a home with just a 5 per cent deposit and avoid Lenders Mortgage Insurance.

There would be no caps on the number of places (currently 50 000 each year), nor on the incomes of first home buyers (currently $125 000 for singles, and $200 000 for couples), starting from 1 July 2026. And property price limits would also be raised to average house prices in each city and region – rising from $900 000 to $1.5 million in Sydney, for example.

The announcement was rightly criticised as the latest in a long line of proposals to put more money in the pockets of first home buyers, especially those already likely to buy a home, which risks pushing up house prices even further.

The best that could be said for the government's plan is that it was marginally less bad than the federal Coalition's pitch to allow first home buyers to deduct the interest costs on the first $650 000 of their mortgage from their taxable income for the first five years after purchase.

More promisingly, the government announced it would invest $10 billion to partner with state governments and private developers to build up to 100 000 homes – with these homes reserved for sale only to first home buyers. If all built, these 100 000 homes would be enough to reduce house prices and rents by up to 2.5 per cent. But much will depend on its implementation.

Where to from here?

Housing – long Australia's national obsession – has become our nightmare. House prices have continued to rise, and renting is far less affordable than it was just three years ago. Did the first-term Albanese Government meet the moment on housing? The answer is clearly no.

As it began its second term, the Albanese Government could point to some important policy wins on housing, including further support to vulnerable renters, and increased investment in social housing.

But its cautious approach to governing hampered its efforts to tackle the housing crisis. As did delays in passing its modest agenda through Parliament, and in rolling it out. As a result, these programs had little impact on Australians' lives during the government's first term.

The government's focus on getting more housing built, especially via its plan for 1.2 million new homes and the $3.5 billion in incentive payments to the states, was admirable. But the plan was undercut by flaws in implementation, sharp rises in interest rates, and the rising cost of constructing new homes.

The most promising steps towards solving the housing crisis in Australia during the first term of the Albanese Government came not at the federal level, but from state government efforts in New South Wales and Victoria to reform land-use planning rules to get more housing built.

References

Coates, B, Bowes, M, and Moloney, J, *Renting in Retirement: Why Rent Assistance needs to rise*, Grattan Institute, 2025.

Greenaway-McGreevey, R, 'Causes and consequences of zoning reform in Auckland', *Cityscape: A Journal of Policy Development and Research*, vol. 26, no. 2, 2024, pp. 413–34.

National Housing Supply and Affordability Council, *State of the Housing System 2025*, 2025.

NSW Productivity Commission, *Building More Homes Where People Want to Live*, May 2023.

Saunders, T, and Tulip, P, 'A model of the Australian housing market', *Reserve Bank of Australia Research Discussion Papers*, no. 2019-01, March 2019.

Smith, A, 'Six more train stations added to high-density housing plan', *Sydney Morning Herald*, 12 April 2024.

CHAPTER 11

HEALTH POLICY 2022–2025: STARTING NECESSARY REFORM

STEPHEN DUCKETT

Hark back to May 2022 when the Albanese Government took office. Former prime minister Scott Morrison and his ministers had waged war on the states, discrediting any public health measures despite a more aggressive version of the Covid virus circulating (Duckett, 2022); bulk-billing rates were in freefall after years of government refusing to index Medicare rebates in line with inflation; under a do-nothing minister, Greg Hunt, health reform had stalled (Huxtable, 2023); and the Commonwealth Health Department had vacated any role in providing leadership to the sector (Public Service Commission, 2023).

The new Health Minister, Mark Butler, had experience in the portfolio as a minister for aged care and mental health in the Gillard–Rudd governments, and indeed, had published a book on policy issues relating to ageing (Butler, 2015). He came into office with perhaps more knowledge of the portfolio than some of its senior public servants, was keen to pursue reform after years in Opposition, and inherited many problems to address.

Public health – mixed progress

A government's primary role is to protect the population, and the first Albanese Government had only mixed success here.

The Morrison Government had left a legacy of a poorly controlled Covid pandemic, and prioritised 'opening up' and ending 'lockdowns' over public health protection. It was aided and abetted in this by a complicit media which added its strident voice to the campaign against public health interventions. The mantra of 'living with Covid' resulted in people dying with Covid: there were more than 10 000 deaths from Covid in 2022, five times the total of the previous two years (Australian Bureau of Statistics, 2024) and five to ten times the pre-Covid annual rate of influenza deaths (Barr, 2024). Government preventive action was minimal, perhaps for fear of attracting opprobrium from the media if any public health measures were proposed.

An inquiry – not a full-blown Royal Commission as recommended by a Senate Committee – was established 'to identify lessons learned to improve Australia's preparedness for future pandemics' with terms of reference which precluded the panel from considering the actions of the major players, the states and territories (Covid-19 Response Inquiry Panel (Chair: Robyn Kruk), 2024). The panel's report, although almost 1000 pages long, was bland, eschewed identifying failures in governance or the response, and sank without trace shortly after its release. Another pandemic will come again in the future, and there is unfortunately no evidence of any learning from how the Covid pandemic was handled in its first years. Sadly, a mooted Centre for Disease Control, which was supposed to re-energise national public health leadership, became yet another public policy unicorn: much talked about but as yet unseen.

Australia has long been at the forefront of tobacco control, and an early challenge for the new government was what to do about e-cigarettes ('vaping'): were they a gateway to smoking for young people or an alternative (Reynolds et al., 2024)? In May 2023, Minister Butler announced that in future vapes would be prescription only: a decision which 'propelled Australia to the forefront of global tobacco control' (Stone et al., 2024: 504) as a 'tobacco control trailblazer' (Freeman, Jongenelis, and Maddox, 2023: 1). Subsequent policy changes restricted sales to pharmacies with other regulatory conditions (Martin and Jegasothy, 2025). Regulating is one thing, enforcing another. Australia's very high excise on tobacco has created an extensive illicit trade in tobacco (Puljević et al., 2024; Martin and Jegasothy, 2025) and there is some evidence of an illicit market in vapes too (Hall, 2024). A regulatory approach employing enforcement which creates criminals out of recreational drug users, including vapers, is antithetical to a contemporary harm reduction approach. Smoking rates are increasing in young people (Roy Morgan, 2025), hinting at early signs that the policy is failing, but the balance of benefits and harms of this approach is still an open question (Stone et al., 2024).

Primary care for a population in transition

Australia, in common with many other countries, is in an epidemiological transition, with increasing prevalence of chronic disease replacing infections and childhood accidents as leading causes of death and burden of disease. The Covid pandemic is the notable exception to this trend.

Australia's healthcare system has not adapted well to these changed needs (Hall et al., 2024). The medical profession has become addicted to fee-for-service as the favoured mode of remuneration and, until recently, fought to keep it as the cornerstone of payment design. Fee-for-service rewards disintegrated care: each visit to the doctor is separately remunerated, with no payment for ongoing responsibility for a patient between visits. It makes team working harder, discouraging sharing care amongst the team because care provided by others does not attract fees to the general practitioner. Primary medical care is therefore now essentially delivered in a mono-disciplinary way with few practices having allied health professionals co-located, and most being structured as a few contracted doctors and one nurse. The needs of patients with multiple comorbidities require a quite different profile of multidisciplinary teams who can oversee patients between visits.

Medicare is a Labor brand, with the public seeing Labor governments as more trustworthy with Medicare and health policy than Liberal governments (Wooldridge, 1991; Duckett, 2008). Much was therefore made of Medicare's fortieth anniversary, which fell on 1 February 2024, with green and yellow cakes cut, and Medicare cards waved around at every opportunity (Albanese, Butler, and Shorten, 2024; May, 2024).

But these celebrations did not mean that the work of reform was not proceeding in the background. One of Health Minister Butler's achievements was to bring the medical profession along to accept a new vision for primary care and a 'blended payment' approach to remuneration, foreshadowing a significant shift in the balance/blend of fee for service and other forms of payment. He quickly established a broadly representative Strengthening Medicare Taskforce and chaired each of its meetings. The taskforce talked through the issues and developed a consensus report which recommended 'a 10-year funding commitment (with the majority of investment achieved by 2032) that includes additional funding for new general practice payments under (a) new payment architecture' (Strengthening Medicare Taskforce, 2023).

The 2023–24 Budget included a hesitant start to this reform with the announcement of myMedicare – a new scheme where patients could register with practices, thus creating an attachment between patients and a practice. Butler's approach here was a long-term one, perhaps predicated on the assumption that the Albanese Government would have more than one term. Flesh was put on the bones of the Strengthening Medicare Taskforce report by a departmental advisory panel, the report of which was still sitting on the minister's desk when the election was called (Review of General Practice Incentives, 2024).

Policy commentators have long bemoaned short-termism in politics, with three-year terms allegedly inhibiting long-term policy development and implementation. But Butler recognised the importance of major reform to primary care and eschewed a 'big bang' approach, rather building support and outlining a 'blueprint' for change over the longer term (Tuohy, 2018). All this was carried out quietly, with little public fanfare.

Meanwhile, general practice was a dumpster fire, at least as measured by financial barriers to access. Bulk-billing rates were collapsing following years without indexation as the Coalition implemented its plan for a copayment by stealth, reinforced by a parallel campaign by the Royal Australian College of General Practitioners to get practices to pull the plug on bulk billing to pressure governments to increase rebates. The combined effect of this undermining was that bulk billing declined from 87.5 per cent of general practice attendances in 2019–20 to 77.3 per cent in 2023–24. The percentage of people reporting they missed out on seeing a general practitioner because of cost increased from 3.7 per cent (one in 27 people) to 8.8 per cent (one in 11) over the same period.

In response, the new government reintroduced indexation of rebates and tripled the additional incentive payment for GPs to bulk-bill certain classes of patients. These new incentives were not enough to lift bulk-billing rates to the old levels and so, as part of the 2025 election campaign, Labor promised to extend eligibility for the incentives to all Australians. A bonus of 12.5 per cent was also offered if practices achieved 100 per cent bulk billing. This promise was matched by the Coalition.

Another 2022 election promise was partly about access and partly about hospital diversion: Medicare Urgent Care Centres (UCCs), which would provide extended hours and bulk-billed urgent care as an alternative to hospital emergency departments. Proposed at the 2022 election, UCCs proved popular with consumers/voters, but were also an alternative to general practice, which led to opposition from GP organisations. An interim evaluation of the urgent care centre program was late in coming and could be interpreted as giving comfort to both proponents and opponents (Nous Group, 2025), but by then the government had committed to establish a further 50 urgent care centres in its next term.

Finally, the government also promised to address difficulties in getting access to a general practitioner out of hours with a new telephone doctor service, labelled 1800Medicare, to provide urgent care, following triage by Healthdirect, with no out-of-pocket cost to the patient.

Mental health care: An inherited mess

Minister Butler, and his new Assistant Minister for Mental Health, Emma McBride, were faced with a different set of problems in mental health. A smelly mess, in the form of an evaluation of the Better Access Program (Pirkis et al., 2022), was deposited on their desks six months after being sworn in. The Better Access Program was introduced in 2006 and provided funding for patients to see a psychologist for up to ten sessions if consistent with a GP-developed mental health plan.

During the first two years of the Covid pandemic the Morrison Government temporarily increased the maximum number of sessions to 20. The review showed the increase was a waste of money: the number of people receiving services from a psychologist or clinical psychologist increased by about 10000 but more than one million extra services were provided (Pirkis et al., 2022, Tables 3.3 and 3.7). The scheme, based on fee-for-service remuneration with psychologists charging large out-of-pocket payments on top of the scheduled fee, was inequitable, essentially only accessible to those who could afford to pay the out-of-pockets. The report showed that although those living in low socio-economic status areas had twice the rate of psychological distress (Pirkis et al., 2022, Figure 4.7), they utilised the scheme at about a 30 per cent lower rate than people in wealthier areas (Pirkis et al., 2022, Figure 4.6).

Butler again prioritised long-term reform rather than accepting the easier but more expensive road of extending the temporary increase in visits indefinitely. He convened a broadly representative forum to discuss the issues and then created another consensus-building mechanism, showing the priority he accorded change in this domain by chairing all its meetings.

What was clearly missing from Australia's mental health infrastructure was a contemporary scheme for people to get access to needed mental health support early. In contrast, the English National Health Service now incorporates 'talking therapy' services for people with specific mild to moderate mental health conditions, providing cognitive behavioural therapy by telehealth. The 2024–25 Budget provided funding for such an initiative in Australia which will be free to the consumer, available by telehealth or online, starting in 2026. It is expected that this new service will address many people's needs and reduce demand for more expensive services.

The unfinished agenda

The two examples here of Minister Butler's successful engagement with stakeholders to build consensus on long-term system reform in primary care and mental health shows his skill as a reforming minister. The overall result is that the Albanese Government has performed well on health – embarking on a significant reform journey in a sustainable way, investing the energy to bring stakeholders along, so that the reform will stick in the long term. The election outcome and Butler's reappointment as health minister provides welcome continuity in the portfolio, showing that Butler's implicit two-term strategy has paid off, allowing consolidation of reform in the areas he identified as priorities.

But, despite the progress recounted here, much remains to be done. Bickering between private hospitals, private doctors (represented by the Australian Medical Association), and private health insurers simmered away during much of the government's first term. The government strategy simply kicked the can down the road with a 'fact check' (Department of Health and Aged Care, 2024), with none of the parties accepting that they needed to work together to fix the industry's problems, and much finger-pointing and blame-shifting between the industry stakeholders that all the problems were the fault of the other players.

Commonwealth-state negotiations on a new funding agreement for public hospital services – the current agreement expired on 30 June 2025 – are at an impasse. The Commonwealth share of public hospital funding has been declining over time and a mid-term evaluation of the current agreement revealed a litany of failures (Huxtable, 2023). The report was welcomed by both the states and the Commonwealth, an example of the triumph of hope over experience as reform aspirations in previous agreements have essentially led nowhere (Duckett, 2025 (in press)).

Despite promises of a significant injection of funds, the Commonwealth was not able to get the states over the line before the election, possibly because the hospital deal was linked to agreement about disability services reform, and possibly because of inadequate caps on hospital funding growth in the deal that is on the table.

Workforce reform – critical to ensuring access to health services into the future – has not progressed significantly. A report on scope of practice reform (Scope of Practice Review (Reviewer: Mark Cormack), 2024) was still sitting on Minister Butler's desk when the election was called. The number of health personnel is also an issue: the current flow of new entrants, falling retention rates, and changing patterns of work with reduced full-time working, mean that the current projected workforce supply will not meet need in the medium term.

The May 2023 Budget saw another reform: extending the length of prescriptions from 30 to 60 days for some medications, saving patients visits to doctors but reducing pharmacy dispensing fees. The change evoked a slew of doomsday predictions and tears in the eyes of the head of the main lobby group for pharmacy owners on TV (Massola, 2024), but no change to the policy. None of the dire predictions came to pass, but pharmaceuticals are again on the agenda at the start of the second term as an unpredictable President Trump threatens punitive tariffs on the import of Australian pharmaceutical products into the United States.

Australia's Pharmaceutical Benefits Scheme (PBS) has long attracted the ire of United States big pharma with its successful push to keep prices paid by governments and consumers in Australia low but, at least in the eyes of the United States companies, at the expense of their profits. President Trump is now threatening the PBS as part of the bargaining over tariffs, because of Australia's 'fourth hurdle' cost-effectiveness requirement before drugs are subsidised through the PBS and pricing which reflects a fairer sharing of benefits to innovators and consumers (Woods et al., 2021). Although the chair of CSL – Australia's largest pharmaceutical exporter – didn't 'think America's demand is an unreasonable demand' (Cranston, Packham, and Dowling, 2025) and the head of Australia's pharmaceutical industry lobby group supported changes to the fourth hurdle (Swannell, 2025), the Liberal Opposition has joined Labor in pledging to support the PBS (Newling, 2025). Nevertheless, the threat to the PBS will remain on Minister Butler's watch list for the duration of President Trump's term.

Butler's remit was extended post-election in the new ministerial line-up to include the National Disability Insurance Scheme, a welcome move which may mean that the stalled negotiations on the new health funding agreement, which are linked to disability reform, might be re-energised. The states will also point out to Minister Butler that 'stranded patients' – patients stuck in hospital because of poor access to more appropriate accommodation in aged care or disability facilities – are strongly driving the increased costs of public hospitals and are now clearly his to fix.

Labor played to its strengths on health during the campaign, also emphasising Opposition Leader Dutton's abysmal performance as health minister under Prime Minister Abbott, as Dutton had been dubbed Australia's worst health minister in 35 years in a poll of doctors a decade ago (Medhora, 2015). Prime Minister Albanese rarely had his Medicare card in his pocket during the campaign, waving it around at every photo opportunity. Fulfilling the health promises made during the campaign and dealing with unfinished business means that the health reform agenda for the government's second term will be a big one and will require negotiating skills of a high order to chart an affordable path forward.

Note: Stephen Duckett was a member of Minister Butler's Strengthening Medicare Taskforce and his Mental Health Advisory Group.

References

Albanese, A, Butler, M, and Shorten, B, 'Celebrating 40 years of world-leading Medicare', media release, 1 February 2024, <https://www.pm.gov.au/media/celebrating-40-years-world-leading-medicare>.

Australian Bureau of Statistics, 'COVID-19 Mortality in Australia: Deaths registered until 31 January 2024', Canberra, 2024.

Barr, I, 'Influenza in Australia before, during and after the Covid-19 pandemic', *Microbiology Australia*, vol. 45, no. 4, 2024, pp. 188–92.

Butler, M, *Advanced Australia: The politics of ageing*, Melbourne University Press, Melbourne, 2015.

Covid-19 Response Inquiry Panel, Report, Canberra, 2024.

Cranston, M, Packham, B, and Dowling, J, 'Trump's bad medicine to cost us $3bn: Albanese should consider tweaks to PBS to avoid Trump tariff', *Australian*, 10 July 2025.

Department of Health and Aged Care, *Private Hospital Sector Financial Health Check – Summary*, Canberra, 2024.

Duckett, S, 'The continuing contest of values in the Australian health care system', in den Exter, A (ed.), *International Health Law: Solidarity and Justice in Health Care*, Maklu, Antwerp, 2008, pp. 177–99.

— 'Public health management of the Covid-19 pandemic in Australia: The role of the Morrison Government', *International Journal of Environmental Research and Public Health*, vol. 19, no. 10400, 2022, p. 1–32.

— 'The National Health Reform Agreement as an instrument of broader health reform', *Journal of Australian Studies*, in press, 2025.

Freeman, B, Jongenelis, M, and Maddox, R, 'Australia: Reclaiming tobacco and e-cigarette control leadership', *Health Promotion International*, vol. 38, no. 4, 2023, daad078.

Hall, J, van Gool, K, Haywood, K, and Fiebig, D, 'Medicare at 40: Are we showing our age?', *Australian Economic Review*, vol. 57, no. 2, 2024, pp. 200–205.

Hall, WD, 'Will Australia's tightened prescription system reduce nicotine vaping among young people?', *Addiction*, vol. 119, no. 10, 2024, pp. 1682–88.

Huxtable, R, *Mid-Term Review of the National Health Reform Agreement Addendum 2020–2025: Final Report*, Canberra, 2023.

Martin, J, and Jegasothy, E, 'Fanning the flame: Analysing the emergence, implications, and challenges of Australia's de facto war on nicotine', *Harm Reduction Journal*, vol. 22, no. 1, 2025, p. 42.

Massola, J, 'This powerful lobby group claimed 665 pharmacies would close. Here's what really happened', *Sydney Morning Herald*, 2024.

May, N, 'Medicare turns 40: Is Australia's "little green card" keeping up with changing health needs?', *Guardian*, 1 February 2024.

Medhora, S, 'Peter Dutton ranked as worst health minister in 35 years in poll of doctors', *Guardian*, 12 January 2015.

Newling, N, 'Labor and Coalition in lockstep as Trump threatens to pull pharma tariffs forward', *Sydney Morning Herald*, 16 July 2025.

Nous Group, 'Evaluation of the Medicare Urgent Care Clinics: Interim Evaluation Report 1 for the Department of Health and Aged Care', Department of Health, Disability and Ageing, 2025.

Pirkis, J, Currier, D, Harris, M, and Mihalopoulos, C, *Evaluation of Better Access: Main Report*, University of Melbourne, 2022.

Public Service Commission, *Capability Review: Department of Health and Aged Care*, Canberra, 2023.

Puljević, C, King, M, Meciar, I, and Gartner, C, 'Smoking out Australia's growing illicit tobacco market: Current trends and future challenges', *International Journal of Drug Policy*, vol. 127, 2024.

Review of General Practice Incentives, *Expert Advisory Panel report to the Australian Government*, Canberra, 2024.

Reynolds, C, Edel, M, Mack, J, O'Connor, L, and McAvoy, H, 'The effects of vaping on children and adolescent health: a review of systematic reviews', *The Lancet*, 2024, p. 404: S87.

Roy Morgan, 'The full picture: A decade of smoking in Australia' (Article 9936), Melbourne, 2025.

Scope of Practice Review, *Unleashing the Potential of Our Health Workforce: Final Report*, Canberra, 2024.

Stone, E, et al., 'Recreational vaping ban in Australia – policy failure or masterstroke?', *The Lancet*, vol. 404, no. 10452, 2024, pp. 504–06.

Strengthening Medicare Taskforce, *Report*, Canberra, 2023.

Swannell, C, 'Is Trump just gibbering or is there a genuine threat to Aussie pharmas?', *Health Services Daily*, 9 July 2025.

CHAPTER 12
AGED CARE UNDER THE ALBANESE GOVERNMENT

DIANE GIBSON

The Albanese Government came into office a year after the Final Report of the Royal Commission into Aged Care Quality and Safety was tabled. In response, the Morrison Government had already commenced a series of reforms. The general consensus that aged care in Australia had suffered a prolonged period of government neglect combined with the truly confronting findings from the Royal Commission meant that the stage was set for continued legislative and policy activity.

While the planned rights-based Aged Care Act remained the centrepiece of the reforms, a number of Royal Commission recommendations were addressed more immediately through the *Aged Care and Other Legislation Amendment (Royal Commission Response) Act 2022*. This Act enabled changes to the residential aged care funding system, the introduction of star ratings for residential care, a Code of Conduct for providers and workers, expansion of the Serious Incident Reporting Scheme to community care, the strengthening of consent arrangements regarding restrictive practices, and governance changes, including the inclusion of pricing control under the renamed Independent Health and Aged Care Pricing Authority. Most of this first tranche of reforms was underway by December 2022. A far-reaching flurry of changes followed across both community and residential aged care, and through diverse spheres – legislation, regulation, governance, public access to service performance metrics, funding models, prudential arrangements, access pathways, workforce, industrial relations and system design.

Among these many areas of change, improved staffing, quality of care and access to care stand out as central areas of the reform agenda, in company with changes to the financial arrangements underpinning the aged care sector.

Inadequate staffing in residential aged care

Inadequate numbers of staff and inadequately qualified staff are key determinants of poor-quality care. The Albanese Government actions to directly address inadequate staffing reversed policy changes made by the Howard Government under the *Aged Care Act 1997* that removed minimum staffing levels from residential aged care, accountability requirements on the proportion of government funds spent on direct care, and later the requirement for a registered nurse to be on duty 24/7. Subsequently, staffing levels fell steadily, as did the proportion of care delivered by qualified nursing staff.

In October 2022 a new assessment instrument, the AN-ACC, replaced the previous system for assessing residents' care needs. The AN-ACC determines the 'care minutes' per day required by each resident, which are in turn aggregated to the service level to create the mandatory care minutes for that service, and the funding that service receives from the government. The introduction of these mandated minimum care minutes and the requirement to have a registered nurse on duty 24/7 in 2023 arrested and reversed this trend. Over a two-year period, care minutes increased by 24 per cent for registered nurses and 14 per cent for all direct care workers combined. Care minutes, which are measured as an average per person per day, reached 42 minutes for registered nurses and 209 minutes for all direct care workers, very close to the mandated average requirements set for October 2024. This increase in overall staffing levels, and the specific designation of registered nurse care minutes, which enhanced the proportion of skilled clinical care, constituted a major step forward in improving Australia's aged care system.

There were two further important steps forward with the introduction of the AN-ACC. First, under the AN-ACC, the initial care needs assessment is undertaken by an independent registered nurse, physiotherapist or occupational therapist, improving accountability, and second, that classification remains the same even if the resident's health improves, providing an incentive for aged care providers to focus attention on rehabilitation. However, the AN-ACC does not include specific allied health requirements; the system relies on the Aged Care Quality Standards that require residential care services to provide appropriate allied health services to maintain or restore a resident's ability to perform daily tasks. In a context where there are mandated minutes for nursing and personal care, but no mandated levels of allied health care, allied health staffing levels in residential aged care have declined. Average levels of allied health care dropped by 25 per cent to only four minutes per person per day by 2024, well below the seven minutes recorded at the time of the Royal Commission and the target recommended to the Commission of 20 minutes per person per day. Access to appropriate allied health services is an important determinant of quality of care and quality of life for older people in residential aged care and one that will require urgent attention under the second term of the Albanese Government (Gibson and Isbel, 2024).

Workforce shortages in residential and home care sectors

While mandated staffing levels were an important step, workforce shortages remained a critical issue – in 2022 one estimate placed the shortfall at 30 000 to 35 000 across residential and home-based care. This was not surprising given aged care workers have been historically undervalued and underpaid, with high levels of casualisation and associated levels of income insecurity. Previous governments have done little to address this issue.

Early in its term the Albanese Government made a submission to the Fair Work Commission supporting the case for increased pay, and also committed to providing increased funding to cover the increased salary costs, bringing the industry on board with improved pay for aged care workers. An interim pay increase of 15 per cent from 30 June 2023 was followed by the final decision in March 2024 of an increase of between 18 and 28.5 per cent for direct care workers and 6.8 per cent for other support service workers to take effect during 2025. The wage increases are significant. Registered and enrolled nurses (a major concern in workforce shortages) will have received increases between 2023 and 2026 amounting to around $370 per week for enrolled nurses and $430 for registered nurses.

Addressing the long-neglected and systematic underpayment of the aged care workforce is an important achievement of the Albanese Government. However, areas for improvement remain. Some workforce categories such as nurse practitioners and allied health professionals were not included and workforce casualisation and associated income insecurity remain largely unaddressed.

A circle of improvement

Increased staffing levels and increased wages do not act alone, but rather interact to improve workplace morale, reduce stress, and contribute to a sense of workplace value. Other factors, such as the Commonwealth's investment in developing expertise in gerontological nursing through the Transition to Practice Program and the Aged Care Nursing Clinical Placements Program as well as the expanded Dementia Training Program, combine to further build enhanced capacity and pride among the aged care workforce.

Enhanced reporting on quality: The 'Star System'

Enhanced reporting on quality of care and public access to that information was a major recommendation of the Royal Commission. Better information on quality of care is important to the public to inform choice of service provider, to providers so they can monitor their own performance internally and compare their performance externally, and to government for monitoring quality of care. It is now possible to review quite detailed information on individual residential aged care services via the My Aged Care website (see breakout box on page 146). Making information publicly available is an important achievement by the Albanese Government for transparency and public accountability.

The star rating system is the headline act, ranging from five stars for 'excellent' care to one star for 'needing significant improvement', and developed to provide 'a simple way of showing information about the quality of care' services provide. Yet there are a number of reasons to question whether the star system is fit for purpose as a meaningful guide to older people and their family members.

First, star ratings offer limited differentiation among homes because 96 per cent are ranked either three or four star – only 3 per cent achieve five stars and less than 1 per cent achieve one or two stars. Second, timeliness is an issue – the overall star rating is a weighted average of four sub-scales (staffing, resident experience, quality indicators and compliance) that draw on data from varying dates – for example a 2025 five-star overall rating may draw on a compliance sub-scale rating from 2023 – giving a misleading impression of recency. Third, there is evidence of a disconnect between star ratings and compliance with the Aged Care Quality Standards. A recent analysis showed that four homes with a 5-star rating and 67 homes with a 4-star rating were non-compliant with at least some of the Quality Standards (Jilek, 2025).

Residential aged care information available on My Aged Care website

Overall star rating: one to five stars summarising compliance, quality measures, residents' experience and staffing.

Compliance star rating for compliance: date, performance against the eight aged care quality standards.

Quality measures star rating: date, performance on five quality measures compared to national average – pressure injuries, restrictive practices, unplanned weight loss, falls and major injury, and medication management.

Residents' experience star rating: performance on 12 resident experience questions, summary of most compliments and most concerns.

Room size and maximum cost.

Food and meals: Dollars spent per resident compared to sector average, resident feedback on food, expenditure on food and catering compared to sector average.

Staffing: star rating, total care minutes and registered nurse care minutes compared to the aged care home's target, compliance with the 24/7 registered nurse requirement, worker wages compared to sector average, expenditure on care and nursing compared to national average.

SOURCE My Aged Care Find a provider: <https://www.myagedcare.gov.au/find-a-provider/search-by-name>

Concerns and criticisms have come from diverse sources, including consumers and consumer peak bodies (OIGAC, 2024; Allen and Clarke, 2024), the major industry peak Ageing Australia (Egan, 2024), and a government-commissioned independent evaluation (Allen and Clarke, 2024). The evaluation report suggested most respondents did not feel that the star ratings had contributed to an improved quality of care, and less than one-fifth of prospective users would use the star system as a primary source of information to guide their choice of residential aged care. The Commonwealth Ombudsman released a public statement noting 'currently star ratings are not sufficiently meaningful to help people make informed decisions about their aged care'. Further developments are anticipated as the government responds to these concerns.

Other quality improvement measures

Other measures have been undertaken under the Albanese Government to enhance available data and public reporting on quality of care. Most notably, the existing National Mandatory Quality Indicators program for residential care was expanded from five indicators to 11 in April 2023, and by a further three indicators in April 2025. The earlier measures had a strong clinical focus (for example, pressure injuries and restrictive practices) with subsequent additions incorporating broader metrics (workforce, consumer experience and quality of life). Development work was undertaken for quality indicators for the new Support at Home Program. The review of the Aged Care Quality Standards, commenced under the previous government, was completed, and the revised 'Strengthened Quality Standards' were released in February 2025, with planned implementation from July 2025 to apply to both residential aged care and the Support at Home Program. Other developments included the expansion of the Serious Incident Reporting Scheme to include home care services in 2022, the establishment of the aged care Complaints Commissioner within the Aged Care Quality and Safety Commission in 2023, and the introduction of published Complaints Reports from November 2023.

The establishment of the statutory position of the Inspector-General of Aged Care and the associated Office of the Inspector-General in 2023 provided an important independent line of oversight of progress in aged care reform. To date the Office and the Inspector-General have taken a firm stance on maintaining their independence, exemplified by the emphasis on continuing problems of access and navigability in the 2024 Report on progress on the recommendations of the Royal Commission (OIGAC, 2024).

Inadequate supply

The new rights-based Aged Care Act specifies a number of rights for older Australians in relation to individual choice, quality and safety, privacy, dignity and respect, and equity. Yet while the Act includes the right to be assessed for care, it does not provide the 'universal right to high quality, safe and timely support and care' recommended by the Royal Commission (p. 78). At the end of the Albanese Government's first term, aged care remains rationed, access remains difficult, and waiting times for care remain unacceptably long.

Home Care Packages
The Albanese Government inherited a waiting list of some 58 282 people in March 2022, a number which dropped by March 2023 to 30 839, only to increase substantially to 82 960 by December 2024. Additional packages were released during this period, and the number of people on Home Care Packages increased, but supply has not kept pace with demand.

For those who do receive a care package, wait times reduced between 2021–22 and 2023–24. In 2023–24, wait time for high-priority clients was 40 days at the 50th percentile and 76 days at the 90th. The comparable figures for medium-priority clients were 138 days and 267 days respectively. These wait times apply to commencement for any care package, which may be at a lower level than approved. While the reduction in wait times is positive, these amounts of time remain unacceptably long. Based on the most recent data for the October to December 2024 quarter, it appears that waiting times will have increased further when 2024–25 data become available.

Assessment

The waiting times described above exclude the period older people may spend waiting to get an assessment – in 2023–24 a person on the 50th percentile waited 22 days for an assessment, and someone on the 90th percentile waited 138 days (over four months). When the Albanese Government came to office (2021–2022) wait times were substantially shorter, at 15 and 69 days respectively (Productivity Commission, 2025).

In 2024 the Australian Government introduced a new aged care assessment tool, combined three separate assessment programs into a Single Assessment System and introduced triage delegates to complete a short triage process within two weeks of referral. These changes, intended to streamline the system, have yet to affect wait times.

Commonwealth Home Support Program

The Commonwealth Home Support Program provides 'entry-level' support to older people living in the community, including a range of services from domestic assistance to allied health care. It is the largest aged care program, supporting 834 981 people in 2023–24, however data availability is poor, and patterns are consequently difficult to track.

From 2021–22 to 2023–24 the rate of service provision in the target population declined slightly from 179 to 170 per 1000 persons in the eligible population. Total Australian Government expenditure (in 2023–24 dollars) also declined, from $3.136 billion to $2.990 billion, as did per-person expenditure (Productivity Commission, 2025). On balance, these data suggest CHSP services contracted slightly under the Albanese Government.

Residential care

Some analysts (Egan, 2024) have suggested Australia may be moving into an undersupply of residential aged care places. Several national data indicators support this view. Growth in operational places slowed from 11 per cent between 2015 and 2019 to only 3 per cent between 2020 and 2024. Occupancy rates increased from 86 per cent to 88 per cent between 2023 and 2024. Both the number and rate of hospital patient days being used by those eligible and waiting for residential aged care increased between 2021–22 and 2022–23, with the rate for 2022–23 being the highest reported over the past decade. Already there are signs of providers being able to pick and choose more desirable residents, and in particular that people experiencing changed behaviours associated with dementia are experiencing difficulties in accessing care. Taken together with long waiting lists for care packages and a shortage of respite care services, problems of access to residential aged care appears likely to emerge as a significant issue in coming years.

Access – finding your way

A key finding of the Royal Commission concerned the difficulties older people and their families faced in obtaining accurate and reliable information about aged care services through the My Aged Care website and associated Contact Centre. Under the Albanese Government, improvements have been made in content and accessibility, and the addition of a fee estimator has increased utility. Nonetheless recent data from the Council on the Ageing indicate that 41 per cent of people who had used the website found it difficult to navigate, and only 17 per cent said it provided all the information they required (COTA, 2024). The Contact Centre remains an important alternative means of access, as do the new developments providing face to face support. Aged Care Specialist Officer positions were established within Services Australia in late 2022 to provide an in-person or video chat basic advice service on access to assessment and aged care and the Care Finder program, which provides more co-ordinated assistance to more vulnerable older Australians, commenced in early 2023.

While these developments are positive, public consultations conducted by the Office of the Inspector-General of Aged Care found evidence of difficulties in securing appointments with Aged Care Specialist Officers, and problems of inadequate capacity, scope and level of support regarding the Care Finder program (OIGAC, 2024). Another indication of inadequate support comes from stakeholder reports of increased reliance on private navigators.

Financial changes to the aged care system

Successive Australian governments have expressed strong concerns about the rising costs of an ageing population, beginning with the first Intergenerational Report prepared by Treasury in 2002. This position has been maintained in political discourse in the decades since, and while health, the dependency ratio and the aged pension remain areas of concern, the focus on the costs of the aged care system has increased. The Albanese Government established an Aged Care Taskforce in 2023 to address the perception that a change in funding arrangements was required. While the Royal Commission had recommended introducing a levy on personal income tax, the Aged Care Taskforce and the Albanese Government opted for a different direction – a focus on increased 'user charges', emphasising the importance of system sustainability and capacity to attract the additional investment required to deliver high-quality care.

The new co-payments system will come into effect from November 2025, with a 'no worse off' principle applying for those already receiving care packages or residential care until or unless their level of care changes. For some groups, particularly those who do not meet means and assets tests, the increase in co-payments for both residential care and the new Support at Home program will be substantial, largely as a result of increased charging for everyday living tasks and non-clinical care, as well as for accommodation for residential care. Clinical care will be fully government funded. The political ramifications of these charging models will remain unknown until the implications begin to have an impact on individual financial circumstances.

What's next

The term of the second Albanese Government will see the implementation of the new Aged Care Act, along with the commencement of the new Support at Home Program, changes to user contributions to care, and the implementation of the Strengthened Quality Standards amongst many other changes. The sheer volume of policy change during this government's first term, combined with the seismic shifts originally scheduled for July 2025, have caused substantial unrest in the sector, as government and industry alike seek to meet demanding implementation deadlines. There has been substantial industry pressure for a more staged approach, and the new Minister for Aged Care and Seniors, Sam Rae, has already responded by delaying implementation until November 2025. It remains to be seen what other changes may follow.

References

Allen and Clarke Consulting, *Evaluation of Star Ratings for Residential Aged Care: Summary Report*, 19 November 2024, <https://www.health.gov.au/sites/default/files/2025-01/star-ratings-evaluation-summary-report_0.pdf>.

Commonwealth Ombudsman, 'Aged Care Star Ratings Public Statement', 31 October 2024, <https://www.ombudsman.gov.au/__data/assets/pdf_file/0020/306083/Public-Statement-Aged-Care-Star-Ratings-October-2024.pdf>.

Council on the Ageing, *Submission to the review of the administration of My Aged Care to Office of the Inspector General of Aged Care*, June 2024, <https://cota.org.au/submission/my-aged-care-submission-inspector-general/>.

Egan, C, 'Aged care sector is 5300 beds short – what now?', *The Weekly Source*, 16 May 2024.

— 'Star ratings have "significant limitations": ACCPA', *The Weekly Source*, 11 July 2024.

Gibson, D, and Isbel, S, 'Reform and reverberation: Australian aged care policy changes and the unintended consequences for allied health', *Australian Occupational Therapy Journal*, vol. 71, no. 3, 2024, pp. 392–407.

Jilek, R, 'Groundhog Day: The continuing failure of the aged care star rating system: 1 July 2024 to 28 February 2025', Aged Care Consulting and Advisory Services Australasia, 31 March 2025.

Office of the Inspector-General of Aged Care (OIGAC), *2024 Progress Report: Implementation of the Recommendations of the Royal Commission into Aged Care Quality and Safety*, 2024, <https://www.igac.gov.au/resources/2024-progress-report-implementation-recommendations-royal-commission-aged-care-quality-and-safety>.

Productivity Commission, 'Chapter 14: Aged care services', *Report on Government Services*, 2025.

Wells, A, 'Once in a generation aged care reforms', media release, 12 September 2024, <https://www.health.gov.au/ministers/the-hon-anika-wells-mp/media/once-in-a-generation-aged-care-reforms>.

CHAPTER 13

BACK ON TRACK? LABOR'S STRUGGLE TO BALANCE NDIS COSTS AND PARTICIPANT NEEDS

HELEN DICKINSON

The National Disability Insurance Scheme (NDIS) featured centrally in Labor's election campaign. They promised to review and reform the NDIS, aiming to restore trust in a mismanaged scheme. Labor accused the Coalition of taking a 'minimalist' approach to administering the NDIS – one that had caused significant damage during their years in government (Shorten, 2021: ix).

Disability advocacy groups saw the election as a 'critical moment'. Many campaigned hard to unseat the Coalition, fearing the scheme would be further unravelled if they continued in government. Labor's victory was widely celebrated by the disability community. For the first time, the NDIS had a dedicated minister: Bill Shorten, one of the scheme's original architects, who had vowed to defend it.

At first, things looked promising. The first half of Labor's term saw the government working largely harmoniously in partnership with the disability community. But this did not last. Under pressure to moderate growth of the scheme's budget, commitments to co-design gave way to top-down legislative change. By the end of the government's term, many within the disability community felt betrayed and worried that the very promises that had brought them hope had been broken. But the broader Australian population saw a government taking difficult decisions and embarking on significant reform to get the costs of the scheme under control.

'A decade of mismanagement'

While the NDIS had bipartisan support, Labor frequently reminds the country it was their government that created it. Legislation was passed in March 2013, and the pilot phase began just four months later – a rapid rollout driven by fears that a change of government might see it cut back. After losing the 2013 election, Labor watched from Opposition as the Coalition Government oversaw the rollout, expansion and administration of the scheme.

Over the next eight years, concerns grew about the scheme's rising costs. Initially projected to cost $13.6 billion per year, by 2022 scheme actuaries estimated it could reach $64 billion by 2030, making it one of Australia's most expensive social programs. While the NDIS is jointly funded by federal and state and territory governments, intergovernmental agreements mean any overspend beyond original projections is picked up by the federal government. By 2024, the federal government was responsible for just over 70 per cent of the costs of the scheme (Gifford, 2024). This makes the NDIS a key concern for federal governments with a focus on fiscal responsibility.

The Coalition Government made some attempts to deal with increasing scheme costs, establishing a taskforce to cut growth in funding packages and participant numbers. But this was met with outcry from the disability community as many NDIS participants experienced significant cuts to their budgets with little clarity about why. Appeals about the NDIS to the Administrative Appeals Tribunal (AAT) increased by 224 per cent from 2021 to 2022. Attempts at reforming how individuals would be assessed and funding levels set, known as independent assessments, were also met with significant resistance from the disability community and eventually shelved (Dickinson and Kavanagh, 2021).

By the 2022 election the disability community had lost faith in the Coalition to administer the scheme and frequently resisted reform attempts. Labor promised that there would be no more arbitrary cuts and that it would rebuild trust in the scheme. 'The NDIS is something that we all, in Australia, can be proud of', Bill Shorten said. 'But a decade of mismanagement means it's in trouble' (Ransley, 2023).

Early moves and emerging fault lines

After taking office, Labor moved quickly to signal a new direction for the NDIS. They brought forward a planned independent review of the scheme by a year to help inform this process. The year-long review would consult extensively with people with disability, their families and experts to assess how the NDIS was working, recommend improvements and remain sustainable. This would be headed by Bruce Bonyhady, who is often described as the godfather of the NDIS and served as the inaugural chair of the National Disability Insurance Agency (NDIA), and former public servant Lisa Paul. Their appointments sent a clear message: the government wanted to listen to people with disability and work with trusted leaders.

But Labor wasn't content to wait for the review findings. In the meantime, it began making targeted changes that were broadly welcomed by NDIS participants and the wider public. Australian Criminal Intelligence Commission chief Michael Phelan warned that as much as $6 billion per year might be lost to fraud (Dickinson, 2022). This striking figure was often cited to contrast Labor's approach with what it described as Coalition mismanagement. But in talking widely and often about issues of fraud and misuse of NDIS funds, the government may have damaged public trust in the scheme.

On closer interrogation the term 'fraud' was being applied broadly. There was evidence of some serious cases of organised crime – including fake clients, invoices for services not delivered and threats of violence against participants. But these practices were likely a small element of the overall fraud estimated. The more common problem was not criminal but exploitative business practices that operated within the rules. This involved service providers charging the maximum allowable price, often operating a two-tiered pricing system with a more expensive price for NDIS participants than non-participants. These behaviours are not technically illegal, but they do expose the structural flaws in how the scheme was designed.

The Albanese Government came to recognise that fixing these issues might require not just better oversight but deeper reform of the NDIS system and structures.

Rebuilding trust from a fractured foundation

Under the Coalition Government, trust in the NDIA had been significantly broken. The agency was seen as having little insight into the challenges and frustrations that people with disability face on a day-to-day basis interacting with the scheme and providers. In Opposition, Bill Shorten was highly critical of both the agency and its CEO, Martin Hoffman, accusing them of damaging the relationship with the community – particularly through the widely opposed independent assessments proposal.

Shortly after Labor's election victory, Hoffman resigned. He was replaced by Rebecca Falkingham, who pledged to rebuild trust through greater collaboration with participants and stakeholders. A new chair was also announced for the NDIA board: former Paralympian Kurt Fearnley, alongside two additional directors with disability. Five board members now had lived experience of disability – a move widely welcomed as a genuine effort to embed disability leadership in the organisation.

Throughout their term Labor grappled with the need to balance fiscal responsibility with participant needs. Although they acknowledged the need for financial control they, initially at least, rejected cuts to participant numbers or budgets. Instead, they focused on strengthening the NDIA's capacity to deliver. The spring Budget included significant funding to recruit more staff. The agency had long been under-resourced due to a staffing cap introduced by the Coalition in 2014. With far more participants than originally forecast – and fewer staff to manage the system – the NDIA has increasingly relied on expensive external contractors.

Labor also invested in clearing the backlog of appeals inherited from the Coalition. A new dispute resolution process helped resolve 60 per cent of legacy cases by December 2022. AAT appeals also dropped 36 per cent since May of that year.

One major challenge in federal–state relations was the growing problem of delayed discharges for NDIS participants. These are cases where a person is medically fit to leave hospital but can't return home safely as appropriate supports are not in place. Since state and territory governments fund hospitals, the backlog became a serious concern.

To tackle the issues, the NDIA launched a targeted program. In

Victoria, average discharge delays fell from 160 days in 2021 to 29 days by 2023 – a shift estimated to have saved the hospital system up to $550 million (Shorten, 2023). This was perhaps a high point in federal–state relations, which would soon become more fractious.

While Labor's reform process was piecemeal, it addressed some pernicious issues: restoring public trust by addressing fraud; reforming the NDIA to rebuild trust; reducing appeals; and working to save states and territories money. Still, media scrutiny over the scheme's growing cost intensified – especially as a national cost-of-living crisis took hold.

In April 2023, Bill Shorten gave a Press Club address announcing a full-scale 'reboot' of the NDIS, outlining systemic reforms across six major areas. Many in the disability community were caught off-guard. The minister had repeatedly said that people with disability would shape the changes – something the NDIS Review was still actively working on. Some of these announcements were not new and were already being worked on, and others were broadly supported. The final would feature in the NDIS Review and be a key area of contest for the remainder of Labor's term – making mainstream services delivered by federal, state and territory governments more accessible.

This reboot came with a bold fiscal goal. At a meeting of the National Cabinet, it was agreed that by 2026 the growth in the NDIS would be moderated, from around 14 per cent a year down to 8 per cent by mid-2026. Many in the disability community were concerned that this might lead to cuts in budgets without a clear, coherent and co-designed plan for how to achieve this.

The NDIS Review finally arrives

In December 2023, the long-awaited NDIS Review was released, setting out 26 recommendations and 139 actions to overhaul and improve the scheme (NDIS Review, 2023).

One of the review's most important findings focused not on the NDIS itself, but on the broader disability ecosystem. The NDIS was never designed to support all Australians with disability, and around 86 per cent of disabled people do not have an NDIS plan. Instead, they rely on mainstream services like schools, hospitals, and public transport. But these services are often inaccessible, leaving many without the supports they need – or forcing them to pay out of pocket (Olney et al., 2022).

The review noted there is not a single issue driving NDIS cost pressures, but the lack of accessible and mainstream services is pushing more people into the NDIS than originally intended. This phenomenon had given rise to a plethora of metaphors about the NDIS being the 'only lifeboat in the ocean' or the 'oasis in the desert'.

To address this, the review proposed foundational supports to fill the gap. But this idea quickly became a flashpoint. While National Cabinet agreed that states and the federal government would jointly fund these supports and added a sweetener of billions of dollars to strengthen Medicare, tensions soon emerged. At the end of January, the federal government committed $11.6 billon over two years to develop and implement the foundational supports strategy. But by March 2024 states and territories were expressing concerns, saying the supports were uncosted and would likely go beyond those indicated at the December meeting (Dickinson, 2024b).

By the end of Labor's term confusion still surrounded foundational supports: who would receive them, what they would cover, and how much they would cost. As intergovernmental disputes dragged on, so did uncertainty over one of the review's central reforms.

Many in the disability community saw many of the review's recommendations as largely reasonable but often short on detail. While the review called for ambitious change, it did not contain any modelling and had few specifics on implementation. The broad proposals lacked the clarity needed to reassure people how the NDIS would achieve sustainability and enhance participant experience along with it.

But one recommendation set off a wave of resistance. The review proposed that all NDIS service providers should be registered. Some providers in the scheme can choose to operate without registration, which can be costly in compliance and auditing requirements. Participants under some plan management arrangements are able to buy services from unregistered providers and around two-fifths of NDIS spending goes to these providers.

The review argued it was important to register all providers to ensure visibility and hold providers to account. It had become apparent that several participants with high support needs, and large budgets, were living in unregistered group homes that were subject to little regulation and the NDIS Quality and Safeguards Commission had lost sight of these individuals.

While many agreed more high-risk services should be registered, the idea of registering all providers sparked backlash. This was seen as heavy-handed and a potential threat to participant choice and control (Bennett and Orban, 2024). Some saw it as a shift that would benefit large providers with vested financial interests and not necessarily participants.

The disability community began to mobilise forcefully, echoing campaigns that had defeated the Coalition's proposed independent assessments.

In response, Bill Shorten made a politically savvy move announcing a taskforce to investigate registration, led by lawyer and disability advocate Natalie Wade. This took some of the heat out of the issue, engaging more deeply with the community and giving leadership to someone well respected in the disability community. Its final report suggested reframing the definition of an NDIS provider in line with community concerns (Wade et al., 2024) – although this was not legislated for within the government's term.

Shock legislation

Despite promising to work in partnership with the disability community, the Albanese Government never formally responded to the NDIS Review – a move that surprised many. The review had suggested sweeping recommendations, and the community was eager to know which would be introduced and how. Then, in late March 2024, came a shock: the government introduced a new Bill aimed at getting the NDIS 'back on track'.

Not only was no exposure draft released, some disability representative organisations had been briefed but only under non-disclosure agreements to prevent them from talking about it (Basford Canales and Convery, 2024). This seemed entirely contrary to the principle of 'nothing about us without us' to which the disability community thought the government was committed.

The government insisted the Bill was simply enabling legislation, designed to create the framework for future changes, with co-design to follow over the next 18 months. But many in the disability community disagreed, seeing the changes as far more substantial.

Mark Pietsch from Physical Disability Australia explained, 'there's a lot of concern in the NDIS space – and a lot of uncertainty … especially given that so few details have been shared with the community in regards to what the future looks like with the NDIS'. The potential implications of this Bill were so significant that Marayke Jonkers, President of People with Disability Australia, stated 'there are people who have said today they're going to end their lives because this takes away the good life they have had for 10 years' (SBS News, 2024).

The Bill proposed significant changes to: how people access the scheme and how plans are created; how participants can spend funds; how the NDIS can step in if they are concerned that funds are not being spent effectively; and the powers of the NDIS Quality and Safeguards Commission. Some of the changes suggested to assessment processes looked remarkably similar to the Independent Assessments the Coalition had attempted to push through.

With an eye to sustainability, the Bill sought to redefine what an NDIS support is in a narrower way. This explicitly ruled out some supports on which participants rely. The Bill also clarified which services should be delivered by states and territories, reinforcing the message that the NDIS would not pick up what others should be delivering (Dickinson, 2024a).

The Bill quickly ran into opposition. Both the Greens and the Coalition pushed back, and the Bill was referred to a Senate committee for review. In what became a familiar pattern, submission timelines were short: hearings took place in May, with a final report due just weeks later in June. Still, hundreds of submissions poured in from the disability community.

A staggering number of amendments to the legislation followed, including how NDIS supports are defined and how human rights are considered. The legislation passed the House of Representatives in early June, but without enough Senate support, it was sent to a second committee hearing.

While the Greens remained firmly opposed, the Coalition's stance appeared more tactical. At times, it seemed their resistance was intended to make Labor feel the heat of a critical disability community – much as the Coalition had during its own tenure. But in the end the Coalition supported the Bill, and it passed.

The response from the disability community was one of anger and disbelief. Many were stunned that a government which had so often spoken about the need to rebuild trust would push through major reforms without consultation. Some expressed disappointment that prominent figures like NDIA Chair Kurt Fearnley had remained relatively quiet about these reforms.

For many NDIS participants and advocacy groups, the legislation marked a turning point – a move toward a more restrictive, top-down scheme that threated to erode the choice and control at the heart of the NDIS. While sharing a concern that the scheme should be sustainable, this felt like fiscal matters winning out at the potential expense of participant experience.

Shorten exits, implications of legislation become apparent

Just weeks after pushing this controversial legislation through, Bill Shorten announced his retirement from politics to become Vice-Chancellor of the University of Canberra. For many it was a jarring moment: the minister who had promised to defend the scheme was leaving after initiating some potentially fundamental reforms.

With legislation passed and a federal election looming, the NDIA started to make full use of their new powers. Reports emerged of participants having their eligibility reassessed, and being asked to provide evidence to justify their ongoing eligibility with just 28 days to respond (later expanded to 90 days in February 2025). For those who needed evidence from a clinical professional, this could be a significant difficulty. Children with disability and their families were particularly affected. In some cases they were told their support needs would be more appropriately delivered by mainstream services – and thus shifted to state or territory responsibility (Morton, 2025).

New foundational supports were supposed to be available to participants who were removed from the scheme or whose supports were reclassified as not being a responsibility of the NDIS. But by the end of Labor's term these had not yet started. There was still widespread confusion within governments and the community about what foundational supports would include, who would fund these and when they would begin.

After initial progress in clearing the backlog of NDIS appeals, cases began to rise again, raising nearly 10 per cent between 2023 and 2024.

Despite repeated commitments to avoid arbitrary plan cuts as experienced under the Coalition Government, many felt that was exactly what was happening. Early efforts to rebuild trust and co-design solutions gave way to a growing perception that fiscal responsibility had taken priority over participant experience. Yet short-term solutions that failed to engage with participants' real experiences and priorities will likely only be a band-aid when significant reform of the system is needed.

For some, the NDIS under the first Albanese Government started to resemble the very system they had campaigned so hard to change. While many in the disability community were still highly wary of the Coalition's track record on the NDIS, Labor's tumultuous term would have made them wary of a return as a majority government with no check on their influence on the scheme. But to the general public this Labor term may have succeeded in demonstrating that they can make tough decisions about important and costly social programs.

References

Basford Canales, S, and Convery, S, 'Greens and disability groups criticise federal government gag on NDIS talks', *Guardian*, 26 March 2024.

Bennett, S, and Orban, H, 'Choice and control: The NDIS was designed to give participants choice, but mandatory registration could threaten this', *The Conversation*, 17 April 2024.

Dickinson, H, 'NDIS fraud reports reveal the scheme's weakest points', *The Conversation*, 16 August 2022.

— 'Choice and control: Are whitegoods disability supports? Here's what proposed NDIS reforms say', *The Conversation*, 12 April 2024(a).

— 'States agreed to share foundational supports costs. So why the backlash now?' *The Conversation*, 26 March 2024(b).

Dickinson, H, and Kavanagh, A, 'NDIS independent assessments are off the table for now. That's a good thing – the evidence wasn't there', *The Conversation*, 10 July 2021.

Gifford, D, *National Disability Insurance Scheme Annual Financial Sustainability Report: 2023–2024*, 2024.

Morton, R, 'Children targeted in NDIS crackdown', *The Saturday Paper*, 11–17 January 2025.

NDIS Review, *Working together to deliver the NDIS: Independent review into the National Disability Insurance Scheme*, 2023.

Olney, S, Mills, A, and Falon, L, *The Tier 2 tipping point: Access to support for working-age Australians with disability without individual NDIS funding*, 2022.

Ransley, E, 'Bill Shorten says he's under no pressure to slash NDIS costs', news.com, 18 April 2023, <https://www.news.com.au/lifestyle/health/bill-shorten-says-hes-under-no-pressure-to-slash-ndis-costs/news-story/0070db94cd6ceb84cb48303d18f2ae08>.

SBS News, 'Disability advocates voice concern over contentious NDIS reform bill', 22 August 2024, <https://www.sbs.com.au/news/podcast-episode/disability-advocates-voice-concern-over-contentious-ndis-reform-bill/as1olhron>.

Shorten, B, 'Foreword – The Hon. Bill Shorten MP' in Cowden, M, and McCullagh, C (eds), *The National Disability Insurance Scheme: An Australian public policy experiment*, Palgrave Macmillan, Melbourne, 2021, pp. vii–ix.

— Address to the National Press Club, 2023.

Wade, N, Borowick, J, O'Halloran, V, and Fels, A, *NDIS provider and worker registration taskforce advice*, 2024.

CHAPTER 14

CHILDCARE, SCHOOLS AND HIGHER EDUCATION

ROBERT BREUNIG, LOUISA JEFFERY, GLENN FAHEY AND ANDREW NORTON

O f the three policy areas discussed in this chapter – childcare, schools and higher education – only in childcare did Labor take significant promises to the 2022 federal election. But by the end of the first Albanese Government, led by education minister Jason Clare with Anne Aly as early childhood minister, it had major initiatives underway in all three areas. Although historically childcare policy was more about family budgets and female labour force participation than education, Clare sought to tie the three areas together to increase educational success and attainment.

A strong childcare campaign, but was it delivered?

Anthony Albanese ran hard on childcare in his May 2022 election campaign. The Liberal Government's moving the childcare system from a combination of price subsidy and refundable tax rebate to the current Child Care Subsidy (CCS) regime had reignited debate about the balance between spending on childcare to boost female labour force participation and budgetary pressures. Earlier that year, in March, data had revealed increased subsidies working as intended, with a 1.4 per cent annual increase in attendance at childcare centres. However, expenditure on the CCS spiked 9.2 per cent over the same period. With this in mind, Albanese pledged a further $5.4 billion to the CCS, to lift the subsidy rate to 90 per cent for the lowest income families and increase subsidy rates for all families earning less than $530 000 a year. He also promised a Productivity Commission review of the sector to consider a universal 90 per cent subsidy for all families.

In his first budget of October 2022, Albanese increased subsidy rates for families earning less than $80 000 to 90 per cent and added generous subsidies for second and subsequent children, at a cost of $4.6 billion.

An Australian Competition and Consumer Commission (ACCC) inquiry report, delivered in December 2023, confirmed that budget relief had reduced out-of-pocket childcare costs by 11 per cent, while cautioning that these costs had increased as a fraction of disposable income for the lowest income households. Damningly, the report noted that temporary gains in affordability were unlikely to endure, with 40 per cent of the largest providers charging above the hourly rate cap. Other analyses confirmed these fears, revealing an historical pattern of increases in the price of childcare outpacing inflation. In general, increasing subsidies flows through to higher prices, albeit with some lag.

The Productivity Commission's interim report of November 2023 and the ACCC both found price pressures to be systemic. The ACCC found contemporary system design effecting little downward pressure on prices and, in particular, that the hourly rate cap does not deter higher prices. In response, the government talked up regulatory intervention, potentially with stronger price controls, a renewed focus on workforce conditions to prevent provider cost-cutting, and an expanded role for not-for-profit and public providers.

During the lead-in to the 2024–25 Budget, Albanese's narrative shifted towards a 'universal childcare' agenda. The government remained vague about what 'universal' meant, but frequently placed more emphasis on *availability* than affordability.

In December 2024, following a recommendation of the 2024 final PC report, Albanese pledged a re-elected Labor Government would scrap the activity test component of the CCS and give all Australian families earning less than $530 000 per year access to three days a week of sub-sidised childcare.

Significantly, Albanese touted childcare as the 21st-century equivalent of public education, 'three days of early education: affordable for every family, funded for every child, building a better education system every step of the way'. This was a diversion from the widely accepted narrative that subsidising childcare was about female labour force participation. In February 2025, this new norm became a costed, central part of the election campaign, with a $1 billion commitment to the *Building Early Education Fund*: 'the next step in creating a universal child care system'.

Concerns about low pay in sectors such as childcare triggered calls for higher wages. In response, the Albanese Government introduced a convoluted policy encouraging providers to increase wages above the award in exchange for government-funded 'worker retention payments'. The policy's complexity and the opacity of the compensation formula mean many providers have ignored it.

Lack of co-ordination between state and federal governments complicates childcare policymaking. States increasingly provide free 'preschool' for three- to five-year-olds who might otherwise be in the federally run childcare system. The two systems do not interact in co-ordinated ways; indeed they sometimes work at cross-purposes.

The returned Albanese Government's next steps in childcare policy, shaped by the broader economic outlook, will be severely constrained by the combination of private provision, heavy government subsidies with little downward effect on prices, low wages, a desire for cheaper childcare, and tight budgets. The hinted-at move towards a universal childcare system remains politically and fiscally fraught and, without nationalising childcare, unaffordable and unachievable. Emphasis on universal availability over affordability suggests the government may seek to expand childcare places and workforce capacity, but that significant new funding for subsidies may not be forthcoming. In a truth not so universally acknowledged, further subsidy increases will do little to increase female labour force participation, with most gains already realised. Most recent subsidy increases (for example, the Cheaper Child Care legislation of 2022) generated little measurable change in female labour force participation.

Challenges in the schools sector

In schools policy, Jason Clare's early profile-building set the tone for his time as minister. Within his first days in the portfolio, Clare visited his alma mater, Cabramatta Public School, where he underscored his identity as a 'proud product' of the public education system, and highlighted his belief in the transformative force of public education. Subsequently, he has described teachers as doing 'the most important job in the world', earning himself kudos from many in education.

In doing so, Clare cemented the traditional support and goodwill that federal Labor has enjoyed within the schools sector, and avoided the sometimes punitive rhetoric of the former government, such as then-acting federal Education Minister Stuart Robert's remark in March 2022 that seemingly attributed Australia's declining performance in international student testing to 'dud teachers'.

Though Clare would not suffer from the same baggage as the Coalition, he would not enjoy a honeymoon period either. The schools sector remained beset by several key challenges, all years in the making.

Student achievement in international assessment was in a prolonged two-decade decline. A widely publicised national teacher workforce shortage raised doubts about future labour supply. University teacher trainers had been shaken by the previous government's Quality Initial Teacher Education (QITE) Review. It concluded that universities routinely failed to prepare teachers for the classroom or support them in their early careers. The schooling system remained slow in returning to normal post-Covid. A decade on from the landmark Gonski Review, funding issues were far from settled.

Of these challenges, Clare settled on four priorities through the government's first term: rebuilding teacher workforce numbers; addressing Initial Teacher Education flaws; lifting school completion rates; and, most consequentially, inking new funding deals with the states.

The first and most immediate challenge was the perceived crisis of teacher workforce numbers. At an August 2022 Teacher Workforce Roundtable, Clare brought together ministers, unions, principals, universities, and other stakeholders to build consensus on next steps, culminating in the National Teacher Workforce Action Plan, agreed by all state and territory education ministers in December 2022.

Though this was badged as an urgent response to a 'crisis', the actual pace and substance of reform in this space has been mixed, not least because the federal government's power to effect change is genuinely limited. By the end of the first term, Clare would be encouraged by relatively healthy teacher workforce numbers, as well as reforms that will likely improve the practical placement of teachers during their training years.

Closely linked to the teacher workforce agenda was Clare's second priority: lifting the quality and consistency of Initial Teacher Education. Continuing the thread of reform initiated by the QITE review, Clare convened the Teacher Education Expert Panel, chaired by Professor Mark Scott – resulting in the landmark *Strong Beginnings* report in 2023.

Most significantly, Clare endorsed the Teacher Education Expert Panel recommendation to require mandatory 'core content' across all accredited teacher education programs – requiring units covering cognitive science, evidence-based literacy and numeracy instruction, and behaviour management. If successful, these reforms could be transformative in better equipping teaching graduates with classroom-ready knowledge and skills.

The third element of Clare's agenda has been more subtle: a commitment to lifting school completion rates. Clare has regularly made this issue personal, through references to his own background as the first in his family to finish high school, and linking his rise – from Western Sydney to the federal Cabinet – to higher education access. Though he has few policy levers (there is no national curriculum for the senior secondary school years), the recording of a slight increase in high school retention rates in 2024 – the first in years – might be considered an early sign of progress.

The fourth, and most consequential, of Clare's policy reforms was the negotiation of new funding agreements with the states and territories, culminating in the Better and Fairer Schools Agreement. Underlying this has been the government's commitment to 'full and fair' funding – a conscious nod to the perceived failing of the Morrison Government to placate public education advocates, states; and a belief that non-government school sectors had unfairly benefited from past funding deals. The headline result of the new Better and Fairer Schools Agreement is that the federal government has accepted a significant increase to funding of government school students – an increase in the share of public school funding from 20 per cent to 25 per cent of what is known as the 'Schooling Resource Standard'.

Clare will chalk up the signed agreements with all states and territories – with the last one in the dying days of the first term – as a political success.

Though the Better and Fairer Schools Agreement resulted in Clare gaining states' co-operation in enacting evidence-based reform initiatives, like universal early reading and numeracy screening, he also suffered some of the same fate as his predecessors. Rather than using the political goodwill afforded to him to press state counterparts into agreements centred principally around reforms to lift education outcomes, Clare was reduced to viewing policy debate almost fully in terms of funding. Moreover, Clare seemed to allow himself to be haggled in his negotiated agreements with states, who leveraged his need for a political settlement ahead of the federal election. This resulted in some states earning a 'reward' for holding out on making early concessions to Canberra.

Through his first term, Clare has made broadly positive steps in school education policy and brought a stability to the portfolio that has been missing in recent years. However, the reform agenda – as Clare himself remarked with the government's return following the 2025 election – is incomplete, but is one he appears willing to see through.

Higher education policy – better for students than universities
In higher education, the Albanese Government's first term was dominated by a major policy review, known as the Universities Accord, student debt, and international education policy.

The Universities Accord idea came from Tanya Plibersek, shadow education minister prior to the 2022 federal election. She wanted to build consensus on key higher education policy issues across universities, unions, students and parents. Jason Clare proceeded with the Accord concept through a major policy review he announced in November 2022.

The Accord review's terms of reference were broad, signalling the government's agenda on skills development, increased access to higher education, smoother connections between vocational and higher education, workplace relations, student funding, university governance and research.

An interim Accord report was delivered in June 2023, prompting several policy changes. Among these was a 'support for students' policy that put detailed new obligations on universities to identify and support students at risk of not successfully completing subjects. While this broad goal was not controversial, Labor's approach suggested it shared its predecessor's doubts about a light-touch approach to university regulation. Since 2011, under a framework established by the Gillard Government, academic matters had been regulated by the Tertiary Education Quality and Standards Agency. The agency's approach used principles but did not prescribe how they should be implemented. It monitored compliance through risk indicators, examining university practices in detail only if these indicators suggested a problem. The more prescriptive 'support for students' policy required universities to report in detail to the Department of Education on how they identified students needing support and what services they provided. It was a move towards an audit- rather than a risk-based system. The policy meant that two agencies, the Department of Education and the Tertiary Education Quality and Standards Agency, regulated the same university activities in overlapping ways.

While the Universities Accord review continued work during 2023, two other major issues emerged. Since 1990 student debt – first HECS and later the broader HELP loan scheme – had been indexed each 1 June to Consumer Price Index inflation. With low inflation, indexation had attracted little attention. But the post-Covid inflation surge pushed the 1 June 2023 indexation to 7.1 per cent. With 3 million Australians owing money under student loan schemes, indexation suddenly mattered financially and politically. But rather than quickly resolving the matter, the government added indexation to the Accord review's already long list of issues.

The government also reacted slowly to another major issue: international education (most international students enrol in universities). In 2022, Labor had continued Coalition policies to encourage international students back to Australia, including a temporary lifting of working hours restrictions. In September 2022, for international graduates with degrees in skills-in-demand fields, the government decided to add two years to the temporary graduate visas they could secure on completing their courses. These graduates could then spend four to six years, depending on their degree level, working in Australia.

Combined with pent-up demand, these inducements triggered an unprecedented international student boom. From March 2022 to January 2024, monthly visa applications exceeded the month-matched equivalent demand in 2019, a pre-Covid comparison year. Between December 2021, when the borders reopened after their Covid-19 closure, and March 2023, the number of student visa holders in Australia increased by 267 000 to 583 000.

In mid-2023 the Albanese Government concluded that rapidly increasing international student numbers had exacerbated a tight accommodation market. It began announcing policies designed to block or deter international students and to send them home more quickly by shortening the temporary graduate visas it had only recently extended. In May 2024 the government introduced a bill that would allow the minister to set formal caps on international student enrolments. It was stopped in the Senate by combined Liberal and Green opposition.

Despite this setback, since mid-2024 the government has successfully brought international student demand down to below 2019 levels. But the prior boom years in commencing students meant that 673 000 student visa holders were in Australia in March 2025, only slightly below a record number set in September 2024.

As international student policy played out, the government began responding to the Universities Accord final report, which was released in February 2024. Although the word 'accord' remained, the concept was gone. The Accord report heralded a new era of technocratic management, to be run by a new organisation, the Australian Tertiary Education Commission. The commission would allocate student places to universities and ensure that the government's equity and skills agenda was implemented, including a goal of 80 per cent tertiary attainment by 2050.

By the time the 2025 election was called, the Australian Tertiary Education Commission had not been legislated. But the government was active on other Accord final report recommendations.

HELP debt indexation was changed to the lower of CPI and the Wage Price Index (WPI). The government went further than the Accord final report recommendation, retrospectively reducing CPI indexation in 2023 and 2024 to WPI levels.

A new National Student Ombudsman (NSO) opened in February 2025. The NSO can examine any university action or omission, recent or historical, other than employment or academic judgment matters. Like the 'support for students' policy, the NSO steps up bureaucratic scrutiny of universities. While the NSO cannot force universities to change policies or practices, if they reject the NSO's recommendations a 'name and shame' process follows.

Universities had expected the Albanese Government to be more sympathetic to their concerns than the Morrison Government. But they were disappointed. Labor's new bureaucratic scrutiny of universities, by the Department of Education and the NSO, signalled a similar loss of confidence in university management. If established, the Australian Tertiary Education Commission will further restrict university decision-making. While Labor's policies on international students were primarily motivated by migration concerns, they will have major ongoing negative consequences for university finances. Labor continued the tough 2020s for universities.

For students and graduates Labor's first term was, by contrast, broadly positive. Some students should benefit from more timely intervention if falling behind. Through the NSO they have more recourse if university teaching or services are not up to standard. Reduced indexation of HELP debt saved students and graduates $3 billion. For students, the Albanese Government's big first-term omission was doing nothing about high student contributions introduced by the Morrison Government. For arts, law and business students these reached nearly $17 000 a year in 2025. Labor sympathised but procrastinated, first deferring the issue to the Accord review and then to the Australian Tertiary Education Commission. Student contributions are a matter for the Albanese Government's second term.

Where to now?

The Albanese Government was active in all of childcare, schools and higher education in its first term. But with only limited 2022 election promises in schools and higher education, the government lacked an immediate significant policy agenda outside childcare. In schools, the government secured major agreements with the states to improve teacher training and school practice. In higher education, the government clearly signalled its approach to future policy, but left much of its agenda to a second term.

In introducing legislation for the three days of childcare, Jason Clare argued that children with early childhood education and care are more likely to start school ready to learn, to finish school, and then to go on to further study. The long-term question is whether these policy areas can, indeed, cohere successfully.

CHAPTER 15

GENDER EQUALITY IN THE ALBANESE GOVERNMENT: FROM THE SIDELINES TO THE CENTRE FIELD

LEONORA RISSE

From the outset of his 2022 election campaign, Anthony Albanese made it clear that an ALP government would place gender equality front and centre in its policy agenda. 'Australia should be leading the world in equality between women and men', he declared.

Once in office, Minister for Women, Senator Katy Gallagher, affirmed 'the Albanese Labor Government is putting women and gender equality at the centre of Australia's economic plan'.

These words were matched by actions.

The positioning of gender equality as a core tenet of government principles and policymaking – not just a special-interest issue – contrasted sharply with the Morrison Government, whose term was marred by widespread public dissatisfaction with its handling of 'women's issues' (Arrow, 2022).

Gender differences in voting patterns prevailed strongly at the 2022 voting booth. Fewer women than men voted for the Coalition, by a margin of 7 percentage points, and more women than men voted for Labor, by a margin of 4 percentage points. This led to the gap between men's and women's average positions on the left-to-right political spectrum reaching its widest on record (McAllister et al., 2022). The election saw a surge in women's representation, including a rise in female independents (Nelson, 2022). The result cemented a mandate – and community expectations – for the Albanese Government to address Australia's flailing performance on gender equality and take more intentional action on the matter.

With women comprising 47 per cent of its candidates nationally, the Albanese Government stepped into office with a record female majority: 54 women and 49 men were elected as part of Labor's 103-member caucus, equating to a 52 per cent female share. Of these, 19 women were appointed to the front bench, and ten of these held roles in the 23-member Cabinet (Grattan, 2022b; *Parliamentary Handbook*, 2025; Sheppard, 2024).

No other previous Cabinet had achieved a female share greater than 30 per cent (Table 15.1). The ALP's female majority fuelled the increase in women's total share of elected parliamentarians, across all parties and independents, to 44 per cent (*Parliamentary Handbook*, 2025).

Table 15.1: Gender composition of Cabinet, 2010–22

Cabinet	Men	Women	Women's share (%)
Gillard 2010	16	4	20.0
Rudd 2013	14	6	30.0
Abbott 2013	18	1	5.3
Turnbull 2016	17	6	26.1
Morrison 2019	16	7	30.4
Albanese 2022	13	10	43.5

SOURCE Williams and Sawer (2023)

In one of its first demonstrations of policy priorities, the Albanese Government convened the Jobs and Skills Summit at Parliament House in September 2022, where gender equality was elevated both on the agenda and in the principles underpinning the summit's design. Women comprised half of all participants. The opening keynote was presented by economist Danielle Wood (then CEO of the Grattan Institute) and the first session on the program addressed the topic of 'Equal opportunities and pay for women' with an all-female panel. This programming was not by accident: it was a signal that gender equality would be a priority of the Albanese Government and interwoven into policy considerations more widely (Risse, 2022).

This set the stage for the policy agenda that followed.

Taking action on policy promises

The Albanese Government delivered a suite of gender equality policies over the course of its first term.

In keeping with the heightened focus on women's safety, integrity and respect that prevailed during the 2022 election, the government committed to fully implementing the recommendations of the Respect@ Work Inquiry chaired by Sex Discrimination Commissioner Kate Jenkins. Recommendations included assigning employers a duty to prevent sexual harassment in their workplace (Grattan, 2022a). The full 55 recommendations had been presented to the Morrison Government in 2020, but not acted on (Golledge et al., 2021).

On women's economic equality, the Albanese Government's suite of policies included incrementally extending government-funded paid parental leave from 20 weeks to 26 weeks by 2026, re-introducing a use-it-or-lose-it paid parental leave component for fathers and partners to encourage a more balanced sharing of leave within households, and adding superannuation to leave payments from July 2025.

To facilitate more affordable childcare, the government's 'cheaper child care' policy increased the subsidy rate and extended eligibility through reducing household income thresholds, consistent with the recommendations of the Senate Select Committee on Work and Care. The government reported out-of-pocket childcare costs fell by over 13 per cent as a result. The activity test, requiring parents to be working, studying or volunteering to gain eligibility for subsidised childcare, was removed in 2024, consistent with the Productivity Commission's recommendations.

Recognising a need to fortify the supply side of the care economy and fully value care workers, the government supported pay rises for female-concentrated sectors, as awarded by the Fair Work Commission, including aged care and early childhood education and care workers.

On women's health, the government brought a concerted focus on endometriosis care. This included expanding more services and treatments for the condition to be covered by the Medicare Benefits Schedule and Pharmaceutical Benefits Scheme and the establishment of endometriosis and pelvic pain clinics. A women's health policy package, announced in 2025, encompassed several other dimensions of women's health needs across pivotal life stages that had previously been overlooked. This included extending the list of oral contraceptives and menopausal hormone therapies covered by the Pharmaceutical Benefits Scheme, and providing Medicare rebates for menopausal and pre-menopausal health assessments.

On domestic violence, the Albanese Government added the right to access ten days of paid domestic violence leave to the National Employment Standards, extending on the previous five days of unpaid leave available for this purpose.

While this suite of policies constituted progressive steps, this was a government that recognised the pursuit of gender equality needed to go beyond simply expansions to policy settings: it required a broader, holistic strategy to redress the gender inequities embedded in existing policymaking, institutional and legislative structures.

These deeper layers of reform took the shape of articulating a foundational strategy and making bold changes to some of the key institutional settings shaping gender equality in our country.

A foundational framework for gender equality

Through the Office for Women within the Department of the Prime Minister and Cabinet, the Albanese Government developed a National Strategy on Gender Equality. The strategy spelt out its vision, principles and policy directions across five pillars: gender-based violence; unpaid and paid care; economic equality and security; health; and leadership, representation and decision-making. This holistic approach contrasts with the Morrison Government's much narrower articulation of portfolios – limited to women's safety and economic security – that did not deliver much past announcement stage.

Released in 2024, the Albanese Government's national strategy drew on elements of the Women's Economic Equality Taskforce, set up at the start of the government's term and chaired by Sam Mostyn. Holistically, the strategy incorporated elements of other key platforms: The Australian Government's White Paper on Jobs and Opportunities, National Plan to End Violence against Women and Children, National Women's Health Strategy 2020–2030, and *Wiyi Yani U Thangani (Women's Voices): Securing Our Rights, Securing Our Future Report*. A distinctive element of the gender equality strategy is the centring of First Nations women and the recognition of the intersectional factors that can amplify the marginalisation of particular communities of women. The government also developed a dedicated Aboriginal and Torres Strait Islander Action Plan in the area of gender-based violence and began developing a *National Strategy for the Care and Support Economy*.

Embedding gender equity into processes

The Albanese Government's approach to gender equality took a bolder approach than previous governments in recognising the impediments and biases that exist within institutional structures and policymaking processes.

A vivid illustration of this is the way the Albanese Government amended the *Fair Work Act 2009* to articulate gender equality as an object of the Act. The Fair Work Commission is now required to consider the need to achieve gender equality and eliminate the gender-based undervaluation of work across all its functions. This legislative change addressed the hurdle faced by previous equal pay cases seeking to rectify the low wage rate of female-concentrated occupations, which required identifying a 'male comparator' (Risse, 2019). To bring this change into effect, expert panels were created and the commission initiated a stream of research and reviews of modern awards focused on redressing historical gender undervaluation and prioritising female-concentrated sectors (Macdonald, 2025).

Taking effect from 2023, these legislative changes to the Fair Work Act enabled the commission to award historic pay rises to aged care workers ([2024] FWCFB 150). Legislated changes to permit multi-employer bargaining also played a role in lifting pay rates in the female-concentrated early child education and care workforce ([2024] FWCFB 461).

Also with a view to rectifying the gender pay gap, the government legislated reforms to the *Workplace Gender Equality Act 2012* that empower the Workplace Gender Equality Agency to publish employers' gender equality metrics, including organisation-level gender pay gaps. It also legislated that large companies must set gender equality targets to be eligible for government procurement. These reforms aligned with the recommendations of a 2021 review of the Act.

In another example of changes to institutional structures to enhance gender equality, the government committed to continuing to invest in the Time Use Survey conducted by the Australian Bureau of Statistics. This survey generates official measurements of gender gaps that are missing from conventional economic statistics, such as the gender differences in time spent on unpaid household work and care.

In terms of embedding a gender equity lens into policymaking architecture, the most substantial reform the Albanese Government has invested in is the reintroduction of Gender Responsive Budgeting (GRB). As articulated in its first Budget: 'The Government is putting gender equality at the heart of policy and decision making through the introduction of gender responsive budgeting, which aims to run the objective of delivering gender equality across the whole Budget process'.

GRB involves systematically applying a 'gender lens' to the design and assessment of policies – including those seemingly unrelated to gender equality – to detect gender-patterned impacts and policy settings that could inadvertently undermine gender equality goals. The Albanese Government's approach to GRB requires all departments developing a Cabinet submission and new policy proposals to undertake a gender analysis. Examples of GRB in action were evident across all Women's Budget Statements:

- Policies to improve safe and secure housing in the 2022–23 Budget were informed by analysis detecting that women were disproportionately affected by the rising costs of living, low vacancy rates and long wait lists.
- The 2023–24 Budget's extension of JobSeeker eligibility, to recipients aged 55 who had been on the payment for at least nine months, noted that women comprised the majority of these recipients.
- Updates to funding indexation in the 2023–24 Budget for programs delivered by community sector organisations acknowledged these programs include services for women and children experiencing violence and are predominantly staffed by women.

- The cost-of-living tax cuts delivered in the 2024–25 Budget were found to deliver a larger tax cut to 90 per cent of women taxpayers, compared to previously legislated settings.
- The Commonwealth Prac Payment for nursing, midwifery, teaching and social work students, introduced in the 2024–25 Budget, recognised that women make up over 80 per cent of students in these fields.
- Changes to the Higher Education Loan Program outlined in the 2025–26 Budget predominantly benefited women, who hold the majority of student loan debt.

Circulated jointly by Senator Gallagher (as the Minister for Women, Minister for Finance and Minister for Government Services) and the Treasurer, Dr Jim Chalmers, the Albanese Government's Women's Budget Statements have been elevated to comprehensive analytical documents substantiated by data, analysis and evidence-based research.

Women in leadership and decision-making

The appointment of Senator Gallagher as the Minister for Finance and the Minister for Women has been an important factor behind the elevation of gender equality policies and implementation of GRB. The combination of these two portfolios is in keeping with GRB best practice that recognises that GRB is more effective when the finance ministry takes a core role. The Minister for Finance sits on the Expenditure Review Committee, which oversees the approval of New Policy Proposals: this is the point of the Commonwealth budget cycle where gender impact assessments are evaluated.

The Albanese Government's first term has been distinguished by the appointment of women into key positions in Australia's economic policymaking institutions – decisions made by Treasurer Dr Jim Chalmers. In 2023 Michele Bullock was appointed as the Governor of the Reserve Bank of Australia – the first woman to hold this role in the bank's 62-year history. In 2024 Danielle Wood stepped into the role of Chair of the Productivity Commission – the first woman appointed to this role in the

30-year history of the commission and its predecessor institutions. Taking effect from 2025, the two newly structured RBA boards comprise a majority of women, including Marnie Baker, Renée Fry-McKibbin, Carolyn Hewson and Alison Watkins on the Monetary Policy Board, and Swati Dave, Elana Rubin, Carol Schwartz and Jennifer Westacott on the Governance Board. Adding to this, at the start of the Albanese Government's second term, Jenny Wilkinson was appointed as Treasury Secretary – the first woman to lead the Treasury in its 124-year history.

Serving as Australia's head of state and representing the monarchy in Australia, in 2024 Her Excellency the Honourable Sam Mostyn AC was sworn in as Australia's 28th Governor-General – the second woman to hold the role in Australia's 124 years of Federation.

The women in Albanese's ministry also bring more demographic diversity than those of previous governments. Among them, Penny Wong is the first Asian-Australian and openly lesbian woman to hold the Ministry for Foreign Affairs, Linda Burney is the first Indigenous woman to become a Cabinet minister and the Minister for Indigenous Australians, and Dr Anne Aly is the first Muslim woman to hold a ministry (Chappell and Annesley, 2022; Williams and Sawer, 2023).

There are potential caveats, however, to these markers of progress. The appointment of women into leadership positions at times when organisations are in precarious states, or need to repair public trust, evokes a 'glass cliff' scenario (Ryan and Haslam, 2005). Bullock's appointment – following a review of the RBA that detected a need for institutional reform – has been characterised as a 'glass cliff' by some commentators (Bahr, 2023). Furthermore, Wood was not the first pick for the Productivity Commission Chair, but appointed only when the initial choice, Chris Barrett, opted for a promotion elsewhere (Clark, 2023). However, a refreshed approach offered by female leadership may be exactly what institutions in crisis need to revitalise and thrive.

Assessing the impact

Women's economic outcomes are improving, by many measures, in ways that reflect the impacts of these changes to policies and processes. Women's labour force participation rate has risen to historic highs and the gender pay gap has shrunk to historic lows.

Australia's ranking in the Global Gender Gap Index, published by the World Economic Forum, has improved notably since the Albanese Government came into power. From 50th in 2021, Australia climbed to 43rd position in 2022, before leaping to 26th in 2023, 24th in 2024 and 13th in 2025. These improvements have been especially driven by the rise in women's share of legislative, senior official and managerial positions in the workforce, and parliamentary and ministerial positions in government.

In policy discourse, this has been a government that recognises that gender equality is an *input* towards economic growth, productivity and wellbeing – not a competing objective. This realisation marks an important shift in economic mindset and policy narrative.

Work remains to be done, particularly for First Nations and marginalised groups of women, and with respect to violence against women and girls, where victimisation rates continue to rise. In policymaking architecture, there is scope to do more to future-proof the gains made, such as legislating the practice of Gender Responsive Budgeting, so that these reforms cannot be unwound by future governments. Recognition is also growing of the need to support men and boys to navigate societal pressures and gender norms, which will also benefit women and girls and advance gender equality across society. The establishment of a Special Envoy for Men's Health in the 2025 Cabinet is one indication of this progressive future direction, as the Albanese Government's pursuit of gender equality unfolds in its second term.

Note: The author serves as a member of the Fair Work Commission Expert Panel on gender pay equity and has undertaken commissioned research for the Workplace Gender Equality Agency.

References

Arrow, M, 'Women have been at the centre of political debate in the past two years. Will they decide the 2022 election?', *The Conversation*, 10 April 2022.

Bahr, J, 'Women are leading Qantas, the RBA and X for the first time. Are they being set up to fail?', *SBS News*, 8 September 2023.

Chappell, L, and Annesley, C, 'Australia has more women in Cabinet than ever before: What difference will diversity make?', *The Conversation*, 1 June 2022.

Clark, B, 'Danielle Wood can rescue the Productivity Commission. But is it worth saving?', *Crikey*, 11 September 2023.

Golledge, E, Anagnos, D, Causbrook, M, and Bowes, S, 'The government's "roadmap" for dealing with sexual harassment falls short. What we need is radical change', *The Conversation*, 8 April 2021.

Grattan, M, 'Employers will have positive duty to prevent sexual harassment in workplaces, under new legislation', *The Conversation*, 26 September 2022a.

— 'View from The Hill: Record 10 women in Albanese cabinet, and surprise move for Plibersek to environment', *The Conversation*, 31 May 2022b.

Macdonald, F, 'A landmark ruling will tackle the gender pay gap for thousands of workers', *The Conversation*, 22 April 2025.

McAllister, I, Sheppard, J, Cameron, S, and Jackman, S, *Australian Election Study 2022: Results from the Australian Election Study*, Australian National University, Canberra, 2022.

Nelson, C, 'Women stormed the 2022 election in numbers too big to ignore: What has Labor pledged on gender?', *The Conversation*, 22 May 2022.

Parliamentary Handbook, 'Gender composition in each parliament', Department of Parliamentary Services, Canberra.

Risse, L, '50 years after "equal pay", the legacy of "women's work" remains', *The Conversation*, 19 June 2019.

— 'How the jobs summit shifted gender equality from the sidelines to the mainstream', *The Conversation*, 4 September 2022.

Ryan, M, and Haslam, S, 'The glass cliff: Evidence that women are over-represented in precarious leadership positions', *British Journal of Management*, vol. 16, no. 2, 2005, pp. 81–90.

Sheppard, J, '2022 Australian Federal Election', *Department of Parliamentary Services Research Paper Series*, 2024–25, Canberra.

Williams, B, and Sawer, M, 'High-vis and hard hats versus the care economy', in Sawer, M, Gauja, A, and Sheppard, J (eds), *Watershed: The 2022 Australian Federal Election*. ANU Press, Canberra, 2023, pp. 79–99.

CHAPTER 16

GOOD INTENTIONS, UNHERALDED SETBACKS: INDIGENOUS POLICY UNDER ALBANESE

BARTHOLOMEW STANFORD

Under the nine years of Coalition government before Labor's election in 2022, Indigenous policy had not moved beyond the conventional neoliberal approach of pursuing Indigenous self-determination through mainstream economic participation. Australia has not made any significant leaps in advancing Indigenous rights since the passing of the *Native Title Act 1993*. Since then, there have been major developments in other countries like New Zealand, where Māori rights have been recognised in the form of legal personhood over the Whanganui River (Crib et al., 2024); although more recently, Māori rights have come under attack from conservative parties in New Zealand.

Australia has not kept up with changes happening internationally and has been fastened to an approach to Indigenous policy that prioritises mostly western-based solutions while offering symbolic gestures, such as the apology to the Stolen Generation, as a way of reconciling the past. Albanese's Labor Government brought a welcome change that looked beyond that dogmatic neoliberal view to envisage a more holistic and substantive transformation to Indigenous affairs. Indigenous rights, decision-making, and truth-telling represented a significant progress in Indigenous policy that aligned with international standards established by the United Nations Declaration on the Rights of Indigenous Peoples (UNDRIP).

Australia's relationship to Indigenous peoples is unique and not for good reasons. For instance, Australia does not recognise Indigenous peoples in its constitution, there are no treaties between the Australian Government and Indigenous peoples, and Aboriginal and Torres Strait Islanders have no dedicated representative body at the national level. It is in this political landscape that Albanese sought to completely reshape Indigenous affairs.

The biggest shift came in Albanese's promise to implement the three principles of the Uluru Statement from the Heart in full. Both the Turnbull and Morrison Coalition governments rejected the Voice component of the Statement, citing fears it would create a 'third chamber of parliament'. Yet, both leaders failed to understand properly the Statement and how the proposed Voice would work alongside parliament and not add to it. Indigenous communities welcomed Labor's position on the Uluru Statement from the Heart, which had strong support from Aboriginal and Torres Strait Islanders across the country. But, as discussed later, the fallout from the referendum has real impacts on Indigenous futures and any possibility of Indigenous rights recognition moving forward.

Indigenous foreign policy

The change in government and approach to Indigenous policy came as a completely new paradigm for international relations. The Department of Foreign Affairs and Trade (DFAT) has introduced a new policy designed to increase Indigenous engagement on the international stage, with the potential to strengthen and enrich Australia's relationships with global communities. Indigenising foreign policy has been on the agenda in Canada and New Zealand for some time, and under Albanese, Labor was intent on reimagining Australia's foreign policy through an Indigenous lens. Work began in DFAT in 2021 to explore how to develop a First Nations Foreign Policy. Once Labor took government in 2022, DFAT had the mandate and support to implement their agenda. An Ambassador for First Nations People role was created to oversee the implementation of this new policy. Justin Mohamed, a Gooreng Gooreng man from Bundaberg, was the inaugural appointee and has led the Office of First Nations Engagement in DFAT since 2023. In a joint media release from Penny Wong (Minister for Foreign Affairs), Linda Burney (Minister for Indigenous Australians) and Patrick Dodson (Special Envoy for Reconciliation and Implementation of the Uluru Statement from the Heart) they outlined the principal aim of this new policy:

elevating the perspectives of First Nations people – this land's first diplomats – enables deeper engagement with many of our closest partners including the Pacific family. (DFAT, 2023)

Aboriginal and Torres Strait Islander people have been engaging with foreign peoples for centuries before the arrival of the First Fleet. Diplomatic trading relations between Aboriginal peoples of Northern Australia and fishermen from Indonesia had been established for hundreds of years prior to Federation, with cultural and commercial exchange occurring in the collection and harvesting of trepang (sea cucumber) (Lee, 2024). In the Torres Strait, Indigenous peoples have intermarried and exchanged culture and customs with migrants from Asia, and the South Pacific. Beginning in the mid-1800s and into the early to mid-1900s, men from Japan, Malaysia, Sri Lanka, the Philippines and Pacific Islands were drawn to the Torres Strait to work in the pearling industry (Nagata et al., 2017). Many of them stayed, creating new linkages between Indigenous communities of Australia and their home countries. It was this history DFAT was hoping to tap into as a way of reshaping how Australia engages with nations in the Asia-Pacific region.

The Ambassador for First Nations People was intended as a new approach to diplomacy that centred First Nations institutions. DFAT has increasingly recognised the role of Indigenous diplomacy in shaping the nation's international engagements, reflecting similar efforts in other settler nations like Canada and New Zealand (Leary, 2024). While this marks a shift towards inclusivity, challenges remain in ensuring genuine representation and influence for Indigenous Australians in foreign policy decision-making. For instance, DFAT promotes Indigenous engagement at the international level, but decision-making power remains largely in the hands of non-Indigenous policymakers.

Australia's promotion of Indigenous foreign policy internationally contrasts with domestic policies that fail to recognise fully Indigenous rights (for example, lack of Treaty, and the rejection of the Voice to Parliament in 2023) (Gockel, 2024). Australia has also yet to recognise fully UNDRIP under domestic law. These contradictions risk undermining Australia's credibility in advocating for Indigenous rights abroad and continued policies that centre Indigenous knowledge and culture in diplomatic relation-building. What is needed, according to Blackwell and Ballangarry (2022), is 'structural reform' to enable greater recognition of Indigenous worldviews and participation in the design of policy, which should be shaped by International Indigenous rights frameworks like UNDRIP.

The referendum and fallout

When the Labor Government took the majority of Lower House seats at the 2022 election, Albanese was able to push forward his vision for Indigenous self-determination. This included holding a referendum to ask the public to establish a Voice to Parliament, a constitutionally enshrined representative body that would enable Indigenous peoples to provide direct advice to parliament on issues that fall within the purview of Indigenous interests. This proposed body would function alongside parliament and provide Aboriginal and Torres Strait Islander peoples a dedicated voice in policy and law-making. Albanese was committed to holding the referendum in his term as leader. Support for the Voice was strong in early polling, but as the referendum was announced and campaigning proceeded, support dropped considerably.

In August 2023, Prime Minister Albanese announced the Voice to Parliament referendum for 14 October 2023. That began a 45-day campaign in which both sides of politics would pitch their position on the Voice to the Australian public. Clear lines were drawn between the parties before the announcement, with Labor and Greens supporting, and Liberals and Nationals opposing. In Australia's history, all successful referendums have relied on bipartisan support (Goot, 2023). In addition, challenges which Australian governments had not faced at a referendum before, such as misinformation and disinformation spread on social media, created insurmountable odds for Labor.

The question put forward to the voters at the referendum was:

A Proposed Law: to alter the Constitution to recognise the First Peoples of Australia by establishing an Aboriginal and Torres Strait Islander Voice.

The 'Yes' campaign started well before the referendum had been announced. Key figures involved in the Uluru Statement from the Heart had been lobbying government and engaging the public on the idea of establishing a Voice to Parliament for years in the lead-up to the referendum. As momentum built to the referendum, individuals, organisations and businesses endorsed the proposal and, in some cases, actively campaigned with the key organiser Yes23. Many independents, business groups, faith leaders, and First Nations organisations were heavily involved in campaigning for the Voice. In an interesting twist, two sitting parliamentarians went against their party lines. Lidia Thorpe, a former Greens senator, opposed the Voice with a group labelled as the 'Progressive No' which had close ties to the 'Blak Sovereign' movement in Australia. Senator Thorpe quit the Greens party in protest. Liberal MP Julian Leeser came out in support of the Voice, citing his previous work on constitutional reform, which included Indigenous recognition, as a key factor in his motivations to support the Voice.

Campaigning for the Voice was centred around a proposal that asked for modest reform to Australia's system of governance, while advancing reconciliation between Indigenous and settler communities. One of the key criticisms of the Yes campaign was its inability to educate the public on what the Voice was trying to achieve. Part of this had to do with time constraints, but also key campaigners spent considerable effort countering and debunking misinformation (Graham, 2024), which may have diverted attention away from opportunities to inform the public.

The 'No' campaign had two main camps, the 'Recognise a Better Way' group which included Senator Jacinta Price and Warren Mundine as key members, and the 'Progressive No' led by Senator Lidia Thorpe. Behind them was a Coalition that was mostly unanimous and vocal in opposition to the Voice proposal. At the state and territory level though, conservative political leaders were split. New South Wales, Tasmania and the Australian Capital Territory were in support, while Victoria, Queensland, South Australia, the Northern Territory and Western Australia opposed. The messaging presented to voters by 'No' campaigners centred on three main arguments:

- The legal ramifications of such a proposal were unclear, therefore the Voice to Parliament would be plagued with uncertainty.

188 | Policy issues

- It would create divisions in Australia across racial groups.
- The Voice to Parliament was only symbolic and did not offer Indigenous Australians real decision-making opportunities.

Most of the language used by the No campaign was drawn from the first two points, such as 'don't know, vote no' and 'dividing the nation'; slogans that were used during the 1999 referendum to play on the public's concerns about the proposition of Australia becoming a republic (Stanford and Evans, 2024). Such messaging may fail to prompt public inquiry or engagement in formal discourse. However, it might still resonate with voters, possibly reflecting gaps in civic education within Australia's school curriculum (Joint Standing Committee on Electoral Matters, 2025).[1] The third point speaks to Indigenous Australians who were unsure about the Voice, and was used by the No campaign to push the notion, more broadly, that Aboriginal and Torres Strait Islanders did not support the proposal.

In the end, the referendum failed to achieve popular support in every state and territory, except for the Australian Capital Territory (see Table 16.1), with many viewing the failure as an indictment of Australia's relationship to Aboriginal and Torres Strait Islander communities in general. The government would stay silent on Indigenous affairs for some time after the referendum, while conservative political leaders began using the referendum result to justify opposing Indigenous rights and recognition more broadly.

In the same week the referendum was resolved, the Queensland Liberal National Party (LNP) walked back their support for a state-based treaty, arguing that the process would create 'further division'. Queensland recorded the lowest support of all Australian jurisdictions at the referendum with 31.79 per cent. Since coming to power at the Queensland election in 2024, the LNP have repealed the *Path to Treaty Act 2023* and scrapped the Truth-Telling and Healing Inquiry which was intended to inform the process of treaty-making in Queensland through accounts of historical and ongoing impacts of colonisation.

In 2024, the Victorian Opposition followed suit and took back their support for Treaty. Their stated reasons for doing so relate to the referendum outcome, but also to their concerns regarding Aboriginal cultural heritage and agreements made under the *Traditional Owner Settlement Act 2010*, which

Table 16.1: Voice to Parliament referendum results, 2023

State/territory	Yes		No	
	Votes	%	Votes	%
New South Wales	2 058 764	41.04	2 957 880	58.96
Victoria	1 846 623	45.85	2 180 851	54.15
Queensland	1 010 416	31.79	2 167 957	68.21
Western Australia	582 077	36.73	1 002 740	63.27
South Australia	417 745	35.83	748 318	64.17
Tasmania	152 171	41.06	218 425	58.94
Northern Territory	43 076	39.70	65 429	60.30
Australian Capital Territory	176 022	61.29	111 192	38.71
Total	6 286 894	39.94	9 125 294	60.06

SOURCE Australian Electoral Commission, 2023

they believe are creating uncertainty for developers, driving up construction costs. This decision by the Opposition came after years of bipartisan support for a state-based treaty. Although Victoria has passed the Statewide Treaty Bill 2025 to enable treaty-making, the Victorian Liberal Party has promised to repeal the legislation and dismantle the treaty process within the first 100 days of forming government.

Pivot to economic initiatives

After the referendum, the government enacted a series of policy changes to encourage Indigenous economic empowerment. The first of these was focused on strengthening the Indigenous Procurement Policy (IPP), with public consultations starting in 2023 and an announcement on revisions to the policy in February 2025. The government elected to increase procurement targets to 4 per cent by 2030, and explore ways improvements can be made to reporting and investigating misuse of the policy.[2] Parliament has also amended the *Aboriginal and Torres Strait Islander Act 2005* to enable

Indigenous Business Australia (IBA) to expand its financial tools to meet the demands of a changing market. Treasurer Jim Chalmers and Minister for Indigenous Australians Malarndirri McCarthy (2024) commented that these amendments were 'part of the Albanese Government's push for greater economic empowerment for First Nations people'. IBA has helped support and grow an Indigenous business sector, now worth approximately $16 billon to the Australian economy (Evans, 2024). It is hoped that these new amendments will further Indigenous business development as well as new investment opportunities for IBA to expand their services. The Australian Government has also committed to investing in remote Indigenous communities to generate increased employment opportunities. In partnership with the Northern Territory Government, $842.5 million will be spent to create 570 new jobs, with over half of those intended for Indigenous Territorians in remote communities (Kellaway, 2025).

As the government pivots to economic initiatives, questions have been raised regarding this change of direction and what it means for Indigenous futures. Indigenous policy since the Howard era has largely been focused on encouraging mainstream economic participation and downplaying the importance of recognising Indigenous rights as a fundamental step in addressing disadvantage. Professor Megan Davis, one of the key architects of the Uluru Statement, has highlighted how economic policies over the past 30 years have not made desired improvements to Indigenous communities. Rather, as she states, such policies are susceptible to 'elite capture and the way in which public resources are galvanised for the benefit of a few individuals in relation to wealth creation' (Williams, 2025). There is a large body of research from Australia and internationally that points to the importance of recognising Indigenous rights as key to enabling Indigenous self-determination (Behrendt, 2001; Sullivan, 2006; Colbourne and Anderson, 2021), thus enabling sustainable economic development that aligns with Indigenous worldviews and priorities.

An uncertain future

The future for Indigenous communities under Labor is uncertain. Any notion of Indigenous rights recognition is off the table for the foreseeable future. Albanese and the Minister for Indigenous Australians have seemingly moved on from the Uluru Statement and are pursuing an economic agenda, but as history has shown, this pathway is well worn and does not include steps towards important issues, such as sovereignty, truth-telling and Treaty. Australia has a long history of denying Indigenous rights. Meaningful changes in Indigenous policy, especially as it relates to land rights, have occurred due to the ceaseless work of motivated Indigenous groups to compel action from governments. With this uncertainty at the national level, Indigenous groups will look elsewhere to push for greater change and rights recognition. As the states and territories explore treaty-making, opportunities may arise for Indigenous political mobilisation at the sub-national level.

References

Australian Electoral Commission, *2023 Referendum National Results*, 2023.

Behrendt, L, 'Indigenous self-determination: Rethinking the relationship between rights and economic development', *University of New South Wales Law Journal*, vol. 24, no. 3, 2001, pp. 850–61.

Blackwell, J, and Ballangarry, J, *Indigenous Foreign Policy: A new way forward?*, Australian Feminist Foreign Policy Coalition, 2022, <https://iwda.org.au/assets/files/AFFPC-issues-paper-Indigenous-Foreign-Policy-Blackwell-Ballangarry-FINAL.pdf>.

Chalmers, J, and McCarthy, M, 'Legislative reform to support First Nations economic empowerment', media release, 25 November 2024.

Colbourne, R, and Anderson, R, *Indigenous Wellbeing and Enterprise: Self-determination and Sustainable Economic Development*, Routledge, Oxford, 2021.

Collin, P, 'Australian students just recorded the lowest civics scores since testing began. But young people do care about politics', *The Conversation*, 18 February 2025.

Cribb, M, Macpherson, E, and Borchgrevink, A, 'Beyond legal personhood for the Whanganui River: collaboration and pluralism in implementing the Te Awa Tupua Act', *The International Journal of Human Rights*, 2024, pp. 1–24, <https://doi.org/10.1080/13642987.2024.2314532>.

Department of Foreign Affairs and Trade, 'Ambassador for First Nations people', March 2023, <https://parlinfo.aph.gov.au/parlInfo/download/media/pressrel/9054886/upload_binary/9054886.PDF;fileType=application%2Fpdf#search=%22media/pressrel/9054886%22>.

Evans, M, et al., *Indigenous Business and Corporation Snapshot Study 3.0*, University of Melbourne, 2024, <https://fbe.unimelb.edu.au/cibl/research>.

Gockel, I, 'Australia's "First Nations Approach to Foreign Policy" does not improve our reputation on Indigenous issues', *Young Australians in International Affairs*, 22 August 2024, <https://www.youngausint.org.au/post/australia-s-first-nations-approach-to-foreign-policy-does-not-improve-our-reputation-on-indigenous>.

Goot, M, 'Support in the Polls for an Indigenous Constitutional Voice: How Broad, How Strong, How Vulnerable?', *Journal of Australian Studies*, vol. 47, no. 2, 2023, pp. 373–97, <https://doi.org/10.1080/14443058.2023.2175892>.

Graham, T, 'Exploring a post-truth referendum: Australia's Voice to Parliament and the management of attention on social media', *Media International Australia*, 2024, <https://doi.org/10.1177/1329878X241267756>.

Joint Standing Committee on Electoral Matters, *From Classroom to Community: Civics Education and Political Participation in Australia*, 2025.

Kellaway, E, 'Labor has pledged $840 million towards improving service delivery in remote NT', SBS, 7 February 2025, <https://www.sbs.com.au/nitv/article/a-landmark-partnership-agreement-has-committed-800-million-for-service-delivery-in-remote-nt/lybdq9r6y>.

Leary, S, 'What does First Nations foreign policy mean?', Perth USAsia Centre, 2024, <https://perthusasia.edu.au/education/indo-pacific-explainer-what-does-first-nations-foreign-policy-mean/>.

Lee, A, 'The Macassan-Aboriginal relationship and the Commonwealth of Australia 1901–1906', *History Australia*, vol. 22, no. 1, 2024, pp. 62–78.

McAllister, I, 'Civic education and political knowledge in Australia', *Department of the Senate Occasional Lecture Series*, 2001.

Nagata, Y, Ramsay, G, and Shnukal, A, *Navigating Boundaries: The Asian Diaspora in Torres Strait*, 2nd ed., Australian National University, Canberra, 2017, <https://openresearchlibrary.org/content/ce178b52-f698-44d8-afb9-29e205c40bbb>.

Stanford, B, and Evans, M, 'What can be learned about Australian values in comparing referendums on Indigenous inclusion and recognition?', *Australian Journal of Political Science*, 2024, pp. 1–13.

Sullivan, P, 'Indigenous governance: The Harvard project on native American economic development and appropriate principles of governance for Aboriginal Australia', *AIATSIS Research Discussion Papers*, no. 17, 2006, <https://aiatsis.gov.au/sites/default/files/research_pub/sullivanp-dp17-indigenous-governance-harvard-project-principles-aboriginal-australia_3.pdf>.

Williams, C, 'Uluru leader says PM's Indigenous agenda is Howard-era status quo', *ABC News*, 2 April 2025.

CHAPTER 17

AUKUS, CHINA AND 'TAKING THE LANE'

DANIEL FLITTON

Labor under Prime Minister Anthony Albanese and Foreign Minister Penny Wong turned a friendlier face to the world than its Coalition predecessor, while essentially preserving the same foreign policy.

Ties with China stabilised – that word 'stabilised' adopted as a mantra for a relationship that had been marred by intemperance and antagonism. But the shift in atmosphere did not result from any concession made on Australia's part following the change of government. Instead, Beijing gradually backed down from its campaign of economic coercion, having been annoyed at the former government over foreign interference laws and technology bans, an irritation that accelerated during the pandemic after China took umbrage at the call for an international investigation into the origins of the coronavirus (McGregor, 2022). Beijing came to realise that its pressure, which also included a freeze on high-level contact, had proved ineffective. Tensions still intruded, particularly over military operations, but the two countries at least got back to talking.

Labor advanced the pledge to acquire nuclear-powered submarines via the AUKUS agreement with the United States and United Kingdom. An 'optimal pathway' was announced in March 2023 whereby Australia would in the next decade obtain three, potentially five, second-hand US Virginia-class submarines, subject to US congressional approval, while aiming, along with the United Kingdom, to build a new type of submarine by the 2040s.

The Albanese Government was not swayed by a gathering chorus of complaints, including from Labor party titans, about cost of the project either in financial terms or to sovereign decision-making. Critics noted that the party had mere hours of notice of the generational commitment by the then Morrison Government and had agreed to back the plan without a debate in Caucus. Labor also had no part in developing a strategic rationale for what would be, at $368 billion over 30 years, Australia's most expensive undertaking in defence.

The August 2023 Labor National Conference shaped as a potential flashpoint for debate. Some union delegates unsuccessfully sought to strip references to nuclear submarines and AUKUS from the party platform, and for their efforts faced trite references to the historical danger of 'appeasement'. But the prospect of an open brawl over nuclear issues, reminiscent of uranium mining debates in the 1980s, was headed off in what unfolded as a largely stage-managed affair. Albanese himself made the case for the nuclear-powered submarines, seeking to emphasise not only the national security considerations, but the economic benefits in jobs for 'Australian workers in Australian shipyards'.

Concerns continued to grow, however, about the reliability of US commitments, British capability, or, indeed, Australia's own preparedness. The biggest theme for critics centred on the question of Australia's sovereign capability. Senior Labor figures such as Paul Keating and Gareth Evans expressed doubt that the Americans would sell the submarines without an undertaking that the boats would fight alongside the United States in the event of war with China. But none of this appeared to dent the Albanese Government's support for the project. It produced a strange spectacle, of former leaders of the party's Right faction driving a campaign against AUKUS, while a Labor prime minister from the Left nutted out the details of the arrangement.

Pacific Island countries received sustained attention over the term, as well as significant financial largesse, only to remain broadly disappointed about Australia's climate change policy and continued support for the fossil fuel industry. Complaints of mistreatment by Pacific Island workers in Australia under the labour mobility scheme also rankled home governments. Southeast Asia won a rhetorical focus, without the intensity of attention applied by previous Labor governments, in part due to the special focus given the Pacific, and also with Indonesia mostly consumed by its elongated presidential election and transition. Ukraine was backed from afar in its war to repel Russia's invasion, against occasional disputes erupting at home over whether Australia could do more.

Events transpired to drive more rancour into domestic debates about foreign policy. The Hamas attack on Israel on 7 October 2023 led to a bitter war in Gaza and beyond, with the spillover of tempers reaching Australia. Anti-Semitic incidents and attacks, particularly in Sydney and Melbourne, fuelled criticism of the Albanese Government's position on the conflict. It also saw considerable tension with Israel. Prime Minister Benjamin Netanyahu declared following an attack on a synagogue in Melbourne that 'it is impossible to separate this reprehensible act from the extreme anti-Israeli position of the Labor government in Australia'. Labor was earlier critical of an Israeli airstrike that resulted in the death of seven aid workers, including Australian Zomi Frankcom, dispatching a special adviser to investigate (Binskin, 2024). Opposition leader Peter Dutton, meanwhile, accused Labor of failing to support a friend in Israel. Dutton slammed the government's voting pattern at the United Nations in resolutions on the conflict and seized on Labor's decision to reverse recognition of 'West Jerusalem' as Israel's capital. The political contest within Australia about the conflict, which broadened to Lebanon, Syria and Yemen, was largely about social cohesion and diplomatic positioning – Australia remained a peripheral player in the Middle East, not one that could sway events. It was, however, the sharpest debate between the parties on international policy. It was also the foreign issue that gave the government the most headaches inside its own ranks, including the defection of a first-term senator.

Donald Trump came to dominate headlines. The timing of his return to the White House in early 2025 in the months leading up to Australia's election underscored that relations with the United States are often more challenging than the familiar and soothing language of alliance allowed. Australia was not spared a punishing US tariff agenda globally, despite longstanding free trade arrangements and past promises of 'deepening' friendship. Debates about the wisdom of relying on America for nuclear-powered submarines grew. Even so, while Labor and the Coalition jostled over which party could better deal with Washington, both went to the May election insisting that the United States remained Australia's principal security partner.

Over the term, Labor appeared driven more by a desire to portray steady management of international relations. Competency and caution seemed watch words. This may have been judged prudent at a time of spiralling inflation and interest rate spikes in the aftermath of the pandemic. The approach perhaps also stemmed from Labor's last experience in government, where a perception of dysfunction, at least during Kevin Rudd's first term, took hold. Nonetheless, the Albanese Government offered little sense of being guided by a broader vision for Australia in global affairs or the 'activist middle power' bent of years past. Ambition was curbed.

The alphabet soup of summits

Albanese and Wong had a fast start, as they jetted to Tokyo within hours of the May 2022 election victory for a meeting of the 'Quad' to join leaders from India, Japan and the United States. The elevation of the Quad to a leader-level summit would illustrate the growing demand placed upon the Prime Minister in the conduct of Australia's foreign policy. Rather than simply being an occasional high-level presence, leaders are increasingly expected to play a frontline role in international talks. In addition, Albanese would be asked each year to attend the East Asia Summit, the G-20, the Asia-Pacific Economic Cooperation meeting and the Pacific Islands Forum. He would also field invitations to the Commonwealth Heads of Government Meeting (CHOGM), the G-7, NATO, the UN General Assembly, annual climate change negotiations, as well as a range of bilateral visits.

Leaders had long sought the international stage, and the number of meetings involving Australia allowed the government to tout its increased prominence. Yet the modern emphasis on the prime minister in diplomacy has a cost, as Albanese discovered.

As a practical concern, gathering busy foreign leaders can make for a scheduling nightmare. Albanese was left disappointed when US President Joe Biden cancelled a planned trip to Sydney at a late stage because of political demands at home, forcing plans for the May 2023 Quad summit to be abandoned. Albanese was himself criticised for skipping CHOGM in Rwanda, climate talks in the Middle East, and a NATO outreach meeting in the United States.

The emphasis on leaders' participation in big diplomatic set-piece summitry creates the perception of a 'snub' whenever circumstances conspire to prevent their participation. This problem will continue until a government is willing to assess which top-level meetings are true priorities (Channer, 2022). Questions about attendance can also easily overshadow whatever outcomes these talks might produce, with a frank judgment about value of attending skewed by fear of causing offence or suffering political criticism at home. By way of example, diplomatic speed-dating also led to paradoxical complaints about the extent of the Prime Minister's travel. Albanese soon earned the nickname 'Airbus Albo'. His two trips to the United States within a fortnight in October and November 2023 didn't help that impression, the first resulting from a special invitation from Biden to attend a state dinner at the White House in a bid by the President to make up for missing the Sydney Quad summit. (The trips did however offer Albanese a further chance to lobby for the United States to drop the pursuit of Australian citizen and Wikileaks founder Julian Assange, held in a UK prison during extradition proceedings, with Assange eventually returned to Australia in June 2024 after pleading guilty to violating US espionage laws.)

The importance of summits – involving leaders in particular – can be easily overstated. The choreographed settings are designed as a showcase for the host, with attendees and an agenda that often overlap. There is also a tendency to graft a new summit event onto the circuit in response to a crisis, rather than working through existing mechanisms and negotiating with stubborn members. Outcomes that justify high-level involvement are hard to quantify, with the most value attributed to personal catch-ups between leaders on the sidelines. Albanese appeared to give voice to his frustration when quizzed about his decision to miss the UN leaders' summit in New York in September 2024, despite being in the United States a few days earlier for a meeting of the Quad. 'I have prioritised the visits that I have to make', he said. 'I know I get criticised for not doing more international travel. And the irony of that, when compared with some of the coverage of when I do travel, is not lost.'

In the end, Albanese's summiteering success would come at home, with his turn to host. Leaders of the Association of Southeast Asian Nations, minus Myanmar, journeyed to Melbourne in March 2024 for an ASEAN–Australia Special Summit. Albanese also invited the prime ministers of Timor Leste and New Zealand. The three-day talks mirrored a similar exercise undertaken by Malcolm Turnbull as prime minister in 2018, allowing Albanese to emphasise messages to the region about trade and investment, clean energy and challenges on the high seas. Language in the final communique was not as strong as Australia had proposed on controversies such as the South China Sea dispute or Russia's aggression in Ukraine. But the inclusion of the issues at all was seen as a win in shaping regional attitudes. Myanmar's conflict, despite being the region's 'hot war', was little more than an incidental focus, with ASEAN itself having struggled to influence the junta. So, Australia raised no initiative to push for peace, having earlier secured the release of economist and adviser to the former Burmese government Sean Turnell after almost two years in a Myanmar prison. The government instead focused on conveying a message to Australia's business community. It urged them not to overlook prospects on their own doorstep while rushing to return to markets in China – as Albanese put it, to recognise the 'opportunity from proximity', with Southeast Asia expected to become collectively the world's fourth-largest economy by 2040. Labor was regularly frustrated across the term that its push for economic diversification in international trade and investment was being ignored, leaving Australia vulnerable to another episode of Chinese displeasure.

Power plays

Albanese met with China's Xi Jinping in November 2022 in Bali, Indonesia, a major signal that relations had thawed. It was the first contact by the Chinese President with an Australian prime minister since a brief handshake conversation with Scott Morrison in 2019 and the first formal bilateral meeting in six years. Beijing had taken the opportunity of a change at the top in Australia to re-engage, writing to Albanese immediately following the election that China stood 'ready to work with Australia to learn from the past [and] look to the future'. The government was careful not to boast about Australia's economic resilience in the face of pressure, lest it further provoke China. But the lesson, to not bend to intimidation, would have been closely absorbed internationally (Brown, 2023).

Gradually over the term China lifted the various restrictions placed on Australian exports, which included barley, beef, coal, lobsters, wine and other goods. The government was also able to negotiate the release of Australian journalist Cheng Lei after more than three years in a Chinese prison on spurious espionage charges. Albanese visited Beijing and Shanghai in October 2023 and a little over six months later hosted China's Premier Li Qiang in Australia, also meeting Xi twice more while abroad.

But friction in dealing with China persisted. Sustained lobbying failed to free another Australian held by China, academic Yang Hengjun. He had earlier been accused of spying and was given a suspended death sentence.

Australia's military presence in the South China Sea also brought its warships and patrol aircraft into proximity with those from China. Several encounters, described as unprofessional conduct, would sour relations. Chinese fighter jets launched chaff into the flight paths of Australian military aircraft, one June 2022 incident coming soon after the change of government, and several similar episodes followed across the term. A Chinese navy ship also deployed a sonar burst while Australian navy divers were underwater in November 2023, risking serious injury. China then dispatched a flotilla of warships to circumnavigate Australia in February 2025, described by analysts as a 'show of force'. The timing, just as the local election loomed, fuelled political debates, particularly after the ships conducted a live-fire exercise in the Tasman Sea without advance warning.

China's shadow would loom in other ways. In relations with the Pacific, Australia increasingly engaged in a contest for influence. The government sought deals with Vanuatu, Tuvalu, Papua New Guinea, Nauru and Solomon Islands, as well as region-wide arrangements, in a bid to remain a 'partner of choice' in security matters. Economically, too, Australia plied the Pacific with aid, the 2023–24 Budget devoting a record $2 billion, approximately 40 per cent of Australia's overall development assistance allocation. PNG was a particular beneficiary, with an additional $600 million commitment to bring a local rugby league team into the Australian competition, reportedly to help scuttle a prospective security pact between PNG and China. The risk of a spiralling bidding war with China was brushed aside. Past concerns about 'chequebook diplomacy' undermining good governance in the region were similarly disregarded. The sense of Australia acting as a junior partner to the United States also lingered. A senior Biden administration official was overheard during a forum in Tonga telling Albanese to 'take the lane' given by the United States to Australia in the region, an echo of the 'deputy sheriff' controversy that arose in the Howard era (Lewis, 2024).

Even so, the China aspect should not eclipse the importance of a sustained effort made to engage with Australia's direct neighbourhood, a region that had long been treated as a diplomatic backwater. Misaligned ambition between Australia and the Pacific Islands nations in addressing climate change did not create enough of an obstacle to a joint bid to host a round of global negotiations in 2026. Wong was a conspicuous visitor to the region, fending off barbs by former prime minister Paul Keating that the effort was a distraction. Australia's bid to ensure a banking presence across the Pacific carried the potential to make a lasting difference in everyday life. The government clearly recognised it could not take the region for granted.

India also presented a delicate challenge. Australia's longstanding hope to strengthen the relationship was bolstered by the increasing size of the Indian diaspora community in Australia, which was also courted as a potential voting bloc. 'Modi mania' greeted a visit by India's Prime Minister Narendra Modi to Sydney in 2023, with Albanese gushing in a sideshow appearance to a man he called 'the boss'. But the public remained lukewarm about the relationship, out of step with official enthusiasm. Lowy Institute polling showed tepid faith in Modi 'to do the right thing regarding world affairs', the measure dropping to 37 per cent in 2024. This could be a result of India's increasing heft and willingness to make its disappointment known. Modi, for example, offered sharp words standing alongside Albanese about vandalism attacks on Hindu temples in Australia linked to a Sikh separatist campaign in India. Mixed feelings may have also stemmed from revelations that India was behind a 'nest of spies' uncovered in Australia, an operation that dated prior to Labor's term in office but was only reported in 2024.

Matters practical

Labor's emphasis lay in functional foreign policy. Challenged during parliamentary hearings to define Australia's 'national interest', Wong eschewed power politics: 'Everything we do – whether it's in our region, in our relationship with China, in our relationships with other powers – is about trying to assure peace and find ways in which conflict and competition can be dealt with in ways that don't threaten peace'. In trade, foreign aid or respect for rights, the government preferred rules and process.

That preference for process also offered a guide to understanding its foreign policy as steady and rarely disruptive. Consular successes, including the return of the remaining 'Bali Nine' Australians imprisoned for 19 years in Indonesia for drug smuggling, allowed the government to chalk up tangible results. Labor was not flustered by a late charge from the Opposition during the election over reports of Russian interest in an airbase in Indonesia, although it did bow to pressure to take back the port of Darwin from Chinese ownership. If there was risk, it was political, in seeking to portray Dutton as Trump-like in his attitudes, even though Albanese would need to work with the unpredictable US President in a second term.

Australia had for years, under both the Rudd–Gillard–Rudd Labor and Coalition governments, been consumed in foreign policy and defence by debates about imagined futures, especially the shape of competition between China and the United States in the decades to come. Drawn-out arguments about the wording of white papers and defence doctrines became common over this period. But these manifestos also quickly dated. The Albanese Government offered its own early prescription, via a Defence Strategic Review, but wisely steered clear of too many crystal ball exercises. The notion of 'using all levers of statecraft' was instead the guiding principle, or, as Wong put it, 'diplomacy [that] signals intent, credibility and even red lines'. An approach less philosophical, more practical.

References

Binskin, M, 'Special adviser public report on the government of Israel's response to the IDF attack on World Central Kitchen aid workers in Gaza on Monday 1 April 2024', 2 August 2024, <https://www.dfat.gov.au/sites/default/files/special-advisers-public-report-israels-response-wck-strikes-august-2024.pdf>.

Brown, J, 'Countering Chinese economic coercion: Enhanced cooperation between Australia and Europe', Lowy Institute, 27 April 2023, <https://www.lowyinstitute.org/publications/countering-chinese-economic-coercion-enhanced-cooperation-between-australia-europe>.

Channer, H, 'Maximising Australia's memberships: Recalibrating Australia's engagement with Indo-Pacific groups', Perth USAsia Centre, May 2022, <https://perthusasia.edu.au/research-insights/publications/maximising-australias-memberships-recalibrating-australias-engagement-with-indo-pacific-groups/>.

Lewis, L, 'US "gives Australia the lane" on Pacific policing – Campbell', *Radio New Zealand*, 29 August 2024, <https://www.rnz.co.nz/international/pacific-news/526460/us-gives-australia-the-lane-on-pacific-policing-campbell>.

McGregor, R, 'Chinese coercion, Australian resilience', Lowy Institute Analysis, October 2022, <https://www.lowyinstitute.org/publications/chinese-coercion-australian-resilience>.

Wong, P, 'Securing our future', Speech to the ANU National Security College, 9 April 2024, <https://www.foreignminister.gov.au/minister/penny-wong/speech/speech-anu-national-security-college-securing-our-future>.

CHAPTER 18

UNCHARTERED TERRITORY: IMMIGRATION RESTARTED AMID POPULATION PANIC

LIZ ALLEN

Prime Minister Anthony Albanese's Labor Government made a rod for their own back on immigration. Political parties tend to talk tough on immigration while in Opposition. Their tough talk and rhetoric continue once in government, while their actions tell a different story, reflecting the nation's reliance on immigration to stay economically afloat. An ageing population means that relatively fewer people of working age are fuelling government coffers. With individual income tax representing the top source of government money (ABS, 2025a), migrants provide a life raft by handsomely funding vital public services they are not permitted to use.

Governments love immigration in practice, but shy away from the optics of being pro-growth. Former prime minister Kevin Rudd made the mistake of publicly welcoming a so-called 'big Australia' in 2010. His party punished him (Allen, 2017) and Julia Gillard came to power promoting population sustainability.

Immigration alongside growing housing, cost-of-living and employment woes presented the perfect storm for the incoming Albanese Government and these big social issues continue to bubble.

Three broad themes framed the first Albanese Government – namely resumption of migration following Covid-related border closure, the migration system review and international student caps.

From Opposition to restarting migration

The actions of the first Albanese Labor government are best understood in the wider context of Albanese himself and the baggage his federal party carried on immigration. Albanese was well placed on population-related matters heading into top office, having cut his teeth on the regional development and infrastructure portfolios during the Rudd–Gillard–Rudd Labor governments. Further, Albanese played a significant role in the country's last population inquiry. After Gillard came into government on the back of 'big Australia' fears, her government initiated the Sustainable Australia – Sustainable Communities inquiry. Infrastructure and regional development were two of the four key initiatives identified in the inquiry report, alongside workforce and migration (Allen, 2011). Albanese oversaw the release of a comprehensive and ambitious infrastructure blueprint. Trouble was, inadequate funding was assigned to achieve the recommendations, and soon after, the Labor Government was voted out.

The aspiring Albanese Government tripped themselves up from Opposition when they failed to factor in that Covid-related border closures would lead to the highest net immigration intake in Australia's history. To be fair, few anticipated the impact Covid-19 would have on immigration once border restrictions eased.

Heading into the 2022 election, Australia's annual permanent immigration had been set at 160 000 in March 2019 by Scott Morrison's government. This figure represented a cut from 190 000 (Martin, 2022). Covid hit and with it border restrictions began. Even Australian citizens and permanent residents were unable to enter the country until restrictions began to ease. Australia's international border reopened via a staged process and fully opened from 21 February 2022. But not before federal Labor had played its card on immigration.

Opining in 2020, then Labor senator Kristina Keneally called for a cut to immigration and an end to the nation's reliance on temporary migrant workers. Keneally suggested the 'cheap supply of overseas, temporary labour … undercuts wages for Australian workers' (Keneally, 2020). The then senator and federal Opposition spokesperson on home affairs and immigration called for restrictions on low-skilled temporary migration, pointing to actions taken by the then British Prime Minister Boris Johnson. The Australia-first rhetoric of Keneally's piece was widely criticised by experts and media alike, especially given evidence showing that immigration had not harmed local workers but in fact contributed a net benefit to the nation (CEDA, 2019). Commentators agreed, however, that Australia's migration system needed an overhaul.

Closed borders during Covid presented a natural experiment of sorts. When net overseas migration was in deficit, housing did not become more affordable (ABC, 2025), wages declined (McCarthy, Ross, Terrell and Wang, 2024) and the need for workers increased dramatically (Cole, 2021). In other words, simply cutting immigration did not ease housing and economic pressures. Moreover, migration was shown to be essential.

Within months of coming into government, Home Affairs Minister Clare O'Neil announced an increase in the permanent migration ceiling to a record 195 000 people annually (Karp, 2022). This was in direct contrast with the rhetoric the spokesperson espoused while in Opposition, but the increase was contextual. The increase was spruiked to alleviate skills shortages that had worsened during the Covid period and aimed to provide greater permanency for migrants. Notably, Home Affairs recruited hundreds more staff to process and clear visa application backlogs that had amassed during the former government. Then Opposition leader Peter Dutton said on the increase in permanent migration, 'the number needs to be higher' (Karp, 2022). Bipartisan support was rare and significant.

Permanent migration, though, is only one aspect of Australia's migration system. Indeed, most people gaining permanency are already in the country. Net overseas migration is a more comprehensive measure of flows of people comprising the population. This number comprises the incoming minus outgoing movements of people who meet the threshold for length of stay, so excludes short-term travellers. In fact, the permanent migration number has little to do with the net overseas migration number, and under the current system the government has limited control over it because it includes Australian citizens and New Zealanders (among others). Taking the year before Covid as an example, the migration program for 2018–19 was set at a maximum of 190 000 and the actual permanent intake was 160 323, while net overseas migration was 241 338 (ABS, 2025b; Home Affairs, 2019). The

Figure 18.1: Net overseas migration, Australia; 2017–2024

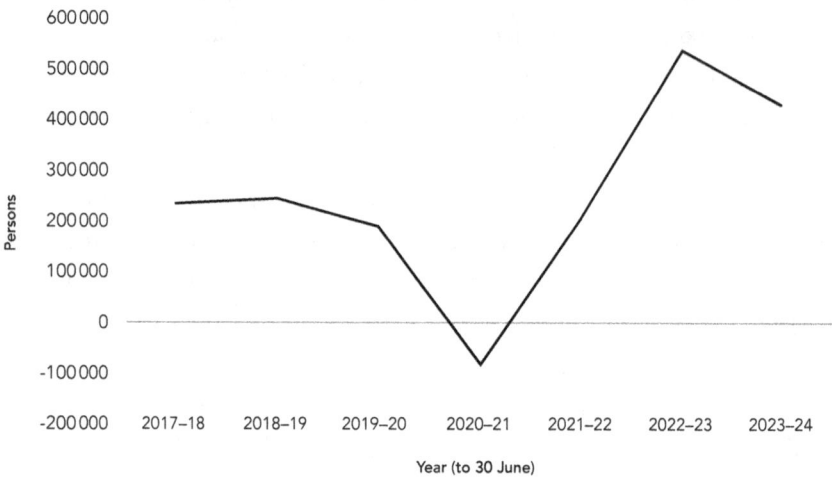

SOURCE Australian Bureau of Statistics, 2025b

permanent program cap reflects political sentiment, not necessarily intent, and least of all reality.

By the time Albanese's government had taken office, the most recent net overseas migration data showed an historic low of -84 930 people for 2020–21. Not since wartime had Australia seen the likes of such negative numbers. There was talk the Australian migration system would fail to bounce back owing to impeded air travel and mounting discrimination toward migrants. Bounce back it did, and then some. Net overseas migration increased to the highest number ever at 538 341 people in 2022–23. The high number was not due to people flooding the country, as the media and the Dutton Opposition had the nation believe. It was a quirk of measurement; people had already left in excessive numbers. Non-residents in Australia during the start of Covid left the country in unprecedented highs; Morrison told them to go home and they did. Students and others on visas left the country prematurely, meaning the usually steady flow of departures was artificially high. Net overseas migration had been disrupted so that when borders reopened the usual flow of people outgoing did not occur, only incoming. The number was high owing to a calculation quirk and if a longer view is taken, Australia actually lost expected people in the long run. This is not what the discourse would have the public believe, and the Albanese Government responded to the increasing concerns about population increase.

Migration system review 2023 and capping temporariness

The Australian Government announced a review of the nation's migration system in September 2022. Citing concerns about Australia's demographic context and the need for skills and labour (Parkinson, Howe and Azarias, 2023), the timing of the review was no mistake given increasing net overseas migration. The Albanese Government needed to show they were serious about ensuring immigration was working in Australia's best interests.

The review made its final report in early 2023, led by the former senior public servant Dr Martin Parkinson and co-reviewed by professor of law Joanna Howe and former Deloitte partner John Azarias. Hundreds of public submissions were received, and the report found 'Australia's migration program … not fit for purpose'. The Minister for Home Affairs, Clare O'Neil, called out the migration system as 'broken' and failing to deliver for Australians or migrants. Parkinson and colleagues went further, stating the 'objectives of the program are unclear, and successive governments and policymakers … responded to challenges through piecemeal reforms which have not addressed fundamental underlying issues' (Parkinson, Howe and Azarias, 2023: 1).

Major wholesale reform was needed to overhaul the clunky and exploitative scheme, according to the review. Of the 38 areas of reform detailed in the review it is hard to see what has come of the suggested wholesale reform. Actions did flow, though. Students, being the largest category of visa holders contributing to net overseas migration, were among the first issues addressed. The Albanese Government, carefully stewarded by O'Neil, did the one thing they could: slow visa processing and seek to cap the number of tertiary students entering the country. Such actions played directly into the public discourse that overseas or 'foreign' students were inundating the country in droves, driving up the cost of living and making housing unaffordable. Blaming outsiders for local, home-grown problems was also an opportunity to shift focus from the long-brewing crises of housing affordability and economic security. The evidence said otherwise, though, with most international students living near or on university campuses and contributing only a small fraction to the private housing composition (Dhanji, 2025). But the government had to act – and in the very least look to be doing something on this front – because Dutton's Opposition was capitalising on population panic, priming the nation for an upcoming election fight on the platform of Australia-first rhetoric.

The Albanese Government was strategically masterful in approaching immigration: showing action while doing little as the numbers settled themselves through the harmonisation of net overseas migration. Immigration was going to decline on its own as the two sides of the equation – incoming and outgoing – settled with time. The government took piecemeal and ultimately ineffectual action but credit for the win. Albanese announced cuts to immigration on the back of a 'once-in-a-generation review' of migration (AAP, 2023).

Student caps were first slated in 2024, off the back of the highest population growth rate on record (ABS, 2021; ABS, 2025b). The intention was to pass legislation through parliament to restrict the number of international students enrolled in universities across the country in line with available campus housing (Ziguras, 2024). In practice, though, it was much cruder. Visa processing was on the go-slow, with the government using Ministerial Direction 107 (MD107) to prioritise universities based on risk of enrolling 'non-genuine students' coming to Australia for the stated purpose of study but actually work (Cassidy, 2024). The reality was that all student visa processing slowed, creating great uncertainty among higher education providers from as early as the beginning of the 2024 academic year. Universities were put on notice and the sector was in a holding pattern while the government sought to make the approach official. But it was not to be; the Opposition blocked the reform, and the government responded with a new ministerial direction, MD111. The government would instead prioritise visa processing to regional universities. These changes created great funding uncertainty for the sector, and in turn the country. Higher education makes a handsome financial contribution to the nation. The impact on prospective students coming to Australia was also not accounted for in the Albanese Government's tough talk.

Alongside the go-slow on visa processing, the Albanese Government instituted a range of measures to increase the hurdles to studying in Australia. Beefed-up barriers were put in place to make Australia a less desirable place to study, including doubling the student visa application fee and tighter English language requirements. Many in the higher education sector also saw the fee increase as revenue-raising to fund the government's higher education review initiatives, which it had foreshadowed (The Accord). Immigration and increasing population growth rates were ultimately at the heart of the crackdown on higher education, with the consequences unrealised for years to come. Easy, but dumb, pickings. Ultimately, net overseas migration numbers would have declined on their own with time as the flow of incoming and outgoing resumed.

The Albanese Government had a much bigger headache on immigration than solely students and net overseas migration. In late 2023, the federal high court found two decades of legal precedent was wrong: indefinite immigration detention is unlawful where an individual cannot be returned to their country of citizenship or resettled in a third country. Around 150 people were released from immigration detention; among them were reported 'convicted murderers, rapists and drug traffickers' (Worthington, 2024). Panicked and unprepared, the Albanese Government responded with restrictions like curfews and monitoring ankle bracelets, many of which responses have been found to be illegal. The High Court decision continues to cause headaches as crimes committed by ex-detainees slowly mount and are reported by media. By 2025, the so-called NZYQ cohort had grown to over 350. Under pressure, Albanese's government began deporting the group to the small island nation of Nauru in a controversial multi-billion-dollar settlement program.

A mandate on population?

The Albanese Government missed some significant opportunities in its first term. Sadly, these included opportunities to show leadership in reframing the populist population panic that periodically comes and goes in Australia. While the Albanese Government criticised the existing immigration structures as broken and reform piecemeal, they have achieved much of the same: making patchy tweaks to a complex and outdated system.

Calls are again growing for population policy to be introduced in Australia. Rather than an ad hoc, reactionary and disjointed approach to population there are opportunities to be more proactive and strategic in the longer term. The Albanese Government's first term was foundational, setting in train what could be done while responding to the unexpected.

Entering his second term, Albanese appointed Julian Hill as Assistant Minister for International Education. This is only the second time in history such a position has existed, and the first time under a more progressive government. Hill was quoted as saying: 'the government has said net overseas migration is too high, and we are working to reduce the overall levels to a sustainable level ... If anyone thinks the government is just going to give up on managing international education, they've got rocks in their head.'

References

Australian Associated Press, 'Anthony Albanese announces plan to reduce immigration levels following Covid influx', *Guardian*, 9 December 2023.

Australian Bureau of Statistics, *Historical Population*, Australian Bureau of Statistics, Canberra, 2021.

— *Insights into Government Finance Statistics, December 2024*, Canberra, 2025a.

— *National, State and Territory Population*, Canberra, 2025b.

Allen, L, 'Sustainable population strategy: Public policy and implementation challenges', *Academy Proceedings*, issue 2, Academy of Social Sciences in Australia, 2011.

— 'Australia doesn't have a population policy – why?', *The Conversation*, 3 July 2017.

Cassidy, C, '"It's very unfair": Australia's visa crackdown is disrupting international students and hitting university finances', *Guardian*, 5 May 2024.

Cole, W, 'Australian job vacancies surge to record, firms struggle to find workers', *Reuters*, 1 July 2021.

Committee for Economic Development of Australia, *Effects of Temporary Migration: Shaping Australia's Society and Economy*, Melbourne, 2019.

Dhanji, K, 'Fact check: Are international students making it harder to find a place to rent as Dutton claims?', *Guardian*, 8 April 2025.

Hare, J, 'Are overseas student caps back on the government's agenda?', *Australian Financial Review*, 22 May 2025.

Home Affairs Department, *2018–19 Migration Program Report*, Canberra, 2019.

Human Rights Law Centre, *Indefinite Detention Continues for People Who Cannot be Forcibly Deported*, 2024.

Karp, P, 'Australia raises permanent migration cap to 195,000 to ease workforce shortages', *Guardian*, 2 September 2022.

Keneally, K, 'Do we want migrants to return in the same numbers? The answer is no', *Sydney Morning Herald*, 3 May 2020.

Martin, P, 'When we open up, open up big: Economists say we need more migrants', *The Conversation*, 20 February 2022.

McCarthy, M, Ross, I, Terrell, M, and Wang, L, 'Developments in wages growth across pay-setting methods', *Reserve Bank of Australia Bulletin*, October 2024.

Parkinson, M, Howe, J, and Azarias, J, *Review of the Migration System: Final Report*, Department of Home Affairs, Canberra, 2023.

Worthington, B, 'High Court immigration detention fallout has Anthony Albanese seeking independence from own government', *ABC News*, 6 May 2024.

Yussuf, A, 'Charts show how Australia's housing market has changed since Covid', *ABC News*, 14 March 2025.

Ziguras, C, 'Why is the government proposing caps on international students and how did we get here?', *The Conversation*, 15 May 2024.

CHAPTER 19

AFTER THE HONEYMOON: THE ALBANESE GOVERNMENT AND THE MEDIA

MATTHEW RICKETSON AND CAROLINE FISHER

P rime Minister Anthony Albanese approached media policy and relations with the media in much the same way he approached government overall – cautiously, methodically and with one eye on reform. If the Albanese Labor Government had lost office after only one term – a prospect that opinion polls suggested was entirely possible late in 2024 – its caution probably would have been marked down as disappointing. As it was, the scale of the stunning victory at the election in May 2025 ensured a second term of office and an opportunity to enact several pieces of media legislation that had been stalled. That is in the future. It is well to remember that after Labor won government in May 2022 it needed to re-set relations with the media which overall had become more than usually fractious, at times almost dysfunctional, during the Liberal/National Party Coalition Government led by Scott Morrison. The Coalition's hostility towards the Australian Broadcasting Corporation (ABC) was palpable.

That said, during much of the 2022–2025 term the prime minister's media performance and relationship with the press gallery were far from steady. Questions about his performance and judgment have been constant companions, whether, most importantly, on how during the Voice referendum he failed to persuade Australians to vote Yes, or less importantly on his tin-eared decision during a housing crisis to buy a $4.3 million clifftop house on the New South Wales central coast.

There was much hope among press gallery journalists that an Albanese Government would prove to be more open and transparent than the Morrison administration. Early signs were promising. Albanese made himself available to the media and returned autonomy to ministers. However, as one press gallery reporter told Fisher, 'We're seeing Albanese with a helicopter-style of leadership, leaving a lot to the ministers. I don't think that'll be able to last as issues become more difficult for the government. But that's what we see now'. As predicted, when the 'honeymoon' period ended, the leader's media operation became increasingly controlled and unresponsive, and the number of staff in his office, including media and policy advisers, grew to 61, which was ten more than under Morrison (Webber, 2024). Trying to control the media is commonplace in government management. Over the past several decades, the significance of this practice has evolved dramatically due to the professionalisation of communication and major advancements in media technology, such as television and social media platforms. These changes have heightened the focus on leaders and raised expectations of their capabilities, resulting in a substantial increase in resources dedicated to centralised media operations (Strangio et al., 2017). As the pressure rises and crises hit, the more centralised prime ministerial media operations become as they batten down the hatches to weather the rolling media storms. The problem is, the more closed politicians' offices become, the lower the trust they engender with the media, which in turn helps to foster cynicism in the electorate. Having strongly performing media advisers to liaise with journalists is key to the press gallery developing and maintaining confidence in a prime minister's office.

With victory achieved, there was an overhaul of the prime minister's longstanding staff soon after Labor won the election in 2022, including the departure of veteran political journalist Matthew Franklin, who had worked with Albanese since 2013.[1] As the new government settled in, questions began to arise about the effectiveness of the prime minister's media operation. As Mizen (2024) reports, after the Voice referendum in 2023, the media director Liz Fitch left, along with former Special Broadcasting Service (SBS) reporter Brett Mason. Former *Guardian Australia* political editor Katharine Murphy and experienced staffer Fiona Sugden were recruited to steady the ship, and the relationship with the press gallery improved. This change in media operations coincided with a wider adjustment in strategic approach to policy as well as to preparing for how to prevent the Coalition parties from wresting power from Labor at the coming election.

The frustration went both ways. To circumvent the tensions and reach voters amid the continuing fragmentation of media audiences, Albanese embraced podcasting, doing 20 in the lead-up to the 2025 election. In two separate podcast interviews he acknowledged the pressures on journalists to produce stories almost instantaneously in a 24/7 digital news environment and lamented the paucity of long-form journalism and the growing reliance on clickbait and commentary. Speaking to former press gallery journalist Mark Kenny (2024) on the Democracy Sausage podcast, the Prime Minister expressed surprise at the 'lack of follow-up' after press conferences or a front-page news article. He worried about 'the state of political discourse and polarisation' fuelled by social media. Albanese told Claire Kimball (2025) from The Squiz that he enjoyed doing podcast interviews because 'it's a format where you're not under pressure to give a quick grab or to stick to a script. So, I quite like it, because it's real'. His lengthy interview with podcaster and influencer Abbie Chatfield (2025) grabbed headlines after she declared her support for the Greens and her clear intention to encourage voters to preference Labor ahead of the Coalition at the federal election.

Albanese's comments on the podcasts were noteworthy for several reasons. First, they were reminiscent of former Labor prime minister Julia Gillard's admonition in 2011 when she told the news media 'don't write crap'. The difference was that her advice was met with hostility by the Canberra press gallery while Albanese's critique was delivered through podcasts rather than at the National Press Club and only the most unreflective journalists did not accept that their standing in society has diminished since 2011. Second, his reflection on the mainstream news media carried the weight of a politician who has witnessed close-up the seismic changes to the business model underpinning media and its negative impact on the state of journalism in general and public interest journalism in particular. Responding to the rise of 'news deserts' in regional and rural Australia, people have been turning to social media for news, while the audiences for TV and newspapers continue to spiral slowly downward (Park, Fisher et al., 2024). The Australian news media is nowhere near as politically polarised as in the United States, but audiences for the right-wing-oriented Sky News Australia continue to grow, up 4 per cent from 2024, especially in regional Australia, and trust in mainstream news hovers in the low 40s (Park, Fisher et al., 2024).

After years of antipathy from the Morrison Government, the Labor

Government ended the hostility towards the ABC. It had promised to introduce five-year funding terms for the ABC and SBS, to ensure funding agreements went beyond a single term of government and so reduce the likelihood of governments using them as a cudgel to cower the ABC or SBS. The government introduced a bill to this effect in 2024, but it had not been passed before the 2025 election. In the meantime, the government had modestly increased operational funding for the ABC from $881 million in 2022 to $1.016 billion in 2025–26, according to analysis by ABC Alumni. The Prime Minister did not, however, change his longstanding approach to News Corp Australia, with whom he maintained cordial relations in the hope he could stave off or at least mitigate attacks from a powerful news organisation customarily antipathetic towards Labor governments. His efforts did not prevent News Corp outlets from reporting and commenting on the government in ways that went well beyond conventional criticism, especially on the fraught issue of the government's response to rising anti-Semitism and Islamophobia following the 7 October 2023 attack by Hamas that killed nearly 1200 people in Israel.

Only late in 2024 did Albanese call out News Corp's negative coverage (Sakkal, 2024). Throughout the term, the Murdoch media outlets continued their support for the Coalition parties led by Peter Dutton until it became obvious that his election campaign in April/May 2025 was misconceived, poorly planned and dreadfully executed. It became apparent that Dutton had learnt the wrong lesson from his success in spearheading opposition to the Voice referendum (Megalogenis, 2024). In private discussions before the referendum in 2023, Albanese warned Dutton that those who would vote 'No' would not necessarily stay loyal to the Coalition and vote for them at a general election but that those who voted 'Yes' would not forget Dutton's actions.

Dutton ignored Albanese. He continued appearing on Sky News Australia where hosts applauded his hard-right pursuit of the culture wars. He aggravated his problem by avoiding the more searching questions he was likely to receive in interviews with the ABC and the Canberra press gallery. Instead, he doubled down, describing the ABC and *Guardian Australia* as 'the hate media', a term lifted from the pursed lips of Donald Trump. After the Liberals' terrible loss in May 2025 a number of commentators were quick to point to News Corp Australia's declining influence, even irrelevance. 'Rupert Murdoch's News Corporation has, for some time, been impotent when it comes to affecting the outcomes of elections' wrote Margaret Simons (2025) in one of the aforementioned hate media outlets. The full-throated support of News Corp was actually damaging those, like the Liberal Party, 'who fly too close to its flame'. This is important. News Corp Australia's advocacy for the Coalition parties does appear to be having the perverse effect of narrowing their electoral appeal, as does its outlets' increasingly loud and extreme efforts to gain audience attention. Politicians may be embracing podcasting and influencers, but they still see News Corp Australia and the Murdochs as powerful and behave accordingly. Until that changes, News will continue to exert outsized influence in Canberra.

Regulation and financing of the media

The government's efforts to address the precarious financial state of Australian news media have had mixed success. The world-leading News Media Bargaining Code introduced by the Morrison Government initially provided a $70 million annual lifeline to the media companies. The relief was short-lived because as several commentators predicted, the digital platforms' dislike of the code ensured they began looking for an exit. In 2024, Meta announced it would no longer cut deals with news outlets in Australia, and deprioritised news on its platforms. The announcement triggered a fresh round of media job cuts and contractions. Google also revealed it was withdrawing from its deals with Australian news outlets by offering less money and shorter contracts.

Rather than use the power in the code to designate the digital platforms, the Communications Minister, Michelle Rowland, announced in December 2024 that the government would introduce a News Bargaining Incentive to address the code's limitations. The incentive would impose a charge on platforms that did not agree to or renew deals with news publishers. The charge would be calculated according to their Australian revenue and cost the platforms tens of millions of dollars. This charge would be on top of corporate income tax and would not be deductible. The proposal was welcomed by a media industry anxious for long-term stable investment to replace their much-depleted sources of revenue. The media commentator Tim Burrowes noted in May 2025, for instance, that in the previous decade the market capitalisation of Seven West Media had plummeted from $1.2 billion to $200 million. The minister's incentive scheme, however, was not implemented before the 2025 election. Even before then, though, the re-election of President Donald Trump loomed as a further hurdle to the government's efforts to regulate the big tech behemoths who have been lobbying Trump to get Australia to relax its laws concerning the digital platforms.

Apart from continuing with the News Media Bargaining Code, the Labor Government had incurred the wrath of the big tech leaders, or 'broligarchs' (Bevan, 2025), by attempting to deal with some of the harms caused by social media. Thanks to Section 230 of the *Communications Decency Act 1996*, passed by the US congress in the early days of the internet, online platforms are not regarded as publishers. They cannot be held responsible for defamatory content, though news publishers whose content was carried on the platforms could still be sued. As digital and social media came to pervade the world over the next three decades, the illogicality of regarding legacy media and new media differently became stark. Not that the broligarchs saw it that way; they wanted to remain free of almost all regulation. The *Online Safety Act 2021* had been introduced in Australia by the previous Coalition Government following public alarm over the livestreaming on Facebook of the killing of 51 people in a mosque in Christchurch, New Zealand. In 2024 the e-Safety Commissioner, Julie Inman Grant, used her power under the act to order Facebook, by then known as Meta, and X, to take down videos of two stabbing attacks in Sydney; the first was a random attack at a shopping centre in Bondi Junction where six people were killed, and the second at a church in Wakeley where bishop Mar Mari Emmanuel was stabbed while delivering a sermon.

Meta complied with the order, but X did not. Elon Musk, who had bought the site known as Twitter in 2022 and re-named it X, assailed Grant as a 'censorship commissar', which may seem an overreaction given the abhorrent nature of the video but in the end the government backed down, uncertain about the enforceability of its powers. Musk's sentiments echoed those of conservative think tanks such as the Institute of Public Affairs, which called Inman Grant a 'global free speech threat' (Hollingworth, 2023). Musk was also critical of the government's Communications Legislation Amendment (Combatting Misinformation and Disinformation) Bill 2024, which he labelled 'fascistic'. The bill sought to balance the need to protect freedom of speech and the need to reduce harms caused by misinformation and disinformation. The government had previously relied on the online platforms to regulate themselves through a voluntary code but Musk's X was the prime example of failure here. Twitter was far from perfect but Musk allowed misinformation and disinformation to run rampant on the platform, with his own account being among the worst offenders. The government withdrew the bill in late 2024. It is unclear whether it will introduce a revised bill in its second term.

The Albanese Government has been boldest in introducing world-first laws to ban children under 16 from social media platforms. Under the *Online Safety Amendment (Social Media Minimum Age) Act 2024*, the onus is on the social media platforms to ensure people under the minimum age cannot create or keep a social media account. The policy was heavily criticised by media experts and youth advocates on the grounds that it was government overreach and would be unworkable, but it also tapped into a growing unease about damage caused to children by social media. How exactly the ban will work is unclear; it is due to take effect by December 2025. In a move that similarly blended populism with addressing a genuine issue, Albanese banned sitting MPs and the public service from having TikTok on their phones out of concern about foreign interference from China. Public servants followed the rule, but politicians circumvented it by using their personal mobile phones to run their TikTok accounts and thereby continue to connect with young voters in the lead-up to the election.

In the meantime, $1.8 million was announced under the Albanese Government's News Media Assistance Program (News MAP) to help local and regional media outlets. News MAP was introduced to develop an evidence-based policy framework to guide government funding to parts of the news media sector identified as particularly vulnerable. The framework focused on four key policy areas: access to news media, diversity of content, quality of content, and engagement with content. Importantly, this exercise also included evaluation of government interventions in the media marketplace. To date, such evaluations have been sorely lacking. Successive governments have provided assistance through inefficient one-off grants schemes that were soon abandoned without their impact being assessed. This has frustrated a news media industry already chary of government assistance for their ailing business model, but willing to accept it as long as they could maintain their editorial independence.

The Albanese Government's approach to the media and to media policy issues has not resolved one of the core communications issues politicians have been grappling with for more than a decade: how to govern in a seemingly ungovernable hybrid communications environment where legacy and digital media outlets battle for influence. It deserves credit for at least trying to reduce the kind of hyper-partisanship that some media outlets have turned to and which floods social media platforms. Unlike some other progressive governments overseas, the Albanese Government has managed to see off populist authoritarian impulses and to distinguish Australia from its progressive allies. The Labor Government survived its first term when other post-pandemic governments in democratic countries did not, which may testify to the prime minister's political and electoral savvy. That his government, and the ailing Liberal Party government in Canada, both benefited from global anxiety over the tumultuous, even dictatorial first 100 days of Donald Trump's second presidency seems significant. Just how significant is too early to tell.

Note: One of the authors of this chapter, Caroline Fisher, is a former Labor ministerial advisor and was married to Matthew Franklin during much of his time working for Anthony Albanese.

References

Bevan, M, 'Australia vs the internet', ABC, 24 April, 1 May and 8 May 2025.

Chatfield, A, 'Prime Minister Albanese: The extended version', *It's a Lot with Abbie Chatfield*, 11 February 2025, <https://podcasts.apple.com/au/podcast/prime-minister-albanese-the-extended-version/id1500849438?i=1000694350921>.

Hollingworth, D, 'Right-wing think tank labels eSafety Commissioner a "global threat to free speech"', *Cyber Daily*, 24 May 2024, <https://www.cyberdaily.au/government/10613-right-wing-think-tank-labels-esafety-commissioner-a-global-threat-to-free-speech>.

Kenny, M, 'Anthony Albanese on two years in the top job', *Democracy Sausage*, 24 May 2024, <https://reporter.anu.edu.au/all-stories/democracy-sausage-anthony-albanese-on-two-years-in-the-top-job>.

Kimball, C, 'Prime Minister of Australia', *The Squiz*, 21 January 2025, <https://www.pm.gov.au/media/podcast-interview-squiz>.

Megalogenis, G, 'Minority report: The new shape of Australian politics', *Quarterly Essay*, no. 96, 2024.

Mizen, R, '"Albo knows best": Inside Labor's discontent with PM', *Australian Financial Review*, 9 December 2024.

Park, S, et al., *Digital News Rerport: Australia 2024*, News and Media Research Centre, University of Canberra, 2024.

Ricketson, M, and Dodd, A, 'In its soul-searching, the Coalition should examine its relationship with the media', *The Conversation*, 4 May 2025.

Sakkal, P, 'News Corp is working with Dutton to bring us down: Albanese', *Sydney Morning Herald*, 10 December 2024.

Simons, M, 'As Australia's election result reminds us, News Corp no longer has the power to sway voters', *Guardian*, 6 May 2025.

Strangio, P, 't Hart, P, and Walter, J, *The Pivot of Power: Australian Prime Ministers and Political Leadership: 1949-2016*, Melbourne University Publishing, Melbourne, 2017.

Webber, M, 'Army of advisers: staffer ranks up in Albanese's office', *Canberra Times*, 6 June 2024.

CHAPTER 20

REALITY BITES: CLIMATE CHANGE AND THE ENERGY TRANSITION

JO MUMMERY AND DARREN SINCLAIR

The Albanese Government commenced its first term on a wave of support for a more ambitious climate change agenda than that of the previous Morrison Government. Heeding the lessons from Labor's loss in 2019 when advocating expansive reforms, Albanese took to the 2022 election credible policy commitments that carefully avoided disenfranchising Australia's powerful fossil-fuel industry. The juggling act in maintaining this vexed position, seeking to address the electorate's desire for more decisive climate action while avoiding a backlash from politically influential fossil-fuel interests, characterised the government's first term on climate change and the energy transition.

The 2022 election

Labor announced a policy plan, Powering Australia, in December 2021 to create jobs, cut emissions, reduce power bills and boost renewable energy. This plan sought to differentiate itself from the Morrison Government's reluctance to progress climate change measures. The plan encompassed targets that were respectable on the global stage: to reduce national greenhouse gas emissions 43 per cent below 2005 levels by 2030, to reach net zero emissions by 2050, and for the share of renewable energy in on-grid generation in the National Electricity Market to reach 82 per cent by 2030. The 2030 emissions target was lower than the 45 per cent medium-term target Labor promised at the 2019 election, and weaker than the targets in the United Kingdom and United States at the time, but substantially up from the 26–28 per cent target in place. Labor also promised electric vehicle (EV) tax breaks to reduce vehicle prices marginally and exempt some EVs below the luxury car tax threshold of $79 659, again a modest proposal to avoid a repeat of the Coalition's successful 'end the weekend' scare campaign in 2019.

Climate change and the energy transition were pivotal for the 2022 election outcome, reflecting a surge of community support for action. Beyond Labor winning a slim majority, the Greens, with core climate and environmental protection policies, quadrupled their seats in the House of Representatives. Climate-committed independents, known as the 'teals', also displaced six sitting Liberal MPs. Albanese asserted 'together we can end the climate wars'.

International leaders welcomed the election outcome. At the May 2022 Quad summit in Tokyo, just a day after Albanese was sworn in as Prime Minister, Australia was praised for raising its ambition on climate change. The Joint Leaders' Statement 'welcomed the new Australian Government's commitment to stronger action on climate change, including through passing legislation to achieve net zero by 2050 and lodging a new, ambitious Nationally Determined Contribution'.

First year of government – an extended honeymoon

Albanese hit the ground running after his election triumph, with diplomatic meetings across the region that spruiked Australia's new climate change commitments, and domestic steps to commence the implementation of Powering Australia. His early governance style was consultative and unifying; at the National Press Club, Albanese criticised the previous government's approach to energy policy, saying that a 'culture of division, dysfunction, and conflict [not only] creates urgent problems in the short term, it stops [Australia] building for the long term'.

Institutional reforms progressed fast. Ministerial and departmental roles and structures were established that overcame divisions in climate change and energy policy and programs. Early attention was given to building the collaborative National Energy Transformation Partnership (NETP), agreed to by all states and territories in August 2022.

In September, the Australian Parliament passed the *Climate Change Act 2022*, which legislates Australia's 2030 and net zero by 2050 targets. It also enhances transparency in government action by requiring the minister to table an annual climate change statement, for the Climate Change Authority (CCA) to advise the minister annually on future emissions reduction targets, and for periodic reviews of the Act's operation. The government's confidence in legislating the 2030 target was based on projections that existing policies, implemented mainly by state governments, would reduce Australia's emissions by around 35 per cent relative to 2005 levels, bringing the 43 per cent target within feasible reach (Hare, 2021).

Funding for Powering Australia was secured through the October 2022 Budget. After a decade of minimal investment, measures included $20 billion in low-cost finance for upgrading and expanding Australia's electricity grid, $157.9 million to support the implementation of the NETP, and $224.3 million to deploy 400 community-scale batteries for up to 100 000 Australian households. EVs were supported with $500 million for national charging infrastructure, as well as $345 million for the EV tax discount.

To incentivise large industrial facilities to reduce their emissions, the government reformed the Safeguard Mechanism, which aims to keep emissions from facilities emitting more than 100 000 tonnes of carbon dioxide equivalent (CO_2-e) per annum below a baseline. The reforms, legislated in early 2023, set declining rates for baselines, initially of 4.9 per cent per year through to 2029–30, to ensure a proportionate contribution from large industrial emitters to achieving national targets.

Internationally, the government was keen to restore Australia's international reputation as an active and trusted leader on climate change. Australia joined the Global Methane Pledge at the UN's Climate Change Conference, COP 27, in 2022, bid to host the conference in 2026 (COP 31), and bolstered funding to strengthen climate change partnerships with neighbours.

Increasing headwinds, honeymoon over

By mid-2023, the honeymoon had ended. International events, primarily Russia's invasion of Ukraine, caused coal and gas prices to skyrocket, shifting the electorate's concerns to cost-of-living pressures that were amplified by increasing interest rates and housing costs. Satisfaction ratings for the government fell. Due to rising wholesale costs and global events, domestic energy prices increased significantly during 2022 and 2023. Government messaging that the energy transition was being driven at least cost, and that renewable energy is an economical energy source, was increasingly at odds with people's experience. The government was perceived as losing touch with community views. Recognising this, an energy price relief plan was agreed in December 2022, which, with some $1.5 billion allocated, imposed temporary caps on coal and gas, and provided rebates to Australians on low and middle incomes.

While the implementation of Powering Australia continued unabated, reports in 2023 showed that clean energy projects were not being rolled out fast enough for Australia to reach its 82 per cent renewable electricity target by 2030. The Clean Energy Council flagged in August 2023 that adequate investment is not flowing into renewable energy projects, and that a huge scale-up is needed of solar and wind farms, transmission lines and big batteries. Similarly, the CCA advised that accelerated and collaborative action was required for the rapid deployment of wind and solar generation, increased network infrastructure and energy storage, as well as an orderly exit from coal-fired generation.

Consequently, the government expanded the Capacity Investment Scheme in November 2023. Initially designed to underwrite 6 gigawatts of renewable dispatchable capacity, the scheme gives investors certainty over minimum revenue levels, aiming to deliver an additional 32 gigawatts of renewable energy capacity (including clean dispatchable power) by 2030. This represents $52 billion in new investment. Its ongoing success will depend on overcoming grid constraints to absorbing electricity generated by solar arrays and wind farms.

At the same time, progress in renewable projects was increasingly hampered by community resistance, particularly to new transmission infrastructure for connecting renewable generation to the grid. While the energy transition attracts broad public support, wind farms have started to generate local protests, especially in New South Wales and Victoria, with community pushback growing in response to the plan by the Australian Energy Market Operator (AEMO) to install 10 000 kilometres of above-ground transmission lines (Aziz and Ahmad, 2022). Findings from a Guardian Essential poll included high support for most renewable infrastructure, but a clear lack of social licence for aboveground transmission, supported by only 35 per cent of respondents. Critically, 70 per cent of respondents felt renewable energy should not be developed 'at the expense of local communities'. Community concerns about the impacts of transmission on endangered species, landscape amenity and values, biodiversity and agricultural practices were arguably ignored within NEM decision-making, which was rigidly based on minimising costs.

Eventually, the government grasped the complexity of, and community sensitivities to, the energy transition underway. Recognition grew that previously held assumptions (for example, that the transition involved a simple switch in sources in a linear pathway from generation to distribution) were naive. A crucial realisation was that consumer energy resources (CER) would be central to Australia achieving its targets; annual reports from the Clean Energy Council had clarified that the uptake of rooftop solar was making the largest contribution to Australia's energy transition. In August 2023, the Australian Energy Market Commission Chair argued that effectively integrating CER into the market is essential for a successful energy transformation.

A policy pivot and wider industry action

The recognition of CER's crucial role led to a (modest) policy pivot. Momentum was provided by a report in February 2024 from the then Energy Security Board, which identified the need to adapt existing regulatory frameworks to enable CER integration into the energy system. Framing a reform agenda to leverage CER's potential to the transition, the Energy Security Board called for urgent collaborative government action.

The National Consumer Energy Resources Roadmap, endorsed by national, state and territory energy ministers in July 2024, recognises that consumers in rooftop solar, household batteries and EVs are driving the rapid transformation of electricity systems. Nevertheless, the scale of action required to meet Australia's energy and emissions targets remains a massive challenge. As modelled by AEMO in 2024, the least-cost pathway requires four times more rooftop solar, 34 times more distributed battery capacity and 135 times more orchestrated battery capacity by 2050.

With Australian passenger vehicles emitting 50 per cent more carbon dioxide (CO_2) (along with other pollutants) than the average in the world's major markets (Smit, 2024), the long-awaited New Vehicle Efficiency Standard (NVES) was approved in May 2024. The standard sets increasingly stringent targets for CO_2 exhaust emissions for new light vehicles sold between July 2025 and December 2029. Seeking to avoid a repeat of the Coalition's scare campaign in 2019, the standard does not prevent a wide range of conventional utility vehicles ('utes') from remaining on the market. The NVES starts slowly, reducing emissions by just 2 per cent for model year 2025 vehicles, rising to 51 per cent for vehicles sold in 2029. However, there are risks associated with assuming rapid EV uptake, such as from insufficient supply, gaps in supporting infrastructure, and unreliability in the electricity grid in many remote regions.

Further developments were $22.7 billion for the Future Made in Australia initiative, announced in the 2024–25 Budget to maximise opportunities to deploy clean energy as we move towards net zero, and the creation of the Net Zero Economy Authority (NZEA) in December 2024. The NZEA will promote and co-ordinate an economically positive energy transformation with benefits shared across regions, industries, workers and communities. Challenges for the NZEA include building social licence and aligning well with state-based transition initiatives targeting areas affected by the closure of coal-fired power stations and coal mines. The NZEA is modelled on international precedents and has a broad remit, albeit one that appears to lack clarity on specific functions. It is too early to assess its impact.

With six years until 2030, and national greenhouse gas inventories showing emissions still rising in some sectors, the government commissioned the CCA to identify opportunities and barriers to decarbonisation pathways in six sectors. The review, finalised in April 2025, will inform next steps in inter-jurisdictional action. The government also amended the *Corporations Act 2001* to require large businesses and financial institutions to disclose their climate-related financial risks and opportunities, with reporting requirements coming into effect from 1 January 2025. These requirements align with the International Sustainability Standards Board, which is used globally by more than 1000 companies and 20 jurisdictions, including the European Union, China, the UK, Japan and Canada.

Policy juxtaposition – fossil fuel developments approved

While multiple initiatives to drive decarbonisation across Australia have progressed since the 2022 election, the politics of preferred ways to achieve targets remained highly contested. The 2024 Senate Committee report on *Energy Planning and Regulation in Australia* is illustrative, with Coalition members arguing strongly for nuclear power to have a central role in Australia's National Electricity Market, and politically divided support for recommendations.

The government's approval of seven coal mines or extensions (with operating lives beyond 2050) in late 2024 exposed deep tensions between climate ambition and mining and financial interests. Following the approval of three coal mines in September, the CCA warned that new fossil fuel projects would undermine the Safeguard Mechanism's promised emissions cap by 30 million tonnes. In December, another four coal mine extensions were approved across New South Wales and Queensland. Collectively, these mines are estimated to release two billion tonnes of CO_2 (predominantly scope 3 emissions) over their lifetime (not to mention clearing threatened species habitat and impacting cultural heritage sites). The public response to these approvals included multiple protests around Australia, with the climate action group Rising Tide drawing more than 7000 people to a blockade of the world's largest coal port, Newcastle, in November 2024.

Further, multiple studies suggest that Australia under-reports its coal mine methane emissions (Sadavarte et al., 2021). Of concern are findings that some companies dramatically reduce emissions reported when switching from a state-based to a company-led emissions measurement approach (Wright, 2024).

The Albanese Government's Future Gas Strategy (FGS), released in May 2024, indicates that gas will remain a central part of Australia's energy and export sectors to 2050 and beyond. Guiding principles in the FGS include that gas production 'must be abated or offset' in contributing to Australia's net zero target, that new gas fields must be found and opened 'to meet demand during the economy-wide transition', and that Liquid Natural Gas will remain a key export market for Australia. The FGS is an extension of the Morrison Government's 'gas-led recovery', and there is a substantial risk that increased emissions will result.

Addressing climate impacts and adaptation – tentative steps

Despite the social vulnerability of many Australians to climate change, it is unclear whether the Albanese Government's adaptation agenda was more ambitious than that of the Morrison Government. Australia's extensive flooding in New South Wales and Queensland in early 2022, resulting in $7.7 billion of loss and damage in Queensland alone, was followed by further extreme events (heat, bushfires, floods and droughts) throughout 2023 and 2024. Responses followed a well-trodden path, with resources predominantly allocated to recovery, and minimal attention to preventative adaptation measures (which entail recognition of trends in the impacts of climate change), regardless of the latter's potential high return on investment.

Nevertheless, the government initiated the National Climate Risk Assessment (NCRA). Charged with identifying exposure and vulnerabilities to climate change over the next century, the NCRA conducted a 'first pass' climate risk assessment in 2024 that identified 56 nationally significant climate risks facing Australia. It also identified a subset of 11 priority risks for analysis in a subsequent 'second pass' risk assessment (which was not released during the Albanese Government's first term).

Work also progressed on developing a National Adaptation Plan, with an issues paper for consultation released in 2024. While a welcome step, the issues paper did not outline a clear vision or direction for adaptation in

Australia, nor did it robustly frame where adaptation is urgent and can deliver significant net benefits. Rather, it presented an overview of existing measures without assessing their actual adaptation outcomes and known gaps. The plan remained a work-in-progress by the end of the government's first term.

Taking stock of progress by early 2025

At the end of the first quarter of 2025, the jury remained out on the effectiveness of Australia's energy transition and climate change policy. While constructive governance reforms have been implemented, much remains to be done to ensure that targets can be met, and the impact of recent initiatives remains unknown. At this point, renewables accounted for 38.9 per cent of the national electricity market, reflecting growth but only marginally higher than in 2023, and a long way from the 82 per cent that needs to be reached by 2030.

In late February 2025, the government released the quarterly update to Australia's greenhouse gas emissions inventory. In the two and a half years since the 2022 election, Australia's emissions have decreased by 3.1 million tonnes, equivalent to a 0.7 per cent reduction in total emissions. Emissions must now fall by 15 million tonnes of CO_2-e per annum on average to reach Australia's 2030 target, a dramatic increase on the 2023–24 reduction achieved.

In claiming to be on track to meet Australia's targets, the government is relying strongly on the projected impacts of future policy measures. For example, the Capacity Investment Scheme, combined with renewable energy targets and other policies, is projected to more than halve electricity sector emissions between 2024 and 2030 – this represents a 39 per cent reduction in electricity emissions in 2025 alone. Similarly, the renewable hydrogen industry, currently in its infancy, is anticipated to produce at least 15 million tonnes of renewable hydrogen per year by 2050 and drive a reduction of between 93 and 186 million tonnes of CO_2 per year by 2050. This is an ambitious target underpinned by, arguably, heroic assumptions from a largely untested technology.

Offsets are also critical to achieving climate targets and are supported by the Safeguard Mechanism and the FGS. Within weeks of the 2022 election, the government commenced an independent review of Australia's Carbon Credit Units (ACCUs), led by former chief scientist Professor Ian Chubb, to respond to emerging concerns and ensure the ACCUs maintain high integrity. Researchers have recently published work claiming that of 143 projects registered under the government's Human Induced Regeneration offset program, the vast majority have seen minimal increases in carbon storage (Macintosh et al., 2024). Further, several big Australian companies have walked away from the government's carbon offset scheme Climate Active (Mazengarb, 2025).

CCA pathway modelling suggests that land-based removals, which deliver ACCUs, will likely play a significant role in Australia's pathway to net zero emissions by 2050. However, estimates of the potential contribution differ widely. CSIRO modelling and government projections indicate that the land sink is expected to increase modestly to 2040, then more than double by 2050, reaching approximately 129 million tonnes of CO_2-e by 2050. This increase would require approximately three million hectares of land converted to forest. The CCA's analysis estimates a much smaller sink of between 32 and 39 million tonnes of CO_2-e, based on lower assumptions of the land area planted.

The good, the (not so) bad and the ugly

The government's first term on climate action and the energy transition reveals a complex story of genuine progress: the good, shadowed by tenuous steps; the (not so) bad; and in glaring contradiction, the ugly. The 'good' is real progress after a decade of climate policy stagnation. The government legislated emissions targets, established the NETP to co-ordinate across jurisdictions, reformed the Safeguard Mechanism with declining baselines, improved reporting, and introduced the NVES in a policy area long neglected. Crucially, policy developments recognised that CER (rooftop solar, household batteries and EVs) drives Australia's energy transformation faster than large-scale infrastructure.

The '(not so) bad' is underdone policy initiatives in the face of deep challenges ahead. Adaptation planning has been largely neglected despite escalating climate impacts, with the promised national adaptation plan still unreleased by the end of the first term. Doubts also exist about the robustness of company self-reporting on emissions, and of the integrity and sustainability of carbon offsets claimed under the ACCUs program. Further, genuine community engagement in energy transition infrastructure has been inadequate. The 'ugly' is contradictory policy decisions undermining climate progress and Australia's energy transition. The approval of multiple coal mines or extensions sits uncomfortably alongside public commitments to net zero by 2050. The FGS that commits Australia to expanding Liquid Natural Gas exports also exemplifies the government having a 'bet each way' on climate action and protecting fossil fuel interests.

In closing, it is important to acknowledge that when the government took office in 2022, it inherited a decade of climate policy inaction, toxic debates, and political polarisation, depleted public service capabilities, institutions poorly equipped to manage the energy transition, and community disillusionment due to a lack of climate action. There has been substantial progress from this position, albeit more of a shift in momentum and direction rather than significant emissions reductions.

Finally, the May 2025 election delivered an overwhelming victory for a second-term Albanese Government. This provides an opportunity to move beyond the promising, but ultimately patchy and sometimes contradictory, juggling act approach that characterised its first term. With many institutional and policy foundations for climate action and the energy transformation having emerged (with varying degrees of implementation), the challenge will be to translate these into tangible and lasting progress on the ground, ideally without further concessions to the fossil fuel industry.

References

Aziz, A, and Ahmed, I, 'A clean energy grid means 10 000km of new transmission lines. They can only be built with community backing', *The Conversation*, 17 August 2022.

Hare, B, 'Yes, Australia can beat its 2030 emissions target. But the Morrison Government barely lifted a finger', *The Conversation*, 16 October 2021.

Macintosh, A, et al., 'Australian human-induced native forest regeneration carbon offset projects have limited impact on changes in woody vegetation cover and carbon removals', *Communications Earth & Environment*, vol. 5, no. 149, 2024.

Mazengarb, M, 'Is Australia's "carbon neutral" scheme being abandoned?', *Tempests and Terawatts*, Substack, 29 March 2025.

Sadavarte, P, et al., 'Methane emissions from superemitting coal mines in Australia quantified using TROPOMI satellite observations', *Environmental Science and Technology*, vol. 55, no. 24, 2021.

Smit, R, 'At last, Australia has fuel efficiency standards – but they're weaker than they could have been', *The Conversation*, 21 May 2024.

Wright, C, 'How an accounting shift could conceal millions of tonnes of coal mine emissions: A proposal for open-cut coal mines to self-report their emissions, without external review, transparency, verification could further undermine reporting standards and reward coal miners in the process', *Ember*, 21 June 2024, <https://ember-energy.org>.

CHAPTER 21

DELAYED AMBITIONS: ENVIRONMENT POLICY

EVAN HAMMAN AND JACKI SCHIRMER

The first Albanese Government had ambitious goals for environmental policy. Election commitments made in the 2022 campaign included reform of the *Environment Protection and Biodiversity Conservation Act 1999* (EPBC Act), 'rescuing' the Murray-Darling Basin Plan, re-establishing a National Water Commission, introducing mandatory sustainability reporting for corporations, action on waste and ocean policy, and increasing funding for conservation action such as protected areas and rangers.

Many of these ambitions were not fully realised, as the government became trapped between the demands of an environmental advocacy sector seeking meaningful and large-scale reform, and the concern of key business sectors who argued reform would place insurmountable barriers to business in a period of already slow economic growth.

These tensions came to a head near the end of the government's first term in the form of an amendment to the EPBC Act, introduced and passed in a small number of days by an alliance of Labor and Coalition votes. The amendment enabled controversial salmon farming in Tasmania's west coast to continue, despite a prior commitment by then Environment Minister Tanya Plibersek to review the 2012 determination allowing salmon farming in Macquarie Harbour. The review commitment was made in response to growing evidence that salmon farming could potentially negatively affect the endangered Maugean skate, a species endemic to the Macquarie and Bathurst harbours. The amendment effectively removed the minister's right to review previous decisions if they had been ongoing for at least five years and had approvals involving state-based regulation. It symbolised the government's prioritisation of economic interest over environmental outcome, and an inability to find pathways to achieve both: the decision reduced the ability to use new scientific evidence to support environmental health, while arguably providing greater certainty to businesses to make long-term investments based on determinations made under the Act.

Stuck between environmental activism and a flailing economy

The Albanese Government's ongoing inability to implement reform of the EPBC Act, culminating in the amendment that ultimately reduced its powers, is emblematic of its overall difficulty in translating its environmental ambitions into meaningful on-ground outcomes. Reform of the 1999 Act was long overdue by 2022. A Senate Committee Inquiry spanning three successive parliaments as well as two comprehensive statutory review processes, first in 2010 (led by Dr Allan Hawke) and then 2020 (led by Professor Graeme Samuel) failed to crystallise meaningful change. Indeed, the Act has been amended only a handful of times over its two-and-half decade history, and only for minor matters. The weaknesses in the legislation in 2022 were thus largely the same as in 1999: limited compliance and enforcement powers that were rarely used; slow and complex assessment and approval processes; a narrow focus that did not enable action on many environmental problems, particularly actions involving cumulative impacts; and 'tokenistic' engagement with Indigenous communities (Samuel, 2020).

In December 2022, Environment Minister Tanya Plibersek released the Albanese Government's much-anticipated overhaul of the legislation. Its Nature Positive plan – to be delivered in tranches – came with the tagline 'better for the environment, better for business' (DCCEEW, 2022). The government accepted the majority of Professor Samuel's (2020) findings and outlined its commitment to making the 'long overdue changes to our environmental laws' (DCCEEW, 2022, p. iii). The first tranche of Nature Positive, legislating a national market for nature repair and expanding EPBC Act requirements to enable greater consideration of impacts on water resources of coal seam gas and large coal mining developments, passed in late 2023.

By the end of 2024, however, the second stage of the reforms – intended to establish a new Environmental Protection Agency (EPA) as a 'tough cop on the beat' (DCCEEW 2024) and create 'legally enforceable' National Environmental Standards (a centrepiece of Samuel's recommendations) – had stalled in Parliament. The Greens refused to support the reforms on the basis they continued exemptions for forestry and failed to adequately address climate impacts (Hanson-Young, 2024). Independent senators David Pocock and Lidia Thorpe also opposed the reforms, with Pocock arguing the proposed EPA lacked integrity, and Thorpe pointing out that the laws failed to adhere to the United Nations Declaration on the Rights of Indigenous Peoples, including the principles of self-determination and Free, Prior and Informed Consent (Pocock, 2024; and Thorpe, 2024). Senator Thorpe's stance made direct reference to the ongoing Juukan Gorge controversy, where Rio Tinto had destroyed Indigenous cultural heritage, laying bare systemic problems with the federal *Aboriginal and Torres Strait Islander Heritage Protection Act 1984* (also administered by the Environment Minister). Despite First Nations peoples specifically asking to be at the forefront of the Nature Positive reforms (First Nations, 2024), Senator Thorpe argued environmental reform should not be passed until amended 'in a way that will genuinely improve the health of Country' (Thorpe, 2024).

In early 2025, the second stage of legislation was officially shelved, an apparent result of 'fierce resistance from West Australian Premier Roger Cook and sections of the mining industry' (Speers and Truu, 2025). The result left many environmental advocates dismayed. The government's last-minute amendment to protect salmon farming in Tasmania's Macquarie Harbour, passed through an alliance of Labor and the Coalition, shattered belief in the government's claimed commitment to environmental reform. The Greens labelled the amendment rushed; The Australia Institute proclaimed it was a 'dark day for the environment' (The Australia Institute, 2025).

The shelving of the Nature Positive reforms, more broadly, put Australia behind much of the world when it came to international commitments. The agreed targets under the Kunming-Montreal Global Biodiversity Framework require Australia to, amongst other things, prevent further species extinctions and restore 30 per cent of currently degraded ecosystems. In fairness to the Albanese Government, prior to taking office, it had inherited a seemingly insurmountable task with regards to these and other international environmental obligations. Climate change had been wreaking

236 | Policy issues

havoc on the Great Barrier Reef with coral-bleaching events increasing in both frequency and severity, and terrestrial Australia was leading the world in mammal species decline (Ritchie, 2022). Previous governments had failed to address ongoing large-scale land clearing, with the cumulative effects of multiple individual instances of clearing unable to be effectively addressed under the existing provisions of the EPBC Act.

Murray-Darling Basin Plan and water reform: Extending time to 'rescue' the Plan

The Murray-Darling Basin Plan is both lauded as world-leading environment policy tackling the complex challenge of reversing decades of over-allocating water for agriculture, and criticised for implementing a complex and sometimes opaque series of actions to achieve its goals of returning water to the environment. In 2022, the Albanese Government inherited the Basin Plan's existing – and by that point effectively impossible – commitment to return 2750 gigalitres (GL) of water to environmental use by June 2024. Previous governments had fallen well short of this target, stalling at just over 2100 GL with little progress for several years. The stalling resulted from factors including limits on the mechanisms that could be used to return water from predominantly agricultural use to environmental use, in particular a cap on purchasing water directly from irrigators ('buybacks') to return to the environment amid concerns from Basin communities about the social and economic impacts of taking water away from local agriculture.

The Albanese Government took a pragmatic approach to addressing its impending failure to meet the 2024 deadline. Publicly acknowledging that the target was not achievable, the *Water Amendment (Restoring Our Rivers) Act 2023* extended the deadline to December 2027, repealed the cap on buybacks, and increased options that could be used to deliver water recovery. The Restoring Our Rivers legislation thus committed to supporting the original intent of the Basin Plan, albeit on the new extended timeframe. By 2025, the Environment Minister announced a rapid increase in water recovered for the environment, far more than under the previous government.

In this area of environment policy, the Albanese Government

demonstrated willingness to challenge those who opposed the changes. The Environment Minister rejected claims by rural communities in the Basin that water buybacks were a major contributor to social and economic decline, while also providing funding to support communities affected by buybacks to invest in other activities.

The legislation also allocated $100 million to support First Nations participation in water markets. While a significant increase from the $40 million announced in 2018 by the then Coalition Government, the $100 million included that as-yet unspent $40 million, meaning much of this funding represented existing commitments. Long-term lack of support for implementation has continued to erode the value of the allocation, with limited progress on translating funding announcements into reality.

While many saw this reform as a policy win, involving sometimes challenging negotiations with the states and territories who are joint signatories to the Basin Plan, it was a necessity: all parties were motivated to come to the table to avoid triggering a statutory deadline which, if not met, would have triggered a halt to direct water recovery. The mechanisms put in place to 'rescue' the Basin Plan did not involve significant new action, but rather a willingness to support actions that had proven successful in the past, namely water buyback.

To support the health of the Murray-Darling Basin, there is a pressing need to invest in enabling environmental water flows to reach the places they are most needed – something which requires overcoming water flow 'constraints' in the form of limits to the volume of water that can flow down key channels without flooding private land and affecting key infrastructure. There is also a need to build climate change adaptation into the Basin Plan: the Basin is experiencing higher temperatures, more extremes of rainfall and streamflow, and more extreme weather events due to climate change. The Basin Plan review, due in 2026, will be the true test of whether the second Albanese Government can identify and implement the changes needed to enable the Basin Plan to deliver on its promise of improved environmental health. This will require amending the Plan to identify explicitly how to achieve its environment goals in a changing climate, and to enable ongoing meaningful involvement of First Nations peoples in water management, all while seeking to ensure high levels of agricultural production continue in a region that is home to 40 per cent of Australian farms, including the lion's share of Australia's irrigated agriculture.

The Albanese Government also promised to establish a National Water Commission (NWC) which would, amongst other things, focus on renewing the 2004 National Water Initiative (NWI), the framework and principles agreed to by all states and territories that guide water trade, management and planning, and seeks to ensure sustainable water allocation. However, the promised NWC was not established, and was conspicuously absent from consultation documents used to inform three rounds of consultation that worked towards a new draft National Water Agreement (NWA). In mid-2024, the Productivity Commission released the findings of its National Water Inquiry, recommending renewing the National Water Initiative with a stronger focus on planning for water security in a changing climate and involving First Nations peoples as active participants in water management, while retaining the foundations of the NWI. The Productivity Commission and many other groups criticised principles the Albanese Government released in 2024 as part of developing the draft NWA, arguing they failed to take on board the recommendations of multiple water inquiries. With a draft NWA released in December 2024, the task of achieving agreement on it was left for the second Albanese Government.

A new nature repair market

The passage of the *Nature Repair Act 2023* established a (voluntary) biodiversity market overseen by the Clean Energy Regulator. The legislation was passed via agreement with the Greens, though it did not receive unanimous support among other crossbenchers. The Nature Repair framework works in a similar way to the existing Australian Carbon Credit Unit (ACCU) scheme, insofar as it requires methods to be approved that outline the rules of eligible projects. Methods must be approved through formal determination by the Environment Minister. In February 2025, immediately prior to the election, Minister Plibersek approved the first methodology, which allows credits to be issued based on revegetation of native forest and woodland ecosystems.

Approved projects that restore or maintain nature will receive biodiversity certificates that can be sold to corporations trying to meet their environmental goals. Initially, the Act had included an option for integrating offsets, but the Greens negotiated for their removal, meaning private developers would not be able to legally rely on a Nature Repair project to counterbalance their environmental impacts elsewhere. Critics of the scheme have argued that 'a lowest-cost approach to generating credits is unlikely to benefit biodiversity' and that it will drive projects 'to marginal areas that do not overlap the ranges of species threatened by habitat loss' (van Oosterzee and Engert, 2024). It is also possible that new methodologies will face similar concerns to those of the ACCU scheme, which critics argue has not meaningfully increased carbon sequestration (Morton, 2022), raising questions about who the repair market truly helps – the environment, or those who benefit financially from the market.

ESG, sustainability reporting and greenwashing

The trend of Environmental Social and Governance (ESG) sweeping the corporate world well and truly made its way to Australia during the first Albanese Government. Spearheaded in Europe and long practised on a voluntary basis by major corporations under frameworks such as the Global Reporting Initiative (GRI) and Carbon Disclosure Project (CDP), ESG is seen by critics as 'woke capitalism' (Levintova, 2024), while supporters view it as increasing corporate transparency, responsibility and action.

In 2024, the Albanese Government made Australia one of the first countries in the world to incorporate mandatory climate reporting. The amending legislation required Australian companies (over a certain threshold) to begin by disclosing their greenhouse gas emissions and assessing the impacts of future climate scenarios on their business. The goal is to improve transparency, consistency and capacity to manage financial risks resulting from climate change. While focused on climate in its first instance, the ambition is to expand to subsequently include mandatory sustainability reporting in other areas such as biodiversity, soil and water, consistent with Australia's position as a funding partner of the Taskforce on Nature-related Financial Disclosures (TNFD) (Treasury, 2022).

The government's embrace of the new reporting requirements (which will sit alongside the company's annual financial reports under the *Corporations Act 2001*) is in line with the position agreed to by the Group of Seven economies in 2021 (Reuters, 2021). In Australia, the new rules are supported by an Australian Sustainability Reporting Standard (AASB S2) created in line with the recommendations from the global Taskforce on Climate-related Financial Disclosures (TCFD).

Quite aside from mandatory reporting, the push from shareholders and customers has led many businesses to make sustainability claims that may in fact be spurious or open to debate. In 2020, the Australian Securities and Investment Commission (ASIC) and the Australian Competition and Consumer Commission (ACCC) announced they would be prioritising the monitoring of 'greenwashing' and enforcing regulations to prevent it. ASIC stated that combating greenwashing was 'critical to maintaining trust in sustainable finance-related products and services' (ASIC, 2024), while the ACCC released guidance noting they consider a business to be greenwashing 'where they use any claim that makes a product or service seem better or less harmful for the environment than it really is' (ACCC, n.d.).

Following increased resourcing from the Albanese Government, ASIC brought three cases to the Federal Court against superannuation companies accused of misleading investors about their ESG credentials. In each of the three cases (Vanguard, Mercer and Active Super) ASIC was successful in establishing false and misleading conduct in relation to financial products or services. Each case resulted in a penalty in excess of $10 million and likely substantial reputational concerns for the trustees and their directors. Immediately following the 2025 election, Energy Australia was also forced to apologise over greenwashing related to its carbon offsetting claims (albeit on the basis of a private suit, not at the hands of ACCC) (Morton, 2025).

With the introduction of mandatory climate reporting and increased fervour from business surrounding ESG, greenwashing and pseudo-sustainability claims are likely to stay on the government's agenda well into its next term.

Business as usual for other environment policy

The Albanese Government continued 'business as usual' for many other aspects of environment policy, with action focusing on minor adjustments and one-off funding announcements rather than significant reform. While some funding was committed to expanding Australia's conservation reserves, there was little attention to meaningfully addressing decades of under-resourcing for managing and maintaining these areas, or for broader natural resource management through Australia's network of natural resource management organisations (including Landcare and others). No meaningful refresh of policy was undertaken in areas including forestry and fisheries management. Consultation processes were conducted for several areas, including to inform development of the Sustainable Ocean Plan (which reached consultation on a draft by the second half of 2024) and to progress to a new National Water Agreement, but did not progress to action by the end of the government's term.

Where to from here?

In its first term, the Albanese Government was successful in environmental policy primarily where implementing change offered either a potential benefit or limited downsides for the business sector, and stakeholder interests were relatively aligned – for example, potential new markets in nature repair, improved corporate reputation with mandatory sustainability reporting, or increasing public trust in claims by businesses about sustainability by clamping down on greenwashing. However, the government was less successful in navigating areas where the interests of environmental advocates and key business-sector interests diverged. Additionally, a desire to progress reform in multiple areas led to considerable activity, but difficulty delivering change by the end of the government's first term.

Time will tell whether the work done by the first Albanese Government will enable it in its second term to pull off what successive governments have been unable to do for the best part of three decades – national environmental law reform. In the meantime, the fate of Australia's threatened species and iconic natural assets hangs precariously in the balance.

References

Australian Competition and Consumer Commission, 'Environmental and sustainability claims', nd, <https://www.accc.gov.au/business/advertising-and-promotions/environmental-and-sustainability-claims>.

Australian Securities and Investments Commission, 'ASIC continues action on misleading claims to deter greenwashing misconduct', media release, 23 August 2024, <https://asic.gov.au/about-asic/news-centre/find-a-media-release/2024-releases/24-185mr-asic-continues-action-on-misleading-claims-to-deter-greenwashing-misconduct/>.

Department of Climate Change, Energy, the Environment and Water (DCCEEW), 'Nature Positive Plan: Better for the environment, better for business', Canberra, December 2022, <https://www.dcceew.gov.au/sites/default/files/documents/nature-positive-plan.pdf>.

— 'Environment Protection Australia legislation introduced to Parliament', Canberra, 29 May 2024, <https://minister.dcceew.gov.au/plibersek/media-releases/environment-protection-australia-legislation-introduced-parliament>.

First Nations Statement, Global Nature Positive Summit 2024, <https://assets.wwf.org.au/image/upload/2410_Nature_FirstNationsNaturePositiveSummit_2?_a=ATO2Bcc0>.

Hanson-Young, S, 'Australian Greens' Dissenting Report, Nature Positive (Environment Protection Australia) Bill 2024', 2024, <https://www.aph.gov.au/Parliamentary_Business/Committees/Senate/Environment_and_Communications/NaturePositivebills/Report/Australian_Greens_Dissenting_Report>.

Levintova, H, 'How "woke capitalism" became a right-wing obsession', *Mother Jones*, Jan–Feb 2024, <https://www.motherjones.com/politics/2024/01/woke-capital-vivek-ramaswamy-esg-capitalism-finance/>.

Morton, A, 'Australia's carbon credit scheme "largely a sham", says whistleblower who tried to rein it in', *Guardian*, 23 March 2022.

— 'Energy Australia apologises to 400 000 customers and settles greenwashing legal action', *Guardian*, 19 May 2025.

Pocock, D, 'Senator David Pocock's Dissenting Report, Nature Positive (Environment Protection Australia) Bill 2024', 2024, <https://www.aph.gov.au/Parliamentary_Business/Committees/Senate/Environment_and_Communications/NaturePositivebills/Report/Senator_David_Pococks_Dissenting_Report>.

Reuters, 'G7 backs making climate risk disclosure mandatory', 5 June 2021, <https://www.reuters.com/business/environment/g7-backs-making-climate-risk-disclosure-mandatory-2021-06-05/>.

Ritchie, E, 'Gut-wrenching and infuriating: Why Australia is the world leader in mammal extinctions, and what to do about it', *The Conversation*, 19 October 2022.

Samuel, G, 'Independent Review of the EPBC Act – Final Report', Department of Agriculture, Water and the Environment, Canberra, October 2020, <https://www.dcceew.gov.au/sites/default/files/documents/epbc-act-review-final-report-october-2020.pdf>.

Speers, D, and Truu, M, 'Labor shelves contentious "nature positive" laws after West Australian backlash', *ABC News*, 2 February 2025.

The Australia Institute, 'A dark day for the environment – and democracy', 27 March 2025, <https://australiainstitute.org.au/post/a-dark-day-for-the-environment-and-democracy/>.

Thorpe, L, 'Senator Lidia Thorpe's Dissenting Report, Nature Positive (Environment Protection Australia) Bill 2024', 2024, <https://www.aph.gov.au/Parliamentary_Business/Committees/Senate/Environment_and_Communications/NaturePositivebills/Report/Senator_Lidia_Thorpes_Dissenting_Report>.

Treasury, 'Climate-related financial disclosure consultation paper', December 2022, <https://treasury.gov.au/sites/default/files/2022-12/c2022-314397_0.pdf>.

Van Oosterzee, P, and Engert, J, 'As Australia privatises nature repair, the cheapest approach won't save our threatened species', *The Conversation*, 18 November 2024.

CHAPTER 22

THE ALBANESE GOVERNMENT'S RELATIONSHIP WITH BUSINESS

STEPHEN BARTOS

The Albanese Government has had a close relationship with business lobby groups and many large Australian companies. This chapter draws out lessons from business relationships, drawing on examples from previous chapters, and concludes that they have been both pervasive and decisive in policymaking.

While in many instances business lobbying or influence has been decisive, it is not simply a question of exercise of power. Financial or political gain has rarely been the sole motivation. It is a more complex relationship. It does not fit the traditional definition of corporatism, where peak coalitions of interest groups including business and unions work hand-in-hand with government; it is based more on connections between individual ministers and specific companies. It is not pervasive enough to warrant the label 'state capture', although some critics have used that term. 'Crony capitalism' as used by US economist Paul H Rubin (2015) to describe similar patterns of government–business relations in the US comes close, although in Australia the term is more often used pejoratively rather than descriptively.

The Albanese Government, unlike previous Coalition governments, has essentially taken a neutral stance, neither pro- nor anti-, towards business as a whole. Instead, it has favoured specific companies or industries based on relationships and politics. The drivers have been circumstances and relationships, not ideology. It is situational rather than general. The influence of peak business peak lobby groups has declined, overtaken by issues-based relationships and individual players.

Business lobby groups, 2022–2025

The Albanese Government's relationship with business peak bodies in its first term was characterised by occasional disagreements but on the whole constructive dialogue and agreement. There are naturally exceptions, given the diversity and range of business lobby groups. Lobby groups representing multiple industries include the Business Council of Australia (BCA), the Australian Industry Group, the Australian Chamber of Commerce and Industry (ACCI), and the Council of Small Business Organisations Australia. Many other business lobby groups represent specific industries. Some of the most powerful include the Australian Food and Grocery Council, the Pharmacy Guild of Australia, the Australian Banking Association and the Minerals Council of Australia.

Collectively these business lobby groups have exercised political influence over governments for many decades in fields ranging from the environment to aged care, manufacturing, tax and health.

There is however evidence that business lobby group influence has been waning. An Australia Institute research report (Browne, 2024) examined 20 of Australia's largest and most influential trade associations. It documented substantial policy wins for business lobbies in the Howard, Rudd and Turnbull governments. It cited only one example for the Albanese Government, minor compared with previous business lobby victories: a decision not to proceed with proposed financial services bills that would have imposed fines on finance executives who failed to act against systemic misconduct.

The Australia Institute report concluded 'in recent years, trade associations and lobby groups have struggled to influence policy', citing the BCA's failure to secure a company tax cut (under both the current and previous government); the Minerals Council, ACCI and other business lobbies' campaigns against the Albanese Government's introduction of multi-employer bargaining, where 'the government proceeded regardless'; and the gas industry warning against the Albanese Government intervening in gas prices, where 'the intervention went ahead'.

The political climate has changed; negative campaigns no longer work as they did for the mining industry in scuppering the Rudd Government's proposed resource rent tax in 2010. A case study is the '60-day prescription' campaign. In 2023 the Pharmacy Guild mounted a vigorous campaign of advertising and automated phone calls against the government's proposed changes to prescription rules to allow patients to buy two months' supply of medications, making them cheaper. Despite the campaign the government went ahead. The guild dropped the campaign after the Albanese Government agreed to bring forward negotiations over the community pharmacy agreement (Pharmacy Guild of Australia, 2023) – a small concession. It indicates that negative business campaigns have lost their power against government policy proposals.

Political donations

Businesses make donations to the Australian Labor Party to obtain influence and leverage with Labor governments. Donations are not based on a crude quid pro quo of donation exchanged for a policy decision – that would be corrupt. Their purpose is essentially access – large donors are likely to be able to meet with and lobby ministers and exercise indirect influence on policy. This applies to all parties in government, no less so with the Albanese Government.

It is impossible to estimate precisely the extent of business donations to the ALP over the past term of government or previous terms of any government. The disclosure regime is opaque. The independent Centre for Public Integrity (CPI) notes 'over the past 25 years, Australia's major political parties have received billions in income – but where much of it comes from remains a mystery' (CPI, 2024). The *Commonwealth Electoral Act 1918*, which governs the conduct of elections in Australia, includes a requirement that donations to political parties must be declared to the Australian Electoral Commission (AEC), which publishes an annual report. Nevertheless, loopholes in the disclosure regime make it far from comprehensive.

The material that is published does however allow a partial analysis of patterns of business donations. The CPI maintains an online political donor database at <https://publicintegrity.org.au/political-donor-directory/> that helpfully summarises large donations based on AEC data. The table below shows the ten largest business donors in each year of the Albanese

Table 22.1: Top ten business donors to the ALP by year, 2021–2024

	2021–22	*2022–23 (i)*	*2023–24*
Donor (ii)	**$'000**	**$'000**	**$'000**
Pratt Holdings Pty Ltd (packaging, recycling and logistics)	1974 and 147	1042	1000
SA Progressive Business Inc. (multi-business)	262		164
Pickard Capital Pty. Ltd (real estate)	223		
Australian Hotels Association	202	115	183
Precision Group (real estate, property)	167		
Pharmacy Guild of Australia	161	143	121
Maurice Blackburn and Co. (law firm)	139		
Australian Stock Exchange Ltd.	134	125	
National Automotive Leasing & Salary Packaging Association	134	125	120
PricewaterhouseCoopers (accounting and advisory)	129	143	
Perth Labor Business Roundtable (a multi-business group in WA)		151	600
Motor Traders Association of Australia		133	
Camufarre Investments Pty. Ltd.		126	
Sportsbet (gambling)		115	
Wesfarmers (agriculture and retail)		115	
Holding Redlich (law firm)			550
Navitas Limited (education)			110
Spirits and Cocktails Australia			99
Honeywell (manufacturing)			94

(i)   There are 11 entities listed in 2022–23 due to three clustered at the low end.

(ii) Note this is not a comprehensive list of donations. It lists large donors (the cutoff at top ten is arbitrary) to indicate their scale and diversity.

Government. The table includes 2021–22 as the first year, although the Albanese Government was elected in May 2022, both because donations increase before federal elections and because donations are often made towards the end of a financial year.

The table has been constructed based on data published by the CPI including only donations to the ALP, and excluding donations made by unions or ALP-associated entities. A notable aspect of the list is that Australia's biggest companies, the large mining companies and banks, do not feature. Their influence with government, and access to ministers, is taken as a given. They see little need to reinforce it with donations. Not all industry associations feature, but some of the largest donors, including the Pharmacy Guild, National Automotive Leasing & Salary Packaging Association, and the Australian Hotels Association, are on the list of top ten donors. These donations ensure that the industry associations concerned can obtain a hearing on concerns affecting their wide and dispersed membership base, who individually would rarely have access to decision-making by governments.

Information on donations is likely to improve considerably in both coverage and detail from July 2026, following parliament's passage of the *Electoral Reform Act* in February 2025. Among other things, the reforms lower the disclosure threshold from the current $17 300 to $5000, cap total donations and require monthly disclosure. They improve transparency, although some critics consider the reforms to favour major parties, and still allow loopholes.

A recent study involving a cross-sectional sample of 135 large firms (Bell, Hindmarsh and Umashev, 2023) found 'only about one third of firms made a political donation or hired an external lobbyist. Our interviews also suggest a downward trend for political donations'. Instead, the study found, companies are investing more in government relations – building relationships and networks of influence. That is the approach taken by mining, banking and financial businesses that choose not to make donations.

Government and business relationships

While the influence of peak lobby groups may be declining, specific industries and businesses have been highly influential in government policymaking. Examples are provided in previous chapters.

On industrial relations there have been some divergences between business and the Albanese Government; for example, on multi-employer bargaining. On the fundamental issue of minimum wages, however, differences between the government and business lobbies have become minimal, to the extent that most business lobbies adopted an identical position to the government on the 2025 case.

The pattern in relation to Australia's largest private sector industries (by revenue, excluding education and health) – mining, banking and finance, retail and construction – is that the Albanese Government has tended to maintain the status quo, albeit with occasional tinkering at the edges. Mining, retail and banking are dominated by a few large players and the government appears reluctant to reduce their market power or influence their positions by taxation or regulation.

Australia's mining companies are among the largest and most profitable in the world. Their business model is based on obtaining rights from government to extract minerals. The review of Australian taxation led by then Treasury Secretary Ken Henry recommended, among many other reforms, the introduction of a resource rent tax (Treasury, 2010). In response, the Rudd Government attempted to pass a resource super profits tax, attracting a negative advertising campaign funded by the mining industry that resulted not only in the tax failing but Prime Minister Rudd losing office. A milder version of the tax instituted by his successor, Julia Gillard, was later abolished by the Coalition Government. Scarred by the experience, the Albanese Government has made no attempt to revive a mining resource rent tax. In 2024 the government did amend the petroleum resource rent tax; the change was minor, increasing tax revenue by less than $1 billion per annum over the forward estimates.

The Albanese Government has examined supermarkets through two inquiries, one by Dr Craig Emerson and one by the Australian Consumer and Competition Commission. The government has accepted recommendations of both inquiries but will make only a marginal difference to improving competition in the sector. Despite considerable public concern, over the first term the major supermarkets successfully headed off reforms that might have cut into their profits. Diversity in the sector is limited: two large supermarket chains, Coles and Woolworths, maintain what many observers consider a duopoly. The ACCC inquiry found Australian supermarkets are amongst the most profitable in the world but had insufficient evidence to conclude this arose from exercise of monopoly power. An indicator that existing regulatory settings are inadequate was provided by the 2025 election campaign where both major parties made promises to improve competition: the Coalition by forcibly breaking up the major supermarkets, and Labor with a promise to make supermarket price gouging illegal. A taskforce will implement the latter; it will be hampered by the lack of a commonly accepted definition of price gouging.

The Albanese Government's investments in skills formation, including making technical and further education fee-free, are very much an industry-driven set of policies. One of the reasons industrial relations is not the point of contention it has been in past decades is that wages and conditions are less of a constraint to business growth than skills shortages. With unemployment at historically low levels, many businesses struggle to attract suitably qualified workers.

Towards the end of the term, a notable win for business over environmental interests came with passage of legislation guaranteeing continuation of salmon farming in Macquarie Harbour on Tasmania's west coast, putting at risk the endangered Maugean skate. This was aimed at supporting salmon farming businesses. The primary rationale advanced by the government was to maintain jobs; the impending federal election was clearly a factor. As shown in the 2025 Tasmanian state election, both major parties see support for salmon farming as a vote winner. Although funding was provided towards improving oxygenation in Macquarie Harbour, it remains to be seen whether this will be sufficient to maintain biodiversity.

Other promised improvements in safeguards and similar regulatory elements of environmental policy have not been implemented, reflecting in large part the interests of affected businesses.

One of the Albanese Government's showcase policies was Future Made in Australia. That signalled the beginnings of a new industry policy. Even though some commentators disparaged the policy as 'picking winners', it was mostly welcomed by business lobby groups. Many of its elements, including financial subsidies through production tax credits, capability building, and investment funding for projects, are likely to benefit businesses that meet investment criteria. An aspect which did raise concern, though, was a commitment, jointly with the Queensland Government, of $940 million (Commonwealth component $466.4 million in debt and equity) to US-based company PsiQuantum to establish a national quantum computing centre. The basis on which the funding was promised remains unclear; the deal lacked transparency. The new Queensland Government is reported to be reviewing it.

A prime example of close business/government relationships is the continuing dominance of Australian passenger aviation by Qantas. As documented by business commentator Joe Aston (2024), Qantas has successfully lobbied not only the Albanese Government but its predecessors to cement its position. Among Aston's claims is that Prime Minister Anthony Albanese would liaise with then Qantas CEO Alan Joyce 'directly about his personal travel' – an assertion the Prime Minister has denied. Regardless of the specifics in relation to prime ministerial upgrades, the book provides ample evidence of Qantas maintaining market dominance and avoiding regulation by doling out favours such as membership of its luxurious chairman's lounge, flight upgrades and special inflight treatment. Qantas is highly profitable, while the travelling public pays the price.

Corporatism, crony capitalism or mateship?

The pattern that emerges from these cases is an Albanese Government that mostly seeks to maintain good relations with business, make minimal change to regulatory settings, and from time to time interrupts the pattern with a large intervention that favours one company or group of companies. It is not simply that those companies are effective at lobbying.

There is an extensive literature on rent-seeking: the propensity of businesses to seek favours from government in the form of handouts or advantageous regulation. The incentives to do this are obvious and the behaviour ubiquitous in advanced economies. Rent-seeking has been analysed for years in the economics literature, from Tullock (1967) onwards, and continues to be observed and documented. It is part of the constant background noise of government/business relations. The many relationships between the Albanese Government and business could not be categorised as 'corporatism', traditionally defined as the coming together of business, union and government interests to make policy. Under the past Bob Hawke Labor Government, the Accord agreement exemplified corporatism for some (for example, Humphrys, 2018). Albanese Government business interventions – and importantly, lack of interventions – do not appear to arise from a planned bringing together of peak interest groups to pursue a reform agenda, nor do they formally involve the union movement.

A more relevant description as applied by Rubin (2015) is 'crony capitalism'; he notes it more usually refers to developing economies, but he uses it to describe a form of rent seeking based on personal relationships and access by businesses to key decision makers in government. He argues it can equally be seen in advanced economies including the United States. Rubin notes it may be a second-best response to 'inefficient interventions – laws, regulations, taxes and subsidies'; he concludes 'reducing cronyism is therefore difficult without limiting the overall size and scope of government'. That is, not all special favours for business have negative outcomes for public policy. Rubin's framing of the concept avoids the connotation of corruption.

An Australian version is 'game of mates' (Murray and Frijters, 2017) – rent seeking in sectors including property, mining, banking and transport, primarily through licences or other special-access entitlements obtained through networks of 'mates'. Murray and Frijters document a long history of the practice from the 1980s under both Labor and Coalition governments.

The Albanese Government in its first term has maintained positive relations with business, largely by adopting business-friendly policies. In some cases, it has intervened to benefit specific industries or companies. Differences over policy have been kept low-key, in keeping with the small-target strategy advanced by the Albanese-led Opposition before the 2022 election. The influence of business lobby groups appears lower than under previous governments; however, the Albanese Government unprompted has adopted many policies favouring specific business interests, often in the interests of job creation.

References

Aston, J, *The Chairman's Lounge: The inside story of how Qantas sold us out*, Simon & Schuster, Sydney, 2024.

Bell, S, Hindmoor, A, and Umashev, N, 'The determinants of corporate political activity in Australia' *Australian Journal of Political Science*, vol. 58, no. 4, 2023, pp. 363–82.

Browne, B, 'Trade associations – the Australian picture', *Australia Institute Research Reports*, December 2024.

Centre for Public Integrity, 'Hey, big spender – what 25 years of political party income disclosures reveal', *Money in Politics Research Report*, December 2024.

Chalmers, J, 'Implementing reforms to the Petroleum Resource Rent Tax', media release, 6 August 2024, <https://ministers.treasury.gov.au/ministers/jim-chalmers-2022/media-releases/implementing-reforms-petroleum-resource-rent-tax>.

Humphrys, E, 'Simultaneously deepening corporatism and advancing neoliberalism: Australia under the Accord', *Journal of Sociology*, vol. 54, no. 1, March 2018, pp. 49–63.

Murray, C, and Frijters, P, *Game of Mates: How favours bleed the nation*, Publicious, Brisbane, 2017.

Pharmacy Guild of Australia, 'Pharmacy Guild and Albanese Government commit to early 8CPA start', media release, 2023, <https://www.guild.org.au/news-events/news/2023/pharmacy-guild-and-albanese-government-commit-to-early-8cpa-start>.

Rubin, P, 'Crony Capitalism', *Supreme Court Economic Review*, vol. 23, no. 1, 2015, pp. 105–20.

Treasury, *Australia's Future Tax System Review: Final Report*, Canberra, October 2010.

Tullock, G, 'The welfare costs of tariffs, monopolies, and theft', *Western Economic Journal*, vol. 5, no. 3, 1967, pp. 224–32.

PART IV
GOVERNING CHALLENGES AND LEADERSHIP

CHAPTER 23

THE ALBANESE GOVERNMENT: AN HISTORICAL PERSPECTIVE

FRANK BONGIORNO

The victory of the Labor Opposition led by Anthony Albanese at the federal election held on 21 May 2022 was unusual in bringing a Labor government to power from Opposition. That had only ever occurred six times in more than 120 years. This chapter seeks to place the Albanese Labor Government (2022–2025) in the broader context of Australian political history. In the late 1980s and early 1990s, there was a debate among political scientists about whether the Hawke Government had, or had not, betrayed 'Labor tradition' (Johnson, 1989, 1991; Maddox, 1989, 1991). It is more difficult, after four decades of neoliberalism, to identify what 'Labor tradition' might actually comprise than it was in the 1980s. Nonetheless, I follow political scientist Graham Maddox (1989) in seeing among its core elements an ethical critique of capitalism, a preference for community over individualism, and a willingness to use democratic methods to transform the existing order into a more just and equal one. I argue here that the Albanese Government has generally been content with moderate institutional reform and piecemeal intervention to modify market outcomes, rather than attempting more ambitious redesign and redistribution.

Electoral support

The unique character of Labor's electoral victory in May 2022 has conditioned its approach to government. Labor won that election with just 32.6 per cent of the primary vote in the House of Representatives. The preferential system has recently worked in Labor's favour by facilitating a large flow of votes from Greens candidates, which in 2022 gave Labor a two-party-preferred vote of 52.1 per cent and a slim majority of three, or 77 seats in a 151-seat parliament. Labor's primary vote was deflated by the presence of highly competitive (and, in several cases, ultimately victorious) independent candidates in multiple divisions. Still, no government had ever won office on such a low primary vote. In the Senate, Labor held just 26 seats in a chamber of 76 following the election, accentuating its normal dependence on crossbench support there.

Unlike every other Labor government elected since 1943, Albanese's would be unable to bear even a modest loss of votes and seats at a second election. Labor had held on in 1946, 1974, 1984 and 2010 in the face of an erosion of support. Similarly, Coalition governments had managed to bear large vote losses in 1998 and 2016 without relinquishing office, on the back of landslide victories at the previous elections (1996 and 2013). The narrowness of Labor's victory in 2022, if considered in relation to the rest of the Parliament and not only the federal Coalition, made it more vulnerable than its predecessors, even allowing for the extension of its majority to five after the Aston by-election on 1 April 2023 (Goot, 2022).

Crises

Since 1910, Labor has had only two periods in office that might be called 'extended' – from 1941 to 1949, and 1983 to 1996. Other Labor governments have ruled for one or two terms, usually lasting between two and three years, with the Rudd–Gillard–Rudd era (2007–13) an exception. Labor governments have come to office in time to face a serious crisis: the First World War, the Great Depression, the Pacific War, the end of the postwar boom, the early 1980s recession, and the Global Financial Crisis of 2007–09.

The Albanese Government has also faced difficult times, if nothing quite on the scale of a world war or depression. The Russo–Ukraine war stimulated global inflation and in combination with pressures associated with the Covid-19 pandemic, created a cost-of-living crisis. Energy prices were particularly troublesome. In December 2022, the government used its powers to intervene directly in the energy market to cap coal and gas prices. The Reserve Bank of Australia (2025) responded to inflationary pressures by raising the official interest rate 13 times from 0.10 per cent in April 2022 to 4.35 per cent in November 2023.

Albanese appears to have thought of his government's agenda as requiring re-election, to the frustration of voters looking for greater ambition. He had seen one of the key reforms of the Gillard Government, notably its Emissions Trading Scheme, abolished when the Abbott Government came to power. Terms such as 'cautious' came to be used frequently in connection with the Albanese Government, sometimes as a compliment. When 'timid' came to replace it as a verdict, that change began to signal a sense of disappointment among those who had looked for a more adventurous progressive government. For its first 18 months in office, at least two terms of government seemed a reasonable prospect, since there had been no one-term federal government since the Scullin Labor Government of 1929–32 and opinion polls favoured Labor.

Policies

The government was not seemingly blamed at first for cost-of-living pressures. The new government implemented its major spending commitments, such as higher childcare rebates, Medicare bulk-billing and energy bill relief. Overall, the government was united, purposeful, low-key and scandal-free. There was an emphasis on order and process, signalled in the first instance by the appointment of experienced public servant, political scientist, and former university vice-chancellor, Professor Glyn Davis, as Secretary of the Department of Prime Minister and Cabinet. On assuming office, the Albanese Government launched multiple enquiries that sought to operationalise an orderly, evidence-based approach to policy. There were enquiries, consultations and task forces on matters such as Immigration, the National Disability Insurance Scheme (NDIS), the Reserve Bank of Australia (RBA), democracy, the universities, and the arts, and a high-profile Royal Commission on Robodebt. The volume of enquiry recalled that of the Whitlam and Hawke Labor governments in their early years.

The new government's systematic approach stood in contrast to post-election revelations that the previous prime minister, Scott Morrison, had taken on five secret ministries; and the Robodebt scandal, the Coalition Government's effort to extract money from welfare recipients by raising fictional debts against their names through a flawed and illegal process.

The actual reform emanating from these processes was mainly modest. There were some changes to the architecture and processes of the RBA. Bill Shorten, as the responsible minister, moved to place the NDIS on a firmer financial footing. There was a new arts policy, Revive: A place for every story, a story for every place, and the commencement of a process of university reform (such as establishment of the Australian Tertiary Education Commission) without unravelling changes made by the Coalition to the fee structure known as Job-Ready Graduates. The Albanese Government established a National Anti-Corruption Commission that has since attracted widespread criticism as ineffectual. It moved to rebalance the migrant intake from large-scale unplanned temporary migration to a smaller number of permanent and skilled migrants. A High Court decision that invalidated indefinite immigration detention created headaches for the government, raising the spectre of former criminals being released into the community amid media sensationalism and Opposition condemnation.

On the night of the 2022 election in his victory speech, Albanese had committed his government to the full implementation of the Uluru Statement from the Heart. Labor had undertaken to hold a referendum on the Voice to Parliament in its first term. In retrospect, it proved ill-judged to adopt the Uluru Statement and the Voice as so conspicuous a part of the government's brand but, since Whitlam, Labor had nurtured a self-image as 'progressive' on Aboriginal rights. Unfortunately for the government, both the National and Liberal parties came out in opposition. The proposal was roundly defeated on 14 October 2023, with more than six in ten voters opposing the proposition. This was devastating to the overwhelming majority of First Nations peoples who supported the Voice, and to Albanese himself. In November 2023, the month after the vote, Newspoll reported a 50-50 two-party-preferred split for the first time.

In its economic and social policy, the government pursued an agenda of modifying market outcomes designed to encourage economic growth, tempered by considerations of social equity and environmental sustainability. Critics of the government have accused it of prioritising powerful economic interests – including the fossil fuel and gambling industries, and wealthy property investors – over the protection of vulnerable people and ecosystems. The government moved quickly after the election to legislate a carbon emissions cut of 43 per cent (from 2005) by 2030, and net zero by 2050. Yet in office it approved large coal and gas projects. Burnt by the perception that it was hostile to the coal industry at the 2019 election, Labor has governed with an eye to votes in Western Australia and Queensland, the two major resource states. It abandoned an environmental protection bill after lobbying by Western Australian premier, Roger Cook, ahead of the 2025 election. Labor has in no way diverged from the developmentalist ethos integral to the party throughout its history. The spirit of Whitlam Government minister Rex Connor lives on in its love of resource development but, unlike that economic nationalist, Labor is now comfortable with large profits being expatriated by foreign companies.

Even when the government has acted to improve equity, such as in its modification of stage 3 income tax cuts, it has been reluctant to defend the policy in terms that explicitly referenced Labor tradition or values, such as promoting greater equality. Labor had voted for this regressive tax reform, which was designed to deliver a windfall to high-income earners, following its 2019 election defeat. Having resisted pressure to reverse its position for almost two years, the government finally did so early in 2024, ahead of the Dunkley by-election (which it would go on to win). The government defended its change of course as motivated by the cost-of-living crisis rather than as a principled defence of progressive taxation.

Despite Albanese's longstanding membership of the Left of his party, the government has not sought to reverse the late 20th-century shift towards government-subsidised market-based provision of key services. A partial exception was a rebalancing of the use of consultants within federal government itself in favour of building greater in-house public service expertise. But across a range of areas, the Albanese Government has pursued the familiar post-1980s technique of assisting people through financial support to gain access to services provided by the market. Albanese nurtures an ambition of achieving universal provision of childcare but his government has provided subsidies to parents and carers to reduce the cost of private provision. The government's housing policy has more explicitly recognised market failure and the need for various forms of government intervention, but there has been no revival of a direct role for government in building public housing for rent. Meanwhile, chastened by Labor's defeat at the 2019 election when it had proposed some winding back of negative gearing concessions for property investors, the government has not revisited this matter. The capital gains tax concession introduced by the Howard Government also remains in place.

Ideologies

Historians of the Labor Party have used a range of concepts to encapsulate its ideology: (democratic) socialism, social democracy, social liberalism, populism and labourism have all figured in the academic literature. The term 'socialism' can contain a range of positions but normally prioritises public ownership and wealth redistribution. Social democracy and social liberalism have often been associated with modernising tendencies that seek to steer Labor away from (socialist) public ownership and towards progressive taxation and welfare provision. Populism has historically been associated with hostility to finance capital or 'the money power' (Love, 1984) and has recently been more associated globally with an insurgent political right than with the left. Populism, however, can also be 'progressive' and champion redistribution of resources towards 'the people' or 'the masses' at the expense of 'elites' or 'the top end of town' (McKnight, 2018).

Labourism remains a useful concept in providing a sense of how these different strands have been mediated within the Labor Party to build a commonsense understanding of 'Labor tradition'. Political scientists Rob Manwaring and Emily Foley (2025: 7) have recently argued that 'thin' or 'new' labourism is apposite as a description of the Albanese Government's approach since it 'emphasises incremental improvements, such as securing better pay for low-income workers and improving conditions for gig economy employees, while treading cautiously around more radical structural reforms'. Traditionally, labourism has at its core the idea that an independent Labor Party, supported by a strong trade union movement, should seek a more just distribution of rewards through the parliamentary system. The focus was traditionally on assisting the working-class family through support for the male breadwinner's 'living wage', supplemented by a means-tested pension. Further benefits, such as the maternity allowance (1912) and the child endowment (1941), were added to strengthen working-class economic security during periods in the life course of greater financial vulnerability (Macintyre 1989: 16–17). Political scientist Francis Castles has called this set of arrangements the 'wage earners' welfare state' (Castles, 1985). From the 1970s, with the end of the family wage concept and a more expansive understanding of social and economic disadvantage to encompass Indigenous people, migrants and women, labourism extended its protections to previously neglected groups without quite shedding the established masculinist assumptions. Its embrace of compulsory but occupationally based superannuation, for instance, has produced better results for men than for women (Millane, 2020: 192–95, 219, 232).

Leadership, images and identities

In her 2022 *Quarterly Essay*, journalist Katharine Murphy suggested that Albanese has many of the instincts of the 'lone wolf': he was 'an outsider who became an avid institutionalist, a Labor parliamentarian fluent in more than a century of tradition in Australia's oldest political party' (Murphy, 2022: 3). The most natural and generally acceptable style of leadership within the party has indeed been collegial. Graham Little, the political psychologist, would probably have seen in Albanese's style an example of 'group leadership' (Little, 1985). 'People are seen as belonging together', political scholar Judith Brett explains of group leadership, 'and the emphasis is on the emotions and experiences that bind – on trust, loyalty, self-effacement, tradition' (Brett, 2021: 300). Albanese's half-serious, half-joking remark that the Australian Labor Party, the Catholic Church and South Sydney Rabbitohs were the three faiths in which he had been raised hints at this idea of local loyalties being microcosms for a wider sense of 'deep, horizontal comradeship' (Anderson, 1991: 7).

The government's emphasis on caution and process takes us some way from the common idea of Albanese as a politician who operates on 'gut instinct' (Murphy, 2022: 9). His mainstreaming as a politician was complete well before he became Labor leader but there were arguably also continuities with his time as activist and apparatchik. In New South Wales, to be on the Left was always to be outnumbered. Albanese was prominent in a subfaction called the 'hard left' which, notwithstanding Albanese's reputation for playing hardball, inevitably engaged in a transactional form of politics in a state branch dominated by the Right (Centre Unity). It was a situation made for a wary battler, the 'lone hand' of Murphy's description – the term also nicely sums up Albanese's status as the Left's man in the New South Wales branch's Sussex Street head office during his years as assistant secretary.

In such ways, Albanese had learned the arts of political circumspection and compromise. On the Gaza War, his government has sought a middle way in an emotionally charged debate; he and foreign minister Penny Wong fell back on the security of Labor's support for a two-state solution. The government, however, also became more critical of Israel as the war continued and evidence of reckless killing mounted. On AUKUS, Albanese has emphasised the economic advantages, in line with the government's 'Building a Future Made in Australia' concept, in a manner that does not so much disarm the critics as avoid engaging them. Albanese similarly refused to provide what he called 'running commentary' on Donald Trump. The government improved relations with China, securing the termination of trade restrictions imposed during the pandemic and the release of imprisoned Chinese-born Australian citizen, Cheng Lei. There was little in Albanese's foreign and defence policy that could be deemed a major departure from Labor tradition in those fields, given its support for the US Alliance in the past alongside Asian engagement and multilateral co-operation. Historian David Lee, however, has argued that AUKUS, in seeming to envisage a kind of 'forward defence', departed from Labor's more usual focus on taking advantage of distance to defend the continent (Lee, 2023).

A steady hand in troubled times

Albanese was a child of the Whitlam era; a young adult – and political staffer – of the Hawke era; a rising politician in the long, barren years (for Labor) of John Howard's prime ministership; and a senior minister during Labor's Rudd–Gillard–Rudd ordeals. He appears to have taken a great deal from each of these experiences, but his government's trajectory has been towards something that has no precedent in any national Labor government.

Labor has often behaved like a state government. Such a judgment need not be pejorative: Labor has been more electorally successful in the states and territories, and it has pursued progressive policies there with positive effects. It is unthinkable that Albanese would see his government in this way and unlikely that there is any conscious emulation. But the style of orderly, cautious, pragmatic and reformist administration is familiar enough in the best of the state and territory Labor governments since Neville Wran's narrow victory in New South Wales in 1976.

Can such an approach produce 'great' and 'transformative' government, as distinct from 'good' or 'competent' government? Perhaps not, but these might not be times for dreamers and visionaries. The uncertainties of the global economic and strategic environment may make voters even more risk-averse than they have been in the past, at the same time as western governments long accustomed to the American imperial umbrella have to confront questions they have long had the luxury of being able to ignore. There is a long-standing discourse of 'security' in Australian politics (Holbrook, 2025), and the times seem likely to suit any government able to craft policies that can be sold as a shelter from a storm.

References

Anderson, B, *Imagined Communities: Reflections on the origin and spread of nationalism*, revised ed, Verso, London, 1991.

Brett, J, *Doing Politics: Writing on public life*, Text Publishing, Melbourne, 2021.

Castles, F, *The Working Class and Welfare: Reflections on the political development of the welfare state in Australia and New Zealand, 1890–1980*, Allen & Unwin, Sydney, 1985.

Goot, M, 'Governments usually win a second term. But could the new Labor government be an exception?', *The Conversation*, 16 June 2022.

Holbrook, C, '"Chifley spells security": Tracing the origins of contemporary Australian security discourse', *Australian Historical Studies*, vol. 56, no. 1, 2025, pp. 6–27.

Johnson, C, *The Labor Legacy: Curtin, Chifley, Whitlam, Hawke*, Allen & Unwin, Sydney, 1989.

— 'A reply to Maddox and Battin', *Australian Journal of Political Science*, vol. 26, no. 3, 1991, pp. 545–49.

Lee, D, 'AUKUS and the Labor tradition', *Arena*, no. 14, 2023, pp. 43–48.

Little, G, *Political Ensembles: A psychosocial approach to politics and leadership*, Oxford University Press, Melbourne, 1985.

Love, P, *Labour and the Money Power: Australian labour populism 1890–1950*, Melbourne University Press, Melbourne, 1984.

Macintyre, S, *The Labour Experiment*, McPhee Gribble, Melbourne, 1989.

Maddox, G, *The Hawke Government and Labor Tradition*, Penguin Books, Melbourne, 1989.

Maddox, G, and Battin, T, 'Australian Labor and the socialist tradition', *Australian Journal of Political Science*, vol. 26, no. 2, 1991, pp. 181–96.

Manwaring, R, and Foley, E, 'The contradictions of the Albanese Labor Government in Australia: The promise and limits of "thin" labourism', *The Political Quarterly*, 2025.

McKnight, D, *Populism Now: The case for progressive populism*, NewSouth Publishing, Sydney, 2018.

Millane, E, 'The Ghost of National Superannuation', PhD Thesis, Australian National University, Canberra, 2020.

Murphy, K, 'Lone wolf: Albanese and the new politics', *Quarterly Essay*, issue 88, 2022.

CHAPTER 24

HOW HARD IS IT TO GOVERN?

MICHELLE GRATTAN

Is governing harder in the 2020s than in earlier decades? The instinctive, and popular, answer would be 'of course it is'. While that's also a correct answer, we should insert some qualifications.

Making the right or best decisions, especially in times of actual or looming crisis, has always been difficult. Consider the choices facing decision-makers, in Australia and abroad, during the Great Depression, when there was less understanding of how financial and economic systems worked than contemporary policy-makers possess. Consider also the choices that confronted leaders in past wars. Wartime prime minister John Curtin, grappling with decisions on which hung the lives of thousands of Australian troops, paced The Lodge grounds at night. And what of the challenges facing public health authorities trying to cope with the influenza epidemic that followed the First World War, compared with responding to the Covid pandemic, that latter in a time when vaccines could be developed quickly?

While keeping history in mind, however, it is undoubtedly true that contemporary governments face extraordinary changes and complexities.

These come from many sources. More demands for the provision of services. An interconnected world but fragmented public squares. Populations in democratic countries that have lost trust in government and in many other institutions. The rise of populism and the desire for instant answers to political and economic problems that do not lend themselves to easy, if any, solutions.

Modern travel, communications and technology have facilitated governing, as well as bringing their own challenges. Easier, faster and more comfortable travel means greater opportunities for face-to-face interaction, while imposing its own burdens. Email and 'virtual' meetings have transformed interactions. The internet is a massive information hub, the scale of which was beyond imagination only decades ago. It is also a monster that disseminates misinformation and disinformation on an industrial scale, and facilitates political intimidation.

Comparing the Hawke and Albanese eras

'It's become a truism of Australian politics that important economic reform peaked in the 1980s and 1990s. Sometimes the first two terms of the Howard government … are given credit as well', John Daley, of the Grattan Institute, wrote in *Gridlock: Removing barriers to policy reform* (2021). That report looked at the fate of a plethora of reforms the institute proposed between 2009 and 2019, finding more than two-thirds of them had not been adopted.

In Australia the Hawke–Keating Government is often looked upon as a sort of 'gold standard' for a reforming Labor government. It is unfair to measure a first-term administration against one that lasted several terms, and especially one that has been so much mythologised. All the same, some critics have argued the Albanese Government in its initial term was not pitching its aspiration high enough – let alone anything like as high as that earlier government.

Leaving aspiration aside, there is the other question. Was it easier in the Hawke–Keating days for a government to get things done – in particular, really difficult things? The answer is, almost certainly. But let us not romanticise the view through the rear vision mirror. Ken Henry, a public servant and Keating staffer during those days, told the National Press Club in 2025, 'These reforms of the 80s and 90s mostly enjoy broad business and political support today, but they were not easy at the time'.

Moreover, some observers see downsides. 'In recent months, there's been a lot of breathless praise for the reforms of the 1980s and 1990s. But where did some of those reforms lead?' ABC economics writer Gareth Hutchens wrote in 2025. 'Some eventually led to appalling scandals that ended in royal commissions (banking, aged care, Robodebt). Changes to Australia's labour market in that period contributed to the rise of underemployment and precarious work.'

Much momentum for Australia's economic reforms in the 1980s, stretching into the 1990s, was imposed from outside. Australia was under pressure from external forces to open its economy to the world. This produced winners and losers, but in many cases the losers (whether from tax changes, or slashing tariffs) could, where considered necessary, be compensated. This didn't prevent pain, but it could ameliorate some of it.

By the time of the Albanese Government, much of the big reform had been done, or tried. The public had become pain-averse; the drag of 'reform fatigue' had been canvassed for years. Trust in government, declining for decades, was down again after a brief revival during the pandemic. The more difficult territory – such as improving productivity, which had languished for years – proved to be harder to navigate than some of the landmark changes under Hawke, Keating and the early days of John Howard. With a tight budgetary situation, there wasn't money to compensate losers – and there was less tolerance for policies where some people would lose.

By the 2020s the community had grown more pessimistic, fractious and negative, uncertain where the country was headed. The 2025 Edelman Trust Barometer's Australian report highlighted the extent of 'grievance'. It found 62 per cent of Australians had a moderate or high sense of grievance. (This was defined as a belief by the person that government and business make their lives harder and serve narrow interests, and that wealthy people benefit under the system while ordinary people struggle.) Fewer than one in five people believed things would be better for the next generation.

Nearly two-thirds (64 per cent) worried that government leaders purposely mislead by saying things they know are false or are gross exaggerations. The barometer found a 'zero sum' mindset increasingly permeating Australian society. 'Those Australians with high grievances are twice as likely to feel that "what helps people who don't share my politics will come at a cost to me" compared with those with low grievances.' An environment marked by distrust and grievance makes governing difficult, let alone the pursuit of reform. Moreover, the modern plethora of well-resourced interest groups will be positioned to exploit grievance – indeed that is often central to their business models. Social media is god's gift to those fanning grievances.

On the whole, people are more trustful if they feel they have agency – the opportunity for a voice, however small. The increasing professionalisation of politics, and the thinning out of the memberships and power within the major parties have further weakened the connection between citizens and the political process. In today's world, for multiple reasons, fewer people are 'joiners' of parties, or other organisations. At the same time, the major parties give less encouragement to the political amateurs who want to be involved. As late as the 1980s and early 1990s ALP rank-and-file members had some clout, with the party's national conference fights over policy (for example, uranium mining and export, reform of the banking system, privatisation) carrying weight. Progressively, however, the extra-parliamentary Labor Party membership declined in importance (with the exception that it gained a 50 per cent say in choosing the parliamentary leader). This is in line with an international trend. John Daley and Rachel Krust write in their *Institutional Reform Stocktake* (2025) that 'major parties around the world have increasingly become "cartel parties" in which members promise each other the benefits of government patronage, part of the machinery of government operated by a professional political class'. As modern ALP national conferences became much bigger in size, they took on the nature of stage-managed rallies, losing policy teeth.

At the 2025 election, for the second time running, only about two-thirds of electors voted number one for Labor or the Coalition. The loss of faith in the major parties has been accompanied by people seeking agency in part through the 'community candidate' movement. Independent candidates ('teals' but others, too) have attracted large numbers of enthusiastic followers. The number of House of Representatives crossbenchers swelled in the 2020s compared with the preceding decades.

This fragmentation, however, does not necessarily promote reform. Crossbenchers can sometimes achieve change by advocacy on particular issues, or by using positions of power to extract concessions (for example, in the Senate). To achieve transformational change, however, may require a government with a substantial, or at least a comfortable, majority. We saw this with John Howard's GST reform, when a big majority went to near defeat.

The 'localism' reflected in the community candidate movement has been matched to a degree in the big parties, which often feel the need to preselect a 'local champion', such as someone who has served as mayor, from the particular electorate, making it hard to get policy-oriented 'high flyers' into seats, especially when these days fewer seats are 'safe' for the party.

Short federal parliamentary terms – a flexible three years – are not conducive to bringing in potentially unpopular policies. Addressing the British Labour conference in 2025, Albanese noted that in the UK, which has five-year terms, they had 'the most valuable resource for any Labor Government' – time. Both sides of politics acknowledge the handicap of short terms but by now have accepted that terms cannot in practice be lengthened, because (on recent history) it would seem impossible to pass the required referendum. Terms could be made fixed by legislation, however there has not been the bipartisan will for that. (After the 2025 election the Special Minister of State, Don Farrell, did ask the parliamentary Joint Standing Committee on Electoral Matters to examine fixed four-year terms and increasing the size of the parliament.)

But the problem is not just the short length of terms. The electoral cycle has progressively become the 'permanent campaign' with the government, especially the prime minister, seemingly never off the election trail, physically or mentally. This may have become so entrenched that longer terms might not significantly change things.

The contemporary phenomenon of the 'continuous campaign' is reinforced by the frequency of opinion polling, and the attention given to it. It shapes much of the media discourse, and the use of it by the parties themselves means their eyes are, much of the time, on what the 'focus groups' are saying. These trends were present in the 1980s but had reached new heights by the 2020s.

Much of the Hawke–Keating Government's success in achieving economic reform was that it could harness the power and co-operation of the trade unions. The formal 'Accord' between the government and unions meant the government could achieve trade-offs with the union movement – wage restraint in return for 'social wage' benefits (Medicare, for example, and later a national superannuation contribution scheme). The union movement of the day covered a much larger proportion of the workforce and had some impressive leaders who were willing to sign up to the government's often controversial reform projects. The Albanese Government delivered significantly to the unions in its first term, including support for wage rises and a raft of changes to industrial laws, but it did not get offsets. The coverage of the union movement had shrunk drastically, and its leadership was not of the 1980s–1990s calibre.

It is hard to recall how different the media landscape was in the Hawke–Keating years. This was the time before social media, and when the mainstream media were more influential for a government that wanted to drive change and achieve ambitious policy outcomes. As a reforming treasurer, Paul Keating was able to skilfully win influential parts of the media to his causes. Keating used to say, with his typical exaggeration, 'If I've got the top five journalists in the press gallery supporting a policy, I've got the country'. In the 2020s not only are the media splintered every which way by the growth of social media, but traditional media are also increasingly polarised and less influential, especially with younger voters who obtain their information elsewhere.

The new round-the-clock, digital media environment has brought extra pressures on governing. How to sell measures has become almost as important in formulating policy as the substance. More generally, the government feels it imperative to fill the media space, which requires deploying ministers to the extensive round of morning TV and radio programs, interviews on the news channels through the day, evening current affairs, Sunday shows, and the like. Arguably, the extent of the media burden on ministers takes away from the time and attention they can focus on detailed policy work.

Reform in any age requires leaders who can identify what needs to be done; grasp the policy challenges; are able and willing to be bold, and can persuade the public. The centrality of leadership in driving reform is crucial. In Bob Hawke, Labor had a leader who could draw on strong personal popularity and was willing to spend political capital (although not be profligate with it – he acted as a restraining hand on his treasurer). Albanese in his first term was a much more cautious brand of leader, mostly unwilling to exceed what he saw as his mandate. He also had a thin majority.

Effective leadership must extend beyond the leader. Paul Keating as Treasurer was willing to stretch the boundaries. Albanese's Treasurer Jim Chalmers began his career by studying Keating attentively, but is still to be seriously tested himself. Importantly, the Cabinet of the Hawke–Keating era was deep in its talent and its ambition. Its expenditure review committee was exceptionally hard-working. While the dynamics of the Albanese Cabinet are more opaque, there is not the breadth of talent or common reform purpose of its predecessor.

With Labor's massive 2025 victory, calls immediately redoubled for the government to set its sights high. Slow economic growth, flatlined productivity and an uncertain external environment added to the push. Stakeholders dusted off their reform proposals. A roundtable on 'productivity', which the Treasurer immediately branded an 'economic reform' roundtable, was summoned by the government. That was the easy part. Whether Albanese's second-term government would have the will to significantly break the reform 'gridlock' will be quite another matter. The Prime Minister might be a restraining hand on those inclined to hasten too fast.

References

Daley, J, *Gridlock: Removing barriers to policy reform*, Grattan Institute, 2021.
Daley, J, and Krust, D, *Institutional Reform Stocktake*, McKinnon, 2025.
Edelman, *2025 Edelman Trust Barometer*, Edelman, 2025.

AUTHORS

Liz Allen is senior lecturer at the Australian National University's Centre for Social Policy Research.

Stephen Bartos is a professor in the Canberra School of Government at the University of Canberra.

Frank Bongiorno is Director of the Vice-Chancellor's Centre of Public Ideas and Donald Horne Professor of History and Public Ideas at the University of Canberra.

Robert Breunig is director of the Tax and Transfer Policy Institute in the Crawford School of Public Policy at the Australian National University.

Stephen Clibborn is associate professor in work and organisational studies at the University of Sydney Business School.

Brendan Coates is director of the Housing and Economic Security Program at the Grattan Institute.

Rae Cooper AO is a professor at the University of Sydney Business School.

Helen Dickinson is professor of public service research at the School of Business in the University of New South Wales.

Stephen Duckett is an Honorary Enterprise professor in the School of Population and Global Health and in the Melbourne Institute at the University of Melbourne.

Uwe Dulleck is dean of the Faculty of Business, Government and Law at the University of Canberra.

Bradon Ellem is a professor of employment relations at the University of Sydney Business School.

Glenn Fahey is director of education policy at the Centre for Independent Studies.

Alan Fenna is a professor in the John Curtin Institute of Public Policy at Curtin University.

Caroline Fisher is associate professor of communication in the Faculty of Arts and Design at the University of Canberra.

Frances Flanagan is a lecturer in the Faculty of Law at the University of Technology Sydney.

Daniel Flitton is managing editor of the Lowy Institute's international magazine, *The Interpreter.*

Diane Gibson is a distinguished professor in the Centre for Ageing Research and Translation at the University of Canberra.

Michelle Grattan is a professorial fellow at the University of Canberra and chief political correspondent at *The Conversation.*

John Halligan is emeritus professor of public administration and governance in the Canberra School of Government at the University of Canberra.

Evan Hamman is a research fellow in the Centre for Environmental Governance at the University of Canberra.

John Hawkins heads the Canberra School of Government at the University of Canberra.

Louisa Jeffery is a research assistant at the Tax and Transfer Policy Institute in the Crawford School of Public Policy at the Australian National University.

Tom King is a retired public servant.

Brendan McCaffrie is a senior lecturer and deputy director of the Public Partnerships and Impact Hub at the University of New South Wales.

Jo Mummery is an associate professor in the Centre for Environmental Governance at the University of Canberra.

Andrew Norton is a professor of higher education policy in the Monash Business School at Monash University.

Matthew Ricketson is a distinguished professor in the School of Communications and Creative Arts at Deakin University.

Leonora Risse is an associate professor at the University of Canberra.

Rebekah Russell-Bennett is associate dean of research in the Faculty of Business, Government and Law at the University of Canberra.

Jacki Schirmer is director of the Centre for Environmental Governance, and professor in the Health Research Institute at the University of Canberra.

Bill Shorten is the vice-chancellor of the University of Canberra.

Darren Sinclair is a professor in the Centre for Environmental Governance at the University of Canberra.

Bartholomew Stanford is a senior lecturer in Indigenous studies at the Indigenous Education and Research Centre at James Cook University.

Josh Sunman is an associate lecturer at the College of Business, Government and Law at Flinders University.

Marija Taflaga is a senior lecturer at the Australian National University and director of the Centre for the Study of Australian Politics.

Alex Veen is senior lecturer and DECRA Fellow at the University of Sydney Business School.

Geoffrey Watson is a director of the Centre for Public Integrity and an adjunct professor at the University of Notre Dame.

Chris Wright is a professor of work and labour market policy at the University of Sydney Business School.

ACKNOWLEDGEMENTS

This is the 15th volume in the *Australian Government Administration* series, which commenced with the end of the first Hawke Government in 1984. The editors wish to thank the University of Canberra for its continuing support for the project and its vice-chancellor (and former Albanese Government minister) Bill Shorten for contributing the preface. Sian Hicks at UC helped bring the project to fruition.

We were delighted to again partner with UNSW Press. Our thanks to Harriet McInerney, Jocelyn Hungerford, Paul O'Beirne and Emma Hutchinson.

We thank all the authors who contributed articles, and Josh Black and Mary Walsh, who read through all the chapters for us. Ben Roper provided excellent research support.

NOTES

1   A cautious first term
1   2022 is the most recent federal election for which there are any fundraising data.

3   The largest crossbench in a century
1   The 2022 'teals' also used orange, coral, light blue, turquoise, purple, yellow, lemon, pink, aqua, navy, peach, olive, purple and burgundy. Zali Steggall had called her campaign colour 'blue with a touch of green'. See Sawer (2007) for a discussion of the use of colours as political signifiers. She pointed out that green, white and violet (the initials represented 'give women votes') were the campaign colours of Vida Goldstein, a proto-teal from over a century ago.
2   Sessional order 65a, *House of Representatives Hansard*, 27 July 2022, p. 74; Berger (2024: 34–38).

4   Reforming the Australian public service
1   Other sources are acknowledged but not specified (APSC, 2024a: 4).
2   Outcomes are defined as: 'the measurable, long-term program objectives describing the intended end-state' (APSC, 2024a: 29).
3   The issues were captured by a Senate report's sub-titles: 'a Calculated Breach of Trust' and 'The Cover up Worsens the Crime': (SFPARC, 2024: 3).
4   The details are: Operational delivery, Policy, Functional (19 professions) and Specialist (10 professions), <https://www.gov.uk/government/publications/ government-professions/government-professions#what-are-the-different- professions>.
5   It is unclear what happened to the APS Policy Project and the APS Policy Capability Roadmap, although secretaries associated with it were purged (Halligan, 2020). New Zealand's policy profession has been maintained and led by the Chief Executive of Prime Minister and Cabinet, <https://www.dpmc.govt.nz/ our-programmes/policy-project/policy-community/policy-system-leadership>.
6   Australian Government website, 'Digital experience policy', <https://www.digital. gov.au/policy/digital-experience>.
7   There was a formal appointment process in 2024 for the head of the UK civil service.
8   Lynelle Briggs, Review of Public Sector Board Appointments Processes, https:// www.apsreform.gov.au/resources/communication/review-public-sector-board- appointments-processes>.
9   The higher the score the lower the corruption.

5   A disappointing start
1   See, for example, 'Public Hearings Sticking Point as National Anti-Corruption Commission Likely to Pass by Christmas', *RN Drive* (ABC Radio National, 10 November 2022).
2   *National Anti-Corruption Act 2022* (Cth) s 73(2)(a).
3   *National Anti-Corruption Act 2022* (Cth) ss 3, 8.
4   Inspector of the National Anti-Corruption Commission, 'Inspector of the National

Anti-Corruption Commission to Inquire into the Decision Not to Investigate Referrals from the Royal Commission into the Robodebt Scheme', media release, 13 July 2024.

5   National Anti-Corruption Commission, 'National Anti-Corruption Commission Decides Not to Pursue Robodebt Royal Commission Referrals but Focus on Ensuring Lessons Learnt', media release, 6 June 2024 ('Referrals Decision').

6   National Anti-Corruption Commission, media release, 6 June 2024.

7   National Anti-Corruption Commission, media release, 6 June 2024.

8   Evidence to Parliamentary Joint Committee on the National Anti-Corruption Commission, Parliament of Australia, Canberra, 22 November 2024 ('Parliamentary Evidence').

9   Referrals Decision (n 5).

10   Referrals Decision (n 5).

11   Referrals Decision (n 5).

12   Parliamentary Evidence (n 8) 7 (Nicole Rose, Deputy NACC Commissioner).

13   Parliamentary Evidence (n 8) 7.

14   Commonwealth of Australia, 'Inspector of the National Anti-Corruption Commission Complaint Investigation: NACC's Decision not to Investigate Referrals from the Royal Commission into the Robodebt Scheme' (October 2024) 13 (Inspector's Report). The Inspector's Report is in substance an adoption of the advice of Mr Robertson, which is provided as Attachment B and contains a clear, clinical analysis of the surrounding events.

15   Commonwealth of Australia, Inspector's Report, 4, 23.

16   Commonwealth of Australia, Inspector's Report, 4, 25.

17   National Anti-Corruption Commission, 'Independent Delegate Appointed to Reconsider Robodebt Referrals', media release, 13 December 2024.

18   National Anti-Corruption Commission, 'National Anti-Corruption Commission to Investigate Robodebt Referrals', media release, 18 February 2025.

19   *Integrity Commission Act 2018* (ACT); *National Anti-corruption Act 2022* (Cth); *Independent Commission Against Corruption Act 1988* (NSW); *Independent Commissioner Against Corruption Act 2017* (NT); *Crime and Corruption Act 2001* (Qld); *Independent Commission Against Corruption Act 2012* (SA); *Integrity Commission Act 2009* (Tas); *Independent Broad-based Anti-corruption Commission Act 2011* (Vic); *Corruption, Crime and Misconduct Act 2003* (WA).

20   For example, the power to compel answers or the production of documents overriding the privilege against self-incrimination and legal professional privilege. These 'exceptional powers' are not necessarily so exceptional – they have been given to royal commissioners since before Federation.

21   See generally, *Law Enforcement Integrity Commissioner Act 2006* (Cth).

22   Parliamentary Evidence (n 8) 6.

23   Alan Robertson, *Report to the Inspector of National Anti-Corruption Commission on the Decision by the National Anti-Corruption Commissioner to Take No Action on the Referrals from the Royal Commission into the Robodebt Scheme Royal Commission* (30 August 2024) 9.

24   Inspectors Report (n 14).

25   An opinion shared by Ms Furness, herself an eminent barrister.

26   Parliamentary Evidence (n 8).

27   See, for example, Parliamentary Evidence (n 12).

28   National Anti-Corruption Commission, *Operation Kingscliff* (Investigation Report, June 2025).
29   National Anti-Corruption Commission, 'NACC Secures Conviction of Corrupt Airport Official', media release, 28 July 2025.
30   Military leaders notoriously have trouble adapting to civilian decision-making: after his first Cabinet meeting as Prime Minister, the Duke of Wellington was heard to remark 'it was the most extraordinary affair. I gave them their orders and they wanted to stay to discuss them'.

7   Inflation, tax cuts and the cost of living
1   The Reserve Bank's forecast was often misrepresented, especially in the *Australian Financial Review*, as a *promise* to keep interest rates 'nailed to the floor' until 2024. But it was always a state-dependent, or data-dependent, *intention* rather than time-dependent. The bank said it would not raise interest rates until after inflation had re-entered the 2–3 per cent target zone and they kept to this.
2   A reconciliation table in the Budget shows that an alternative measure of the budget deficit is expected to be around $20 billion a year larger. Eslake (2025) provides further discussion.

16   Good intentions, unheralded setbacks
1   The Australian Curriculum, Assessment and Reporting Authority has found that Australian students' civics knowledge is at its lowest level since testing began 20 years ago (Collin, 2025). And, as McAllister (2001: 5) notes, 'levels of political knowledge within the electorate are low'.
2   'Black cladding' is a process whereby non-Indigenous peoples exploit Aboriginal and Torres Strait Islanders to gain access to contracts reserved for Indigenous businesses and this issue is increasingly being highlighted as undermining the purpose of the IPP.

INDEX

OTHER TITLES IN THE AUSTRALIAN COMMONWEALTH ADMINISTRATION SERIES

Kouzmin, A, Nethercote, ,J and Wettenhall, R (eds) *Australian Commonwealth Administration 1983: Essays in Review*, Canberra College of Advanced Education, Canberra, 1984.

Nethercote, J, Kouzmin, A, and Wettenhall, R (eds) *Australian Commonwealth Administration 1984: Essays in Review*, Canberra College of Advanced Education, Canberra, 1986.

Wettenhall, R, and Nethercote, J (eds.) *Hawke's Second Government: Australian Commonwealth Administration 1984–1987*, Canberra College of Advanced Education, Canberra, 1988.

Halligan, J, and Wettenhall, R (eds) *Hawke's Third Government: Australian Commonwealth Administration 1987–1990*, Canberra College of Advanced Education, Canberra, 1992.

Stewart, J (ed.), *From Hawke to Keating: Australian Commonwealth Administration 1990–1993*, University of Canberra, Canberra, 1995.

Singleton, G (ed.), *The Second Keating Government: Australian Commonwealth Administration 1993–1996*, University of Canberra, Canberra, 1997.

— (ed.), *The Howard Government: Australian Commonwealth Administration 1996–1998*, UNSW Press, Sydney, 2000.

Aulich, C, and Wettenhall, R (eds) *Howard's Second and Third Governments: Australian Commonwealth Administration 1998–2004*, UNSW Press, Sydney, 2005.

Aulich, C, and Wettenhall, R (eds) *Howard's Fourth Government: Australian Commonwealth Administration 2004–2007*, UNSW Press, Sydney, 2008.

Aulich, C, and Evans, M (eds) *The Rudd Government: Australian Commonwealth Administration 2007–2010*, ANU e-Press, Canberra, 2010.

Aulich, C (ed.), *The Gillard Governments: Australian Commonwealth Administration 2010–2013*, Melbourne University Press, Melbourne, 2014.

— (ed.), *From Abbott to Turnbull: A New Direction?*, Echo Books, Geelong West, 2016.

Evans, M, Grattan, M, and McCaffrie, B (eds) *From Turnbull to Morrison: The Trust Divide*, Melbourne University Press, Melbourne, 2019.

McCaffrie, B, Grattan, M, and Wallace, C (eds) *The Morrison Government: Governing through crisis, 2019–2022*, UNSW Press, Sydney, 2023.

www.ingramcontent.com/pod-product-compliance
Lightning Source LLC
Chambersburg PA
CBHW020503270326
41926CB00008B/719